POLLING UNPACKED

Polling UnPacked

The History, Uses and Abuses of Political Opinion Polls

Mark Pack

REAKTION BOOKS

Published by
REAKTION BOOKS LTD
Unit 32, Waterside
44–48 Wharf Road
London N1 7UX, UK
www.reaktionbooks.co.uk

First published 2022
Copyright © Mark Pack 2022

Printed and bound in Great Britain by Bell & Bain, Glasgow

A catalogue record for this book is available from the British Library

ISBN 978 1 78914 567 0

CONTENTS

'Without data, you're just another person with an opinion.'
– W. EDWARDS DEMING, statistician

'Polls are essential in a democracy which is sensitive to citizens' sentiments, opinions and attitudes.'
– HAROLD MENDELSOHN, sociologist

'The Gallup Poll has been described as "a cross-section of public opinion", but I regard it as a very dangerous constitutional precedent, and one which may undermine the independence of the House of Commons.'
– 1ST VISCOUNT STANSGATE, politician

'Boys, I think we're in trouble.'
– GEORGE GALLUP, pollster, as election results from the 1948 U.S. presidential election came in, showing the pollsters had the winner wrong

INTRODUCTION

'While the individual man is an insoluble puzzle,
in the aggregate he becomes a mathematical certainty.
You can, for example, never foretell what any one man
will do, but you can say with precision what an
average number will be up to.'

– SHERLOCK HOLMES[1]

There is one lie many politicians cheerfully admit to. They tell the world they do not pay attention to polls, yet in private they pore over the details of polls, commission their own and fret about everyone else's.

Despite this coyness from politicians, paying attention to the polls is desirable. Just as it is natural for a meteorologist to look at today's weather, for the manager of a sporting team to look at the current state of the league table or for an author to consult the book sales charts (perhaps), it should be natural for a politician to look at the polls. Polls – if done well – tell you what is going on. They inform you what those outside your bubble think. They tell someone who is there to serve the public what the public says it wants. If, that is, you can tell the good poll from the bad, and separate the useful insight from the dodgy extrapolation.

That is where this book comes in. As well as explaining how polls work, and showing how they can be done right, it also looks at whenpolls go wrong. Do they go wrong so badly and so often that it is best to ignore them? (Spoiler: no, they don't.)

Before we delve into such questions, a little definition is in order. The book explains opinion polls: the systematic posing of a series of questions to a group of people with the answers adjusted to make them representative of a wider group. That wider group might be Tennessee, New South Wales or the United Kingdom. The point is to use the small group of people quizzed to measure that larger population's views.

More specifically, this book explains political opinion polling. That is, polls whose questions are primarily political: voting intentions, attitudes towards measures in the government's latest budget, approval ratings of politicians and so on. Much of the methodology of political and non-political polling is the same, so much of this book will also help you to understand polling in general. But there are specific twists to political polling which this book covers.

The word 'pollster' itself was first used by *Time* magazine in 1939. In one of those beautiful coincidences which light up life, the term was conjured up for a story about how the most famous pollster of the day, George Gallup, was polled at home by the first-ever campaign pollster, Emil Hurja.[2] Like the word, Gallup's fame lived on, while Hurja descended into obscurity. This book tells the story of Gallup and Hurja, their predecessors, their successors and how to make sense of their work.

1

THE FIRST POLITICAL POLLS

'A political leader in a general election, apart from being chronically
overworked and unable to study even the daily press very carefully,
is like a warrior or a pilot operating in almost total fog...[and so]
market research has a valuable role to play.'
– HAROLD WILSON, prime minister[1]

P olitical polls are part of the basic rhythm of democratic politics.
But it was not always that way, for political polls are a much more
recent invention than democracy. Democracy dates back over two
millennia, while political polling dates back only two centuries to
one particular election in the United States of America.

The United States

The U.S. presidential election of 1824 was odd. Only one party contested
it. Yet a contest it was, with four different candidates from that one
party competing for the public's votes. Those votes, however, did not
decide the election. Instead, with no candidate winning a majority in
the electoral college, the decision went to the House of Representatives.
The winner to emerge from there – John Quincy Adams – had led in
neither the electoral college vote nor the popular vote.

Adams's victory was a watershed in the development of the U.S.
party system. The Democratic-Republican Party (not to be confused

with either the later Democratic Party or the later Republican Party) had been dominant, and at the previous election in 1820, its candidate, James Monroe, did not even face a significant opponent.

The party had given the power to pick its candidates for president to its congressional delegation. With little in the way of rivalry from other parties threatening the success of the candidates it picked, that meant the presidential election had, in effect, become a small, closed choice by its congressional delegation alone.

That transfer and concentration of power in the hands of a small caucus was by 1824 widely mocked as 'King Caucus', in reference to the sort of monarchical power that the founders of the USA had deliberately tried to avoid. As a result, in 1824 only a quarter of the congressional delegation chose to take part in selecting the party's official candidate for president. Moreover, three others from the party ran for president.

This shift of power away from elite decision-makers was enhanced by individual states increasingly moving to let the public vote in presidential elections. Previously, individual state legislatures had picked their state's national electoral college members, and the electoral college then voted between candidates for president. But increasingly, states allowed public votes to determine the make-up of their electoral college members. In 1800 only 5 out of 16 states had such voting. By 1824 this had risen to 18 out of 24, and in 1836 South Carolina was the only holdout.[2]

These three factors – a proper, albeit confusing, contest with a real doubt over the outcome; the fracturing of the power of the Democratic-Republican Party's congressional delegation; and the increasing use of the popular vote to decide the outcome in individual states – meant that there was more interest than usual in what the public (or, at least, the subset of men allowed to vote) thought about the candidates.

As a result, the contest also saw the precursors to modern political opinion polls. These were straw polls, simple tallies at various events, such as Fourth of July celebrations, of how many people supported each candidate. In some cases, books were left out in a public place for several days, with people writing in their voting choice. The primary locations for straw polling, however, were local militia meetings. Militia musters were ideal occasions for such votes since the enrolled militia covered all white males aged 18 to 45 and the annual musters were popular events that attracted large crowds. Asking about elections at them fitted with the militias' democratic and political traditions. Most state militias elected their lower offices and some even elected higher ones. They were a natural and relatively straightforward way of testing public opinion. In a foreshadowing of later polling controversies, however, there were arguments over how typical those attending militia meetings were of the broader public, given that one candidate, Andrew Jackson, was a hero of the militia.[3]

There were none of the techniques described elsewhere in this book to ensure a representative sample. Although some reporting tallied up scores from different events to help give a picture of which candidate could claim to be the 'public's' choice, these were much cruder affairs than modern polling.[4]

The exact details of these straw polls are often misreported, sometimes described as organized by newspapers and sometimes giving the credit to newspapers that were actually just re-reporting what other papers had already covered. But it appears that three newspapers – the *Raleigh Star and North Carolina State Gazette*, the *Wilmington American Watchman and Delaware Advertiser* and the *Star and North Carolina Gazette* – deserve the credit for the most pioneering reporting of the straw polls.[5]

In another foreshadowing of later disputes about political polling, there was a pattern of different newspapers liking or not liking straw polls depending on how the results did or did not line up with their own editorial line. The *Raleigh Register*, for example, was a supporter of candidate William H. Crawford and attacked the act of 'prematurely collecting the opinion of people'. Those collections of opinions were showing Crawford lagging.[6] Political polling, in its earliest form, was up and running.[7]

The next significant development again came in the United States, this time in the late nineteenth century with the *Columbus Dispatch*. In a step up from the straw polling that had continued since 1824, the paper trained its interviewers, sending them out across the city. It even considered the age and occupation of those interviewed to (try to) make the results representative. But these pioneering efforts did not catch on, and although straw polling continued, with increasing numbers of votes being counted up, the *Dispatch*'s methodological sophistication remained the exception. Moreover, such results remained geographically constrained. There were no attempts to gauge support across the whole country.

This changed in the early twentieth century with the *Literary Digest*, a national magazine. It can be credited with both the introduction of the idea of seeking national results by asking people across the whole country and then, years later, the embarrassment of a failure so significant that it helped establish modern polling.

The *Literary Digest* started posting out questions to people in selected areas in 1916, later spreading to the whole country.[8] As with the *Columbus Dispatch*, the *Literary Digest* showed some understanding of the need to make sure that the people asked were representative of the wider public. But it mainly selected people from limited lists, such as those with telephones or club memberships, or those who had registered cars.

What appeared to give the magazine's surveys authority, and what made them famous, was the exceptionally large number of responses involved. Questions about Prohibition in 1930 got answers from 5 million people. This impression of trustworthiness was reinforced by the *Literary Digest*'s record at elections. At five presidential elections in a row (1916, 1920, 1924, 1928 and 1932), its survey correctly called the winner.

The *Literary Digest* therefore became the most famous straw pollster. But it was by no means the only one. Nor was the straw polling carried out by dullards who did not understand the risks of biased results. Far from it. Comparisons between straw poll findings and election results were common and there were many variations in methodology as straw pollsters sought to get the best results. This even included what we would now recognize as methodological rigour, such as sometimes posting out a ballot to every tenth person on the electoral roll. Those undertaking such surveys may not have understood the mathematics of sampling, but they were groping towards doing the right thing, just as medicine has often seen treatments evolve before a proper understanding has been acquired of what makes them effective.

For careful observers, however, there were signs of frailty. As one pre-1936 critic pointed out, only one of the five elections for which the *Literary Digest* had accurately predicted the winner – the election of 1916 – had been a close contest. It is much easier to get five in a row right when four of them are landslides. Moreover, the *Literary Digest*'s record on predicting vote shares, rather than just the winner, was less impressive.[9] Despite those signs of frailty, the involvement of millions in its surveys and its record of picking the winners meant that by 1936 the magazine claimed that 'the *Digest* poll is still the Bible of millions.'[10]

Then came the 1936 U.S. presidential election. Ten million people across the country were mailed, and 2,266,566 returns were received. They showed a landslide for Republican Alf Landon, with a 57–43 per cent lead over Democrat and incumbent president Franklin D. Roosevelt. As the magazine reported,

> For nearly a quarter century, we have been taking Polls of the voters in the forty-eight States, and especially in presidential years, and we have always merely mailed the ballots, counted and recorded those returned and let the people of the Nation draw their conclusions as to our accuracy. So far, we have been right in every Poll . . . The Poll represents the most extensive straw ballot in the field – the most experienced in view of its twenty-five years of perfecting – the most unbiased in view of its prestige – a Poll that has always previously been correct.[11]

The *Literary Digest* further boasted that its numbers were unadulterated. It made a virtue of this in a way redolent of how food manufacturers now boast of products being natural and additive-free: 'these figures are exactly as received from more than one in every five voters polled in our country – they are neither weighted, adjusted, nor interpreted.'

But this was the pride before the fall.[12] For the actual election result was a crushing landslide – for Franklin D. Roosevelt. Rather than losing by 43–57 per cent, he was easily re-elected by 61–37 per cent. Both his vote share and his electoral college result were the best for any candidate since 1820.

As, to its credit, the magazine's later headline put it, 'Is our face red!' – although a bombastic determination to continue with such surveys followed: 'Should the University of Minnesota, with the greatest record in modern football, give up the sport because it finally lost one game, after a string of twenty-one victories?'[13]

What had gone wrong? Part of the answer is that the people asked to take part were more Republican than voters overall are. Sources the magazine used, such as car owners, skewed towards those with more money. This particularly mattered in 1936 because the election was held during a severe economic downturn and contested between candidates with very different platforms for helping the poor. However, this explanation on its own is not sufficient as, for example, in Chicago the *Literary Digest* mirrored modern sampling by asking every third registered voter. Yet its forecast of Landon's support was too high there as well. The other part of the answer was an issue with how willing each candidate's supporters were to participate in such surveys. This early form of the 'non-response bias' contributed roughly twice as much to the overall error as did the problem of asking people who were more Republican than voters overall.[14]

Yet while the *Literary Digest* was spectacularly wrong, a new entrant was spectacularly right, using the results from a smaller number of people – a much smaller number: around 50,000 compared with 2.3 million. Those results were, however, not left unweighted, unadjusted and uninterpreted as if raw data was a virtue. They were instead weighted, adjusted and interpreted to create the truth.

The new entrant was George Gallup, armed with a novel scientific method based on understanding the statistical theory behind sampling. His critical insight was that the number of respondents is not what makes a poll accurate. Rather, it is how representative those respondents are of the population you are looking to measure. We will look at the science – and art – of sampling in more detail later. For the moment, it is enough to know that if, say, you want to discover what football clubs people support, standing outside Newcastle United's St James' Park to ask your question will not give an accurate picture. It will be skewed, very heavily, towards Newcastle and whichever team they happen to be playing that day. Other clubs will come out badly in the results not due to actual lack of support but because of whom you asked and where. This is why requests on Twitter to 'retweet for a larger sample' based on the claim that this makes a Twitter poll better than a proper poll with a much smaller sample are so misplaced. Twitter users, and all the more so the limited number of followers of whoever shared the poll, are not typical of the wider population, just as those outside a particular sports ground are not typical of all sports fans, let alone the whole public. A huge, low-quality sample will lose out to a small high-quality one.

George Gallup understood this. He was not the only pollster to do so. He had two rivals who, like him, had developed polling expertise for business research and also applied it to politics: the *Fortune* survey, masterminded by Elmo Roper (whose commencement of polling for the magazine pre-dated Gallup by a few months), and Archibald Crossley, who masterminded surveys for Hearst Publications. Ironically, Crossley was formerly of the *Literary Digest*. He had then gone on to pioneer random sampling by telephone to generate radio audience data. These two rivals of Gallup both also got the 1936 election result right. But Gallup, with his flair for publicity, scooped the attention despite *Fortune* being closer on the vote shares.[15]

Incongruously, Gallup's PhD had been in analysing newspaper readership, looking at finding a superior way of understanding how people read newspapers than by merely asking them, as doing so was too unreliable. The person who became the world's most famous pollster obtained his doctorate from doubting the answers people gave to surveys.[16]

Gallup later became director of research at the advertising agency of Young & Rubicam, and got his start in political polling helping his mother-in-law, Eunice Miller. In 1932 she accepted the nomination from the Democrats for Iowa Secretary of State. Expecting to lose a post seen as safely Republican, that year's Democrat landslide swept her to an unexpected victory, becoming Iowa's first female Secretary of State. Gallup's unpublished polling for her campaign had correctly predicted her win. Further unpublished work followed in late 1933, when he conducted national sampling to foretell the 1934 congressional election results. In the Gallup corporate retelling, his work was spookily accurate, though it is worth noting that polling conducted nearly a year ahead of an election can only be so close thanks to luck.[17] Then in 1935 he founded the American Institute of Public Opinion (AIPO), which later became the polling firm that is still with us today, Gallup. On 20 October 1935 the first syndicated newspaper column appeared carrying his polling figures in around three dozen newspapers across the country, including the *Washington Post*.

The following year, he bested the *Literary Digest* in the presidential election. Until then, the media had been in thrall to the *Literary Digest*. So much so that the *New York Herald* newspaper, which was paying Gallup for polls, gave as much space to the *Literary Digest*'s numbers as to his.[18]

Yet Gallup was extremely confident in the superiority of his methodology over that of the *Literary Digest*. He went so far as to predict cheekily what figures the *Literary Digest* survey would produce ahead of it commencing. The *Literary Digest*'s editor, Wilfred J. Funk, was outraged:

'Never before has anyone foretold what our poll was going to show even before it started!' he snapped. 'Our fine statistical friend' [Gallup] should be advised that the *Digest* would carry on 'with those old-fashioned methods that have produced correct forecasts exactly one hundred percent of the time.'[19]

Gallup was right on that too: he predicted the *Literary Digest* would have it as 56 per cent Landon to 44 per cent Roosevelt, remarkably close to the actual figures they came up with of 57–43 per cent. All of this caught the media's attention.[20] The sparks between them raised

Gallup's profile and, when the results matched Gallup's numbers, his reputation.

Gallup getting it right, and also getting right how wrong his rival would be, is as far as the histories usually go. But dig into the details and you find an important twist to the story. Gallup produced his figures *six weeks* before the *Literary Digest* survey had yet started, and the magazine's gathering of responses for its poll lasted several weeks. Therefore, for Gallup to be so close required a large degree of luck, as the support for candidates can change over time. Even had Gallup's polling been perfect and his understanding of the *Literary Digest*'s flaws been spot on, there was no way he could be sure that reality would not change between his poll and the conclusion of that of the magazine. It was not so much a brilliant prediction as a lucky guess. Data made it an informed guess. But a lucky guess it still was, turned by luck and a flair for publicity into apparent brilliance.[21]

That flair for publicity which boosted Gallup, and which elevated him above Roper and Crossley, also had another effect. It created a myth about just how different the new 'scientific' polling was from what had gone before. Gallup played up to this, promising the newspapers that paid for his polls that he would refund their money if he got the 1936 election wrong. It was as if he had found a new and perfect way of calling elections. Yet, as mentioned, straw polling had in parts become quite sophisticated, including limited use of random sampling. And Gallup knew that no polling methodology could be guaranteed to get an election winner right owing to the vagaries of sampling, which we will look at in the next chapter. The more you peer at the details, the less Gallup, Roper and Crossley look like a sudden change. They were a new generation of people with a much more rigorous use of statistics and performing better than their predecessors, yes, but those predecessors were not all innumerate fools. Rather, their predecessors had already been groping towards the insights that made the new generation so successful and famous.[22] Nor were the new breed perfect. In an interview in 1968, Roper himself paused, chuckled and added a caveat when speaking about how 'scientific' their early polls were.[23]

By 1948 Gallup – and the other of the new pollsters – had followed up their 1936 successes by correctly calling the 1940 and 1944 U.S. presidential elections. Such was George Gallup's reputation that he featured on the front cover of *Time* magazine on 3 May 1948 as the 'Babe Ruth of the polling profession'. The appellation was meant as a compliment, given Ruth's stunning brilliance at baseball. However, it came with an unintentional irony – for Ruth spent most of his life getting a basic number (his own age) wrong. In a twist worthy of a novel, that year also brought Gallup's greatest public failure: another U.S. presidential election and another polling prediction. Gallup predicted a win for Republican Thomas Dewey by 5–15 per cent. Yet Democrat Harry S. Truman won by just under 5 per cent. In a mirror of 1936, once again Crossley and Roper also polled this election and got the same result as Gallup, and once again, their role is frequently overlooked.[24]

Highlighting the humiliation, the *Detroit Free Press* ran the front-page headline 'Truman: 304 Pollsters: 0' in reference to the number of electoral college votes won by Truman.[25] Next to it was another head-line: 'Man on Street, REAL Expert, Explains Vote.' Wilfred J. Funk, remembering his 1936 humiliation at the *Literary Digest*, admitted, 'I get a good chuckle out of this.'[26]

A report published in 1949 found four causes of the 1948 polling miss by Gallup, Crossley and Roper: ending their polling too far ahead of polling day; interviewers skewing those whom they polled towards more educated and better-off people without the methodology of the time correcting for this; an assumption that those undecided over how to vote would in the end vote in the same proportions as those who had already made up their minds (but in practice the undecideds broke heavily for Truman); and turnout varying between supporters of Dewey and Truman, again something the methodologies of the day did not try to account for.[27]

The 1948 election also gave us a photo of Truman holding up a copy of the *Chicago Tribune* with its headline 'Dewey Defeats Truman'. The headline even has a Wikipedia page of its own and is often used to illustrate stories of polling misses.[28] Those erroneous polls were probably in part responsible for that famously wrong headline. The first edition of the *Chicago Tribune* went to print before many election results had come in. Therefore, it went with the prediction from its senior journalist, Arthur Sears Henning, who had a good record of predicting earlier elections. In a rush to get to print – with the story itself so hurried that several lines were printed upside down thanks to a typesetters' strike – it is very likely that those polls influenced his opinion, as did the widespread expectations of a Dewey win.

Typical of those expectations was the *Washington Post*, which reported on 2 November 1948, '[If] Mr. Truman be the winner, the polltakers and the prognosticators would be forced into the greatest crow-eating debauch in the annals of American politics.' *Fortune*, with its own erroneous polling, had reported, 'Barring a major political miracle, Governor Thomas E. Dewey will be elected . . . Such is the overwhelming evidence of Elmo Roper's fifth pre-election Survey.' It also said, in October 1948, '[we] plan no further detailed reports on the change of opinion in the forthcoming presidential campaign unless some development of outstanding importance occurs,' so clear was the margin. *Kiplinger Magazine* sent out a special issue that November. With a front cover confidently stating, 'What Dewey Will Do', it was full of content about how a President Dewey administration would work. The magazine gave advice that turned out to be wise, but not in the way intended: 'Perhaps you should put a copy away for your children or grandchildren. Or perhaps you should get additional copies.'[29] Adding to that, the *Chicago Tribune* was pro-Republican, a factor likely to have encouraged Henning's misjudgement. Besides, he had spotted an error in the early election reports filed by the Associated Press, which wrongly reported that Truman had won in New York. That likely pushed him towards overconfidence in his own judgement.

At 3 a.m., when the newspaper realized its error, staff rushed out to buy up every copy they could find of the edition with the embarrassing front page. In a possibly apocryphal twist, the headline only got its infamy because a rival newspaper sent someone to the *Tribune*'s own offices and picked up a copy of the first edition from there, where *Tribune* staff had forgotten to remove it. But as many other copies had already been sold by that point, this may be more a good story than the truth. Certainly, the owners of a newspaper distribution company carefully preserved their own copy of the first edition.[30]

The most egregiously wrong newspaper report in 1946, however, was a less famous one. The German newspaper *Münchner Merkur*, lured by the need to go to print before results were in, had run the headline 'Thomas E. Dewey America's New President'. It also claimed to report that 'President-elect Dewey expressed his gratitude to the American people in a radio address from headquarters at the Roosevelt Hotel in New York City.'[31]

However, Truman, relishing the embarrassment of a vocal media supporter of his opponent, took the chance to immortalize the *Chicago Tribune*'s error by posing for a photograph with the faulty headline. That the photograph led to the *Chicago Tribune* being the newspaper most closely associated with polling errors is an ironic fate as it had also been one of the pioneers of recognizably modern door-to-door sampling (for market research surveys) from 1916.[32]

Moreover, Truman's famous photograph in some ways does a disservice to the 1948 polls. As pollster Nick Moon has pointed out,

> Because the polls called the wrong winner, the election is usually described in such terms as 'a disaster for the polls', but the actual error of the polls – the gap between the predicted and actual share of the vote for each candidate – was less than it had been in 1936, the year of the pollsters' first great triumph. This was an important lesson for the polls . . . Pollsters will judge themselves more by how close they came to the actual scores for each party, but the media and the general public will not . . . In objective terms, then, the American polls performed better in 1948 than they had in 1936.[33]

This pattern has often repeated since. Predict the winner incorrectly, and it does not matter how close you are on the vote share; the verdict will be a negative one. But predict the winner correctly, and you can miss by a wide margin and still be called a success.

Despite this 1948 polling trip, by then the concepts of political polling and of using relatively small samples, carefully chosen and adjusted, were well established. The events of 1948 were an embarrassment rather than terminal for that approach. In another forerunner of future patterns, this blunder led to a decline in interest for a while in political polls, reducing business for political pollsters. But political polling bounced back.[34] It steadily grew in importance in U.S. politics in the succeeding decades, helped by its parallel spread in marketing, social science research and the public sector.[35]

There is one – initially kept tightly secret and later mostly forgotten – waypoint in that subsequent growth worthy of special mention. It is the case of the secret internal campaign polling operation that became the basis of a novel that spent more than four months in the best-seller charts in the United States. Better still, the election involved was the 1960 U.S. presidential election between John F. Kennedy and Richard M. Nixon. It was a famously close election in which Kennedy outpolled Nixon by less than one-fifth of one percentage point (0.17 per cent). Kennedy only won the electoral college because of two states he took by less than 1 per cent. (Had Nixon won both, neither would have had a majority in the electoral college, sending the election to the House of Representatives to decide.) Eighteen states were settled by less than 3 per cent, with Kennedy winning twelve of them to Nixon's six.

The election is famous too for the impact of the first TV debates, and the contrasting styles and fates of the two candidates. Kennedy, the youthful, charismatic and optimistic one, launched America's Moon programme and had his term of office tragically cut short by assassination. Nixon went on to win two presidential elections himself, before leaving office prematurely, as the Watergate scandal overwhelmed him and his administration.

The only thing the 1960 election is missing in terms of drama is an Oscar-winning dramatization. But it did spawn a best-selling novel by another talented, charismatic figure whose life ended tragically early: Eugene Burdick. Burdick was a surfer before surfing was cool, a man who danced a Tahitian hula on national TV, a seaman decorated for swimming through flames to rescue colleagues in the Second World War, a friend of Marlon Brando, a Rhodes scholar, a TV pundit and political scientist, and 'the greatest teacher they ever had', in the eyes of many students.[36] A political scientist famous and glamorous enough to feature in scuba diving gear in an advertisement for ale ('undersea explorer ... literary man ... Ale man'), Burdick died young of a heart attack on a tennis court in 1965, aged just 46.[37]

His political science work included exploring how people decide how to vote. For example, readers of the *Washington Evening Star* on 13 May 1956 were presented with a twenty-question quiz with questions on topics such as employment, location and whether they read a foreign-language newspaper. It got readers to tally up their scores, promising that 'assuming that both candidates are fully acceptable personalities, the way you will vote in November can be predicted with a very high degree of accuracy right now!'

Burdick had also been the author of multiple Hollywood screenplays and best-selling novels. Among Burdick's most successful novels is the 1962 Cold War nuclear drama *Fail-Safe*, co-written with fellow political scientist Harvey Wheeler. In it, a series of blunders result in a U.S. nuclear bomber force heading off to obliterate Moscow. Made into a successful film directed by Sidney Lumet and starring Henry Fonda and Walter Matthau, its subsequent obscurity (save for a televised play in 2000 with George Clooney) was primarily due to bad luck. In the year of the film's release, 1964, Stanley Kubrick's *Dr Strangelove or: How I Learned to Stop Worrying and Love the Bomb* also hit the cinema with a very similar theme. *Fail-Safe* may have been a good film, but *Dr Strangelove* was an all-time classic.

Burdick's next novel, about a fictional 1964 election campaign, was *The 480*, its story of data, computers, polling and campaign consultants having been inspired by what had happened in 1960. As the preface states,

> There is a benign underworld in American politics. It is not the underworld of cigar-chewing pot-bellied officials who mysteriously run 'the machine'. Such men are still around, but their power is waning. They are becoming obsolete though they have not yet learned the fact.
>
> The new underworld is made up of innocent and well-intentioned people who work with slide rules and calculating machines and computers which can retain an almost infinite

number of bits of information as well as sort, categorize, and reproduce this information at the press of a button ... They are technicians and artists; all of them want, desperately, to be scientists.

The title refers to the real world: to the 480 categories the American electorate was divided into for the 1960 Kennedy campaign, based on polling and other data – categories such as 'Rural, Eastern, Female, Protestant, Professional & White Collar Democrat'. Simulmatics Corporation, whose president, Edward L. Greenfield, Burdick had previously worked for, did this segmentation for the Kennedy campaign. The firm used computers to analyse 63 pre-election polls, along with information such as election results, creating those different electorate segments and then polling issues and policy positions to see how they went down with the segments.

Despite its commercial success, Burdick's novel slipped from collective political memory, and, fearing public hostility to the idea that a candidate might do what polling and computers, rather than their conscience and principles, told them, the team around Kennedy did their best to keep Simulmatics' work secret.

In response to *The 480*, Simulmatics produced their own book, attempting to disabuse people of the notion of 'a number of sensationalized newspaper and magazine articles, even a work of fiction'.[38] The book ostentatiously claims an importance for the work of Simulmatics with an opening dedication to John F. Kennedy – 'the man for whom we worked' – and thanking Robert Kennedy in the acknowledgements. Although an interesting early account of attempts at simulating elections based on polling data, the presence of sentences such as the one starting 'Let us consider balance among three objects, one of them a cognizing human being whom we will call "P" ...', gives a clue as to why the book did not secure a notable place for Simulmatics in histories of the election.[39] So despite its pioneering efforts to scientifically predict the future for business, government and political purposes by using data and simulations, the company too slipped out of memory. It was only in business between 1959 and 1970, its offices later becoming a hamburger restaurant.

Due to those pioneering efforts, the *New Yorker* was only slightly over the top with its headline about the firm in a rare feature in 2020: 'How the Simulmatics Corporation Invented the Future'. Its subheading rightly asked, 'When JFK ran for president, a team of data scientists with powerful computers set out to model and manipulate American voters. Sound familiar?'[40] That feature and a fascinating book on Simulmatics by the piece's author, Jill Lepore, along with a brief reference in the best-selling book *The Victory Lab*, has given the secret polling analysis for the Kennedy campaign a little more profile in recent years.[41]

It is still mostly a forgotten secret, but there are many shades of what was to come in politics in this novel and the real work of Simulmatics, all the way through to the Cambridge Analytica scandal in the following century. As with Cambridge Analytica, quite what the impact of Simulmatics was on election results is hard to judge. It is possible, even likely, in both cases that the pioneering technology did little to change the result, though Kennedy's margin was so wafer-thin that the case for Simulmatics is easier to make.[42]

Nevertheless, *The 480* is – in ideas and prescience, if not in its writing style and attitude towards women – the best novel about political opinion polls. And while there is no brilliant film of the 1960 presidential election, Simulmatics did inspire *The Matrix*.[43]

The Global Spread of Political Polling

Following the start of modern polling in the USA, it spread to other countries, especially thanks to George Gallup's international business ambitions. The global spread of Gallup's empire included Denmark and Sweden in 1939, followed by both Canada and Australia in 1941.[44] In Australia, Roy Morgan started up a Gallup affiliate operation after his boss, newspaper editor Keith Murdoch (father of Rupert), sent him to the United States to learn polling so that he could then conduct polls for Murdoch's newspaper.

Although Morgan started public political polling in Australia, polling on behalf of politicians had already started with Sylvia Ashby. In 1938 she claimed to be 'the only woman conducting a market research organisation in the British Empire', and was carrying out private constituency polling for the ruling Labor Party from 1940.[45]

The Australian experience soon mirrored that of the USA, with getting the winner right mattering more for reputation than did accuracy over vote shares. The best of Morgan's early general election polls in terms of smallest vote share error was in 1954. Yet that was also the election he got 'wrong', as although his polling rightly pegged the Australian Labor Party at just over 50 per cent of the two-party preferred vote share (the standard measure in Australia's alternative-vote elections), the Labor Party won fewer seats than its Liberal or National rivals.[46]

Elsewhere Gallup's indirect but very real influence was felt with the founding immediately before the Second World War of the first French polling firm, the Institut français d'opinion publique (IFOP), by Jean Stoetzel. He had just come back from a year at Columbia University in New York, where he had picked up Gallup's polling techniques. Stoetzel's first political survey was run in July 1938, although his efforts were then delayed by the war. Political polling resumed in summer 1944, with a survey of liberated Paris showing that 61 per cent of Parisians thought the USSR was contributing the most to defeating Germany but that 69 per cent expected the USA to contribute most to France's recovery.

French political polling had a dramatic hiccough in 1946, when it got a constitutional referendum badly wrong in both vote share and result, predicting a 54 per cent approval vote when the result was only 47 per cent in favour. But it recovered and Charles de Gaulle himself became so impressed with IFOP's work that he offered to give the company either official status or state funding. It declined both.

French polling's 1936 moment came in 1965 when IFOP's run of polls showed falling vote share for incumbent president Charles de Gaulle and even, controversially, that by the end he would not obtain a majority in the first round of the presidential election. When the votes were counted, IFOP was right: de Gaulle got 44 per cent compared with IFOP's final estimate of 43 to 45 per cent. French political polling's reputation was made.[47]

Across the border in Germany the U.S. High Commission had instigated political polling after the war in the American-occupied sector. In the French-occupied sector, the American influence was also felt as political polling started up with the critical input of Elisabeth Noelle-Neumann, who had learnt the science of polling by studying American techniques.[48] Noelle-Neumann went on to have a distinguished post-war career and received the Order of Merit of the Federal Republic of Germany in 1976, although her reputation was tarnished by her involvement with the Nazis and her antisemitic writing.[49]

Political polling came late to Ireland, with the first polls not until 1961. Gallup started polling that year, but the *Irish Press* beat Gallup to the honour of the first political poll. It commissioned one earlier that year which asked about Ireland's possible membership of the European Economic Community.[50] By then, polling had spread widely elsewhere, including to countries such as Japan, Italy and the Netherlands.

Due to Franco's dictatorship, Spain was still later to start political polling, although the first poll did appear for the 1966 local elections – nine years before the end of Franco's rule.[51] (It was a 'crashing all-round failure', with the poll way off.[52]) One of the most recent countries to introduce political polling is China, where the absence of a multi-party democracy continues to hinder its development. However, the ruling Communist Party has permitted some polling, particularly for its own use.[53]

The United Kingdom

Political opinion polling came to the UK in the 1930s, when Henry Durant ran the British arm of Gallup, its first overseas affiliate, which was originally called the British Institute of Public Opinion (BIPO).[54]

As in the USA with the *Literary Digest*, in Britain too there was a high-profile predecessor that valued size over quality for its sample. In the British case, this was the Peace Ballot, a privately organized nationwide door-to-door referendum held in 1934–5, with five questions and in which 11,640,066 people took part.[55] It made great play of the size of the response as reinforcing the message about people wanting arms reductions and peaceful resolutions to international disputes. But the partial nature of the organizers (including the League of Nations Union, a pro-League of Nations outfit and hardly neutral in a ballot about that institution) made this more like an enormous petition – remarkably large given the absence of the Internet to gather signatures online, but still more a petition than a poll. That petition flavour was reinforced by its official full name, 'A National Declaration on the League of Nations and Armaments' – note, a 'declaration', not a 'survey'. Its impact is debated by historians, not because of questions about its methodology but rather because of what Hitler and Mussolini were doing at the time: multiple steps in German military rearmament in breach of the Treaty of Versailles and the Italian invasion of Abyssinia. Japan also renounced two international arms control treaties: the Washington Naval Treaty and the London Naval Treaty.

Proper polling was, though, soon on the way. With the help of British-born Harry Field, who was sent by Gallup to the UK to establish the enterprise, Durant started experimenting with polls in 1936, and the first publication of results came in 1938 in the *News Chronicle.*[56] One of the earliest questions was:

If you had to choose between Fascism and Communism, which would you choose?
Fascism: 49 per cent
Communism: 51 per cent[57]

By including those 'don't knows' in the headline figures, however, the results could also be given as:

Fascism: 26 per cent
Communism: 28 per cent
No opinion: 46 per cent

It is an early example of the difference that excluding 'don't know' or 'no opinion' answers can make to the headline figures.

The Gallup polls soon started attracting interest from others, as Durant explained: 'People constantly asked us to put questions on our regular surveys, and at the beginning I was stupid enough to regard these as a nuisance: then I suddenly realized that this was a beautiful way of making money.'[58]

October 1938 saw the debut of a question asking if people were satisfied with the prime minister (51 per cent satisfied, 39 per cent dissatisfied).[59] Parliamentary by-election polls also began in 1938, when a Gallup poll correctly foresaw the Labour Party winning the Fulham West by-election in the face of widespread expectations that the Conservatives would succeed. The Gallup poll was remarkably close to the actual vote shares, leading Durant to comment, 'By a miracle I got it on the nose within one percent; beginner's luck.'[60]

This initial success was followed by getting the winner right in four out of the next five by-elections, including another very close set of figures in the famous Oxford by-election of 1938. Held soon after the Munich Agreement, it was fought on the issue of appeasement. This poll's target sample size was three hundred, and the sampling was carried out on the two days before polling day. Contrary to what later became a problem for polling, in this one it was richer people who were hardest to reach, due to servants often answering the door. The figures had to be weighted to adjust for this.[61]

The first national voting intention question came in February 1939, dividing results between government, opposition and 'don't know'. The first voting intention question breaking down results by party (Conservative, Labour, Liberal) came in June 1943.[62]

The point made by American pollsters in 1936 – that a good small sample beats a much larger bad one – took time to be accepted in Britain. The relative merits of the Gallup and the *Literary Digest* approaches went as far as to dominate a wartime debate in the House of Commons. On 1 August 1940, as the Battle of Britain was fought above them and on the day in which Hitler published Directive 17, ordering an intensification of air and naval operations as a prelude to invasion, MPs in the House of Commons argued over sample sizes. The trigger was the Ministry of Information's research approach for a social survey. In response to critics of the small, scientific sampling approach, one MP, Derrick Gunston, said,

> Here have been many scoffs at new scientific methods, especially at those which have been used in America to find what public opinion is thinking, but there are always scoffs at scientific progress . . . Our party have been accused of being stupid and opposed to progress and scientific endeavour, but . . . I believe that we can use these new scientific methods to get to know what public opinion is really thinking.

He went on to give an example of the merits of small samples:

> The interesting part of these surveys is that they do not depend so much on the number of people questioned as on the scientific differentiation of the cross-section. There was an interesting example in America in 1936, when they took a survey on a certain question. They examined 30,000 people. The answer was 'No.' The first 500 voted 54.9 per cent 'No' . . . the first 1,000 voted 53.9 per cent against; and the 30,000 voted 55.5 per cent against. The actual degree of inaccuracy between the 30,000 and the first 500 was only .06 per cent. This shows how accurate these methods can be. I know it may be said that we do not want American methods in this country, but we are very glad to have American aeroplanes.[63]

He and other defenders of 'new scientific approaches' did not win over everyone. A complication in the UK was the existence of Mass Observation, a vast social science research project run from 1937 into the 1960s. Its more qualitative methodology, using a mix of diaries and open-ended questions for its research, gave other grounds for critiquing the new scientific polling.[64]

But only a few years later, British polling had its breakthrough moment. In the general election of 1945, there was a widespread expectation of a Conservative win, primarily due to the party's leader being Winston Churchill, who had just successfully led the country through the Second World War. Churchill himself told the king that he expected to win, with a majority of between thirty and eighty seats. Key figures in the Labour opposition also expected Churchill to win, with Hugh Dalton, the Labour MP who, as it turns out, was about to become chancellor of the exchequer, predicting 'a Tory majority or a deadlock'. Nor was his party leader, about to become prime minister with a landslide majority, expecting it. Clement Attlee believed Labour was unlikely to get within as much as thirty seats of victory, let alone any sort of majority.[65] The limited evidence we have shows the public expected a Conservative win too.[66]

However, the result was a Labour majority of 146. A shock to others, it was not a shock to Gallup, as a Gallup poll got the general election right. It had been commissioned by the *News Chronicle*, which was sufficiently surprised by the poll's findings to heavily caveat them in its pre-polling day coverage. The figures were an 'interim forecast', it said. The poll, according to its account from 4 July 1945, 'does not pretend to foretell the results of the election' and 'it must be emphasized that it is impossible to base upon these results any forecast as to the probable distribution of seats in the new House of Commons'.

Despite its paymaster's caution, the Gallup poll was vindicated, demonstrating the value of polling over other forms of political prognostication: 'The General Election of 1945 was many things. It was the Waterloo of the Liberal party. It was the Waterloo of the Conservative party but, beyond everything else, it was the Waterloo of the political meteorologists.'[67]

As in the breakthough moment for polling in the USA at the 1936 presidential election, historical accounts of polling at the 1945 British election focus on Gallup, although Gallup was not the only pollster. But unlike in 1936, the other pollster – the Centre of Public Opinion, established by the *Daily Express* newspaper in 1942 – got the election wrong.[68] Where Gallup had a clear Labour lead, the rival had the parties neck and neck.[69] However, that was still more accurate than the widespread expectations of a Conservative win.

The subsequent growth of political polling was helped by the existence of a clutch of national newspapers in Britain, unlike in the United States. They were more natural instigators of national polls than their sub-national colleagues in America. Polling expanded at the 1950 general election, with more frequent polls from both Gallup and the *Daily Express* plus the first election poll for the *Daily Mail*. The final polls from all three were reasonably close to the vote shares, but Gallup once again had more to crow about, being the only one of the three to, correctly, put Labour ahead.[70]

The following 1951 general election, however, brought the first collective failure of British pollsters. All three pollsters – Gallup included – wrongly put the Conservatives ahead on vote share, when, in reality, Labour polled more votes. Luckily for the pollsters, this mistake was not so prominent as the 1948 U.S. failure, thanks to the British electoral system giving the Conservatives the most seats and so making them the winners anyway.

Modern political polling, for both good and ill, had firmly arrived on both sides of the Atlantic. Polling had also become, at least for the Conservative Party, a part of the regular flow of intelligence that politicians relied on.[71] Nevertheless, as late as 1959, the *Daily Express* proclaimed that it 'has no confidence in its own poll, although it is conducted with complete integrity and all possible efficiency'.[72] It should have had confidence: in that year's general election, its final poll had both Labour and Conservatives to within one point of the actual result.

Polling also brought some other unexpected benefits:

When one Gallup Poll interviewer knocked at the door of a house in South London the housewife opened it and said: 'I'm so glad you knocked; I was just going to commit suicide'. The interviewer followed her into the kitchen and there, sure enough, was the cushion in the oven and the farewell note written. The interviewer took out the cushion, shut the oven door, tore up the note and made the woman a cup of tea.[73]

The establishment of political polling in Britain and many other countries did not, however, put a stop to controversies over how much attention politicians should pay to pollsters. There is a tension between the roles of politicians as leaders, telling the public what they think is right, and as listeners, letting the public determine what happens. For some politicians, and their supporters, ignoring what the public wants is a virtue, as it can be dressed up as principled leadership. Of course, this virtue is easier to appreciate when you agree with what the politician is saying. Part of these controversies also is the extent to which polling, along with market research and social science more generally, helps politicians try to win support through means other than promoting the merits of particular policies. Understanding the extent to which political support is driven by policy-light factors, such as whether voters warm to candidates, is, in the eyes of some, a form of cheating.

This is why in Act I of his play about two men rivalling for the Democratic presidential nomination, *The Best Man* (1960), Gore Vidal had the hero attack opinion polls:

RUSSELL (*firmly*): I don't believe in polls. Accurate or not. And if I may bore you with one of my little sermons: life is not a popularity contest; neither is politics. The important thing for any government is educating the people about issues, *not* following the ups and downs of popular opinion.

REPORTER #3 (*in for the kill*): Does that mean you don't respect popular opinion? Do you think a president ought to ignore what the people want?

RUSSELL (*serenely*): If the people want the wrong thing, if the people don't understand an issue, if they've been misled by the press (*politely*) – by *some* of the press – then I think a president should ignore their opinion and try to convince them.

Later in the play, speaking of his rival to the current president, Russell says,

> Suppose the Chinese were to threaten to occupy India and we were faced with the possibility of a world war, the *last* world war. Now that is the kind of thing you and I understand and I think we could handle it without going to war and without losing India. But what would [rival candidate] Joe do? He would look at the Gallup poll.[74]

There will always be controversy over the extent to which politicians should lead or follow public opinion. But while it may be up to politicians to decide how and when to pay attention to what the public thinks, it is up to pollsters to make such information as accurate as can be.

Let's see how that works for the most fundamental job of political polling: asking about voting intention.

2

HOW POLITICAL
POLLS WORK

'Here is the secret ugliness of the polling industry
… We rely on the kindness of strangers, that is when
the phone rings that they will answer it, that when
they find out what the call is about that they do not
hang up and that they will stay and complete the
interview all the way to the end.'

– ANN SELZER, pollster[1]

Political polling suffers from being counter-intuitive. It seems that
a poll with millions of responses should be better than one with
just a few thousand. Yet as the *Literary Digest* found out, that isn't the
case. Rather, one of the merchants in *Don Quixote* was right when he
said, 'By a small sample, we may judge the whole piece.'[2] So to understand polling, and to retune those misleading intuitions, you need
to understand sampling: how pollsters decide whom to ask for their
polls and how many of them to ask.

Sampling

In 1947 the American town of Grandville became the location for a
secret opinion-polling operation. Former basketball player turned
pollster Lawrence 'Rip' Smith was facing disaster. His firm was about
to go out of business, the desks already gone and the telephones left

sitting on bare floors. But then he hit the jackpot when he discovered that Grandville's population exactly matched that of the whole United States. Rather than the time and expense of national polls, he could quickly and cheaply poll the residents of Grandville alone.

But he would have to do so secretly for he understood the risks of the 'panel effect' – that is, how the act of repeatedly asking a fixed group of people their views can result in those very views changing, because the act of being repeatedly asked about something means you end up paying more attention to it. So Smith and two colleagues headed off in secret to Grandville – the 'mathematically perfect town [that] reflects the nation's thinking' – posing as life insurance salesmen to give them the excuse to speak to many people, every day.

That, at least, is the set-up for the movie *Magic Town* (1947), starring James Stewart as Smith and Jane Wyman as the local newspaper editor. One of Stewart's accomplices was played by Ned Sparks, who was so well known for playing characters with dour faces that in a publicity stunt Lloyds of London offered $100,000 to any photographer who could catch him smiling. The other accomplice was played by Donald Meek, who died during filming. His absence from later scenes is poignantly excused in a railway scene with the comment that he 'took the earlier train'.

The scriptwriters included impressively plausible polling details in the film, such as the way Grandville is compared with the nation as a whole using the criteria real pollsters use, including gender and Democrat or Republican affiliation. The fear of the panel effect, used to set up the salesmen's duplicity at the heart of the plot, is also real. Genuine pollster Gallup gets several mentions. (And once again, Crossley and Roper are left out.) Even the idea of studying only the one town was inspired by real research, the 'Middletown studies'. These were a long-running piece of sociological research into the white residents of Muncie, Indiana. The results were published as two books, *Middletown* and *Middletown in Transition*, the names chosen to indicate that it was a typical place – a typical town, at least.[3]

A few years after *Magic Town*, science fiction author Isaac Asimov took the idea even further: from just one place to just one person. In his 1955 short story 'Franchise', Asimov imagined a future, set in the far distant 2008, in which computer modelling had become so refined that elections involved only the one person voting.[4] The story sees Norman Muller selected as the one voter for an election, getting quizzed by the Multivac computer before it calculates 'all the elections, national, state and local'. He is asked questions such as 'what do you think of the price of eggs?' and connected up to health monitoring equipment so that for each answer, 'from the way your brain and heart and hormones and sweat glands work, Multivac can judge exactly how intensely you feel about the matter'.

In the real world, however, you cannot copy Grandville or Multivac. No one person or even one place can capture all the varieties of young and old, urban and rural, religious and non-religious, rich and poor or the many other characteristics that make us all so different. You need instead to select a diverse group of people who are representative of the overall population whose views you are after. The science, and art, of selecting such a group of people is known as sampling.

Because picking such a group of people is not a perfect process, the results need to be adjusted to make up for its flaws. That process of adjustment, called weighting, comes with its own risks. Yet for all these risks, concentrating on the quality rather than the size of his sample is what made George Gallup triumph over the *Literary Digest*. The large, pure unadulterated, raw figures of the *Literary Digest* were inferior to the smaller, refined, adjusted, transformed figures of Gallup.

With that in mind, let's dig into how weighting and, first, sampling work. Prior to the rise of sampling, the idea of systematically trying to count everyone or everything to understand the state of things

better has a very long history, including all the way back to the censuses of the Roman Empire, such as the one that took Joseph and
Mary to Bethlehem.[5] As early examples such as that or the Domesday
Book in Britain show, the initial concept was that everything needed
counting to ascertain the truth. So too with the first censuses, such
as the one in New France, the French colony in North America, in
1665–6 (in which counting 'everyone' meant counting colonists but
not indigenous people or some religious orders). The 1790s saw a
wave of further developments, with similar activity in Sweden (which
at the time included Finland) in 1794, along with the USA, starting
in 1790 (where whether or not indigenous people were included in
the census depended on whether or not they paid tax, a key distin-
guishing feature built into Article 1, Section 2 of the U.S. Constitution).
This era also saw other pioneering collections of statistics such as John
Sinclair's first successful use of a nationwide questionnaire for the
Statistical Account of Scotland, collated during the 1790s.[6]

However, during the nineteenth century, the idea of sampling
began to take hold. That is, rather than having to count everything,
counting a representative sample would still enable you to reach the
truth – more quickly, cheaply and easily. A pioneer was Statistics
Norway, the country's official statistics organization, created as an
independent body in 1876. Its first director, Anders Nicolai Kiær,
faced growing requests for data. When asked to study what the population thought about a proposed new pension and social insurance
system, he therefore opted for a survey rather than attempting to ask
everyone. The success of this 120,000 sample meant that for his next
survey, he was happy to cut it back to 10,000.

These samples were not picked at random. Rather,

> Kiær promoted the idea of drawing samples as if to create
> the world in miniature; he would purposively select areas

of the country (districts, towns, etc.) in a seemingly 'representative' way, and then systematically sample units within those strata (e.g., choosing particular ages and first letters of surnames). His samples were constructed so that they 'agreed in important characteristics with the population at large' – these characteristics being findings from earlier censuses. Kruskal and Mosteller note that, 'for example, if a sample had a deficiency of cattle farmers, he would add more of them'.[7]

Kiær was well connected and his proselytizing spread this approach internationally. That is why his role in the history of sampling is more important than that of French mathematician Pierre-Simon Laplace, who had understood the principle of sampling much earlier. But being active at the time of the French Revolution and the Napoleonic Wars, Laplace's opportunities to spread ideas internationally were circumscribed. Other than provoking a statistical dispute in Belgium, in which the idea of sampling lost out, Laplace's ideas faded out of sight. It was Kiær whose ideas spread.

Among those who were persuaded and took up the approach was British statistical expert Arthur L. Bowley. He developed many of the mathematical approaches to work out rigorously how good a sample was and what the errors between the sample and the truth might be. By 1912 he was using scientific sampling to investigate social and economic conditions in Britain, later writing what became a standard text on sampling.[8]

The use of sampling spread to the private sector, particularly in the USA, with the rise of market research serving commercial firms, commencing in 1911 when pioneering researcher Charles Coolidge Parlin started working for the Curtis Publishing Company. Like governments and social science investigators, companies wanted to know what was going on around them, quickly and cheaply if possible. Surveys using sampling fitted the bill.[9]

But how can you decide whom to ask if you are going to sample only a selection? One way of doing this is to select people entirely at random. That, however, is very difficult. Not everyone is equally willing to respond to a poll or survey. Unless you have the power of the law to force people to take part, you end up with a non-random group. Then there are other problems, such as if you ask questions of people during the day, you miss people who work night shifts and are asleep. Achieving complete randomness is like drawing the perfect circle. If you try hard, you can get close. But the closer you look, the more apparent the deviations from perfection become. In practice, just getting close to random is hard, and therefore slow and expensive.

Moreover, even if you source a completely random sample, it may not be typical. Imagine flipping a coin. The true state of affairs is that if you flip a coin, there is a 50:50 random chance you will obtain heads or tails. Now toss the coin ten times. Did you obtain precisely five heads? The chances are that you did not. You will obtain precisely five heads only just under one time in four (24.6 per cent of the time) although five heads is the 'correct' outcome. The rest of the time, you will obtain either more heads than you 'should', such as six heads and four tails, or fewer, such as three heads but seven tails.[10] So it is with your hoped-for random sample for a poll. You might, by bad luck, obtain – say – far more men in the sample than the true picture over-all. If political views between women and men vary, that will skew your sample in a problematic way.

Statisticians and pollsters have developed solutions to these problems with attempted random sampling. One solution is to use quotas. Select the key criteria – age, gender, occupation and so on – and work out a quota for how many people of each type you need in your poll. With this approach, you interview people until you fill up each quota.

As you reach the end of doing the poll, that can mean turning down many would-be participants, as they only fit criteria for which you have already hit your quota. This method has its own flaw, which is part of what went wrong for Gallup and others in the 1948 U.S. presidential election. The interviewers or the process may let other biases slip in when attempting to fill up their quotas. For face-to-face interviewing in which people are stopped on the street, that may mean stopping people who look less busy – and so ending up with more shoppers and fewer office workers on their lunch break, perhaps.

The answer to that is to mix attempted randomness and use of quotas (pre-stratification) with weighting of the results afterwards (post-stratification) to fix the problems that have come from the earlier steps. For example, require the interviewer to try to stop every Xth person and then afterwards weight the results by age, gender and so on. Weighting is sufficiently important that we will return to it specifically in the next section.

As polling has moved from face-to-face or the post to, as the twentieth century entered its final decades, the telephone and then in the twenty-first century to online panels, new obstacles have had to be overcome. The core ideas of sampling and weighting, however, remain the same.

When applying these core ideas to political polling, there is the question of quite who should be sampled. 'The people' works as a shorthand answer but not as a detailed brief to a pollster. For questions about, say, how happy people are when out and about to hold on to their rubbish until they can find a bin for it, then 'the adults in the country' suffices. For political questions, the answer more often is some variation of 'those who are going to vote at the next election'. That raises issues about whether or not pollsters should check if someone is formally legally registered to vote and also about potentially adjusting answers based on how likely someone is to vote. In the USA, in particular, a distinction is often drawn between some polls that are of 'likely voters', and others of the larger category of 'registered voters' (which, in turn, is a smaller category than 'people who could be registered to vote if they wished'). In contrast, in the UK pollsters generally aim for the equivalent of 'likely voters' for voting intention questions, which results in the need for turnout weighting, as discussed below. But for other types of political questions, such turnout weighting is often omitted.

All of this becomes still hazier under close examination because pollsters tend to take at face value people's answers about whether or not they are a registered voter, or indeed whether or not someone is legally qualified to register to vote. Or they just don't ask about these issues at all. An illegal immigrant unable to vote who gets polled may be able to answer questions honestly and still end up being counted. Or for another anomaly, the fact that dead people can legally vote in well-run democracies (someone who has a postal vote, or an early vote, can vote, promptly die and still have their vote counted on polling day) means they are a category under-represented in pollster's samples as polling day nears.[11] Yet these sorts of anomalies are usually too small in number to really matter. Some curios remain just curios.

This has not always been the case, though. Histories of political polling glide over a grim wrong turn in its development, giving George Gallup a pass on polling techniques that were racist and sexist. Gallup's early sampling was overly focused on white men. Women and non-whites were not properly sampled. In as much as this can be justified, it came from Gallup's focus on predicting election results, and hence wanting to measure the views of voters rather than adults overall. But this meant that the widespread, deliberate suppression of the voting rights of African Americans was, via Gallup's focus on voters, translated into a polling methodology that therefore also deliberately downplayed their views. Even if justifiable when purely trying to measure electoral popularity, the problem was that Gallup then slipped from polling focused on voters into rhetoric referring to the American public as a whole. The title of the syndicated newspaper columns that first covered his polling results was 'America Speaks', not 'White Male America Speaks'. Caveats, warnings or regrets about how his polling did not fully represent the views of Americans other than white men are notably insufficient in Gallup's exhortations to value polling as a way of understanding the public.[12]

To make matters worse, Gallup's reasoning appears to have been not only about polling voters but a commercial reaction to fears that Southern newspapers would not run his polling if they gave proper prominence to the views of African Americans.[13] As for his over-sampling of men (two-thirds of Gallup poll respondents were men in 1936–7), that was not compensated for by reweighting the figures (a particular problem for voting questions, though issue questions were partially reweighted).[14] The best excuse for this is that it was driven by an erroneous belief in low female turnout, though Gallup's record of sexist comments suggests there may have been more to it than just a misreading of data.[15] It was a dark start to political polling.

It was also an episode that should be remembered, as that distinction between 'the public' on one hand and 'likely voters' or 'voters' on the other is still one that can be relevant to questions on topics such as immigration, where the former may include immigrants who have not acquired citizenship but the latter exclude them.

Weighting

As we have seen, weighting is a vital part of polling: to guard against the risks of randomness and to compensate for the failure to achieve pure randomness. For example, as U.S. polling pundit Nate Silver puts it:

47

One dirty little secret about polling is that if you randomly call people on the phone, you will not get a truly random sample. Women are more likely to answer the phone than men; older people more than younger people; white people more than Black and Hispanic people. So, you have to weight your poll to population demographics to basically say, 'we know we only got 5 per cent of Black people in a state where they are going to be 12 per cent of turnout, so let's count every Black person two and a half times.'[16]

The better you get at such weighting, the more you can cope with samples that are a long way from being close to random. In fact, pollsters these days place much more emphasis on getting the weighting right than on trying to be random. There are still gold-standard surveys, especially for social research, in which a lot of time and effort goes into getting very close to random. These sorts of surveys, in which names are picked at random and repeated attempts are made to persuade them to complete a survey, are slow, expensive and therefore rare.

Yet if weighting is necessary, weighting is also a sign of failure. The more you have to weight, the more that says your original sample was off. Pollsters will often comment about how they like to see weighting only having a small impact on their results. Some weighting may be inevitable, but heavy weighting suggests a problem with the original sample – and also therefore that it could be wrong in ways that the weighting does not compensate for. It also means you can end up being very dependent on what only a tiny number of people said if their answers are weighted up to be a significant part of the overall figures. Then you have to cross your fingers, hoping that those tiny number were indeed typical of many others.

Good polling weights need three characteristics. First, the weights need to be relevant. That is, they need to capture the differences that may make your sample's political views different from that of the population you want results for. Political views often vary by age, making age an obvious one to use. Age alone, though, is not enough. The exact mix of which ones to use is the polling equivalent of a cook's special sauce recipe. Different recipes can produce very different results, as a neat experiment in 2016 illustrated. The *New York Times* gave the raw data from one of its Florida presidential polls to four different pollsters and asked each of them to convert it into headline voting intention results.[17] The five results – four from the pollsters and the fifth from the paper itself – varied between a one-point Trump lead and a four-point Clinton lead. None of them had a big lead for Trump or Clinton, but there was enough variation to remind us to be cautious about close races and to show the value of understanding weighting.[18]

Even if right at one election, a pollster's special recipe may need to change as politics changes. A set of weightings that perform brilliantly at one election can be undone at the next if the structure of support for parties or candidates changes. What wasn't necessary to weight for in the past can become necessary to include now. U.S. pollsters were caught out this way by education in the 2016 presidential election: previously, having too many better-educated people in their samples had not caused problems, but in 2016, with a new political cleavage along education lines, it did.

It is a continual risk for pollsters that a similar problem happens again. As an illustration of what might go wrong, consider the example of household size for the pollster YouGov, one of the largest and longest-established Internet pollsters. At the time of writing, YouGov does not weight by household size.[19] As a result, a YouGov sample may have too many people in single-person households, and its weighting would not adjust for this. YouGov does this because the risk of being out on household size has not, so far, turned out to be a problem. Yet we also know that household size affects political behaviour, such as turnout.[20] So it is certainly possible that at a future general election, there may be a change in political patterns that makes getting the single- versus multi-person household balance more important than it used to be. Several things would have to go wrong for this to knock the polls at such an election – the changing pattern *and* samples being off *and* other weightings not compensating via another route. But, as we will see, that is how the polls go wrong – when a series of different factors all pile up.

Second, good weights need to use information that it is possible to get. They need to use information that people are willing to hand over and to be honest about. It might seem useful to weight poll results based on people's wealth, especially ahead of an election in which one party is promising a wealth tax and another vociferously opposing it, but will everyone be happy to tell a pollster their wealth? And how many people will actually get right the net total of their debts and assets off the top of their head? Even if your mental arithmetic skills and financial confidence are up to being able to quickly tally up and subtract away totals such as bank account balances and credit card accounts, it also requires knowledge such as the total amount currently outstanding on a mortgage or the total value of a pension pot. That is asking a lot for people to get right, and get right quickly, when put on the spot by a pollster.[21]

Finally, the pollster needs to know the true value of a weight to target with their weighting calculations. Past vote recall is an example of how this can be harder than it seems. Asking people how they voted at the previous election and using that to weight the sample so that it is made up of the right political mix of people may seem a good way to obtain a representative sample. Leaving aside the issues around how in the interval some people will have died or emigrated while others will have reached voting age or acquired voting rights with citizenship, making last time's election figures not quite the perfect template, there is also the problem that people are not very accurate in recalling their previous vote.

Some of this is about a winner bias. People are more likely to say they voted for whoever won. Some of this is about forgetting last-moment voting switches, with a sudden and brief change of mind then being forgotten. Some of it is about a tendency to bring memories into line with current views, as we like to think we are consistent. Some of it is just memories fading.[22] (You may wonder how people could forget as important a choice as for whom to vote. The wonder and the curse of democracy is that you do not have to pass any attention test to vote.)

Whatever the mix of reasons, pollsters have consistently found that even samples that are as perfect as they can otherwise conjure up – and produce accurate pre-election polls – do not have past-vote recall that matches exactly with what the truth should be.[23] There are two responses to this problem. One is to tweak adjustments for past vote recall to deal with the fallibility of such answers. The other is to worry that such adjustments end up requiring so many assumptions and situation-specific calculations that they are too risky. Better instead to take it on the chin and trust to randomness that if one sample ends up with too many supporters of one party, the next will be different, as will the one after that – and so across your polls, you will end up right anyway.

This is one respect in which online polling using panels has an advantage, as they can take a third route: record the answers people give at election time. Then, instead of having to rely on past-vote recall, the pollster can use what people actually said at the time to the pollster. This approach is not without risks. If there was a problem with the sample at the time of that election poll, it then bakes that error into future polls. At least there was the actual election result to compare with to help catch faulty samples. But what if a faulty sample that caused an error one way was hidden by some other error the other way? You may still be baking in permanent error. And you still have to deal with people who did not vote at the last election but are going to do so next time. It is not all straightforward for online pollsters either.

For all pollsters there is another tricky problem with weighting: turnout. Not everyone votes. What is worse, not all who say they are going to vote, vote. People consistently give over-optimistic answers. Fewer people vote than say they will. That may be because events get in the way of good intentions. It may be because people think they should vote and so say they will, even if they do not always live up to their own standards. Or it may be that people do not want to give an answer they fear is socially unacceptable. Whatever the mix of causes, the problem persists even with online surveys, in which the answers are given to a (less judgemental?) computer rather than to a person.

But pollsters need to find a way to factor turnout into their voting figures, as political views often vary with likelihood of voting, and enforced compulsory voting, which makes this problem moot, is rare.[24] If pollsters do nothing to allow for turnout, then the lower the turnout, the greater the potential mismatch between what a pollster finds and reality. That mismatch can then skew the results.

The pattern is usually that the less likely someone is to vote, the more likely they are to be towards the left of the political spectrum. Therefore, the pushes for action to increase turnout in elections usually come disproportionately from politicians and parties on the centre-left or left. (An odd historical exception to this was the introduction of compulsory voting in Australia. There, politicians on the right feared that the organization of those on the left meant lower turnout would benefit the left, not the right. As a result, it was the right who pushed most for its introduction.[25]) However, there are some signs that the traditional turnout patterns may be changing with both Donald Trump and the Republicans in America and Boris Johnson and the Conservatives in Britain. In both cases, non-voters now seem to be more slightly right wing than the country overall. Changing patterns like this are always risky for pollsters as they can break methodologies that used to work.[26]

Hence, pollsters need to adjust their data for turnout – and do it well: 'Put simply, it is essential to do. The question is how you do it,' says pollster Anthony Wells.[27] The difficulty in doing so accurately is shown by a global study looking at pre-election polls over many decades, showing that the lower turnout is, the higher the average error in pre-election polls.[28] Because of this difficulty, pollsters have created many different solutions to adjusting for turnout. They generally involve some form of asking people if they will vote and then some form of adjustment of those raw figures. The methods are one of the more frequent causes of differences in results between pollsters – and differences between what pollsters find and what elections then produce. In particular, because the turnout patterns do *sometimes* change between elections, and can change quickly, turnout adjustments are a brittle part of the pollster methodology. As far back as the 1940 U.S. presidential election, turnout adjustments by George Gallup made his final poll more accurate but Archibald Crossley's turnout adjustments made his final poll less accurate.[29]

The polling industry is split on the best way of tackling this knotty problem. One school of thought is that you should use the past to help predict the future. Pollsters of this school use data from earlier elections and polls to figure out how best to model who is likely to vote this time around. That may sound obviously the right approach: use as much data as possible from the past to help predict the future. But it comes with a risk. What if the future is different from the past?

The alternative is to be driven just by what those polled say here and now about their likelihood of voting.

That is the approach taken most notably by Ann Selzer, often viewed as the gold standard among gold standards for pollsters for her Iowa polling. Although she specializes in polling what is but one small state within the United States, being good at polling in Iowa is a stage for international fame, given the high-profile role of the Iowa caucuses in the U.S. presidential selection contests. As she puts it, her approach is one of polling forward, not polling backward. She simply includes the people if they say they will 'definitely' or 'probably' vote, and discards those who answer otherwise. This means her results can reflect dramatic changes in turnout patterns, as described later when this methodology delivered the goods in 2008 by correctly picking up the large number of first-timers in the Democrat caucus who propelled Barack Obama to victory. Nearly two-thirds of Democrat participants were taking part in their first caucus. As Selzer puts it, 'There is not a likely caucus-goer model on the planet that would predict, based on past caucuses, that more than half of the people would come to their first caucus.'[30]

Yet this is also a risky approach because there is plenty of evidence about the limitations of the accuracy of self-reporting likelihood to vote.[31] This is why some pollsters prefer instead to pull on other information to help improve the methodology. And so on, round in circles, the debate goes, propelled by the generation of both high- and low-quality polling results from either approach.

There is a touch of arguments over food about all this: natural food, with minimal human intervention, sounds great – until it goes off and preservatives start to sound appealing; you suffer a vitamin deficiency and added vitamins seem useful; or you try to feed a child properly and added goodness in cereals starts to matter. Then you see all the added sugar and high fat and start wondering again about the virtues of simple and natural food produce.

The risks of tinkering help to explain why there does not appear to be a clear relationship between experience and quality when it comes to pollsters. New entrants can be among the best performers at an election, and old hands can bomb. One of the best pollsters in the 2010 UK general election, for example, was Indian firm RNB. New to polling in the UK, it had a straightforward methodology – and in this case at least, simplicity and lack of experience came out top. The successful inexperienced political pollsters often come with skills honed on other types of polling and research, such as detailed social science research or large-scale commercial market research. The budgets and timescales for those often allow the development of skills that political polling far less frequently gives space for. Moreover, the problem is that the more experienced you are, the more things you can spot that tempt you to tinker. Tinkering can work, and tinkering can go spectacularly wrong.

All of this means that second-guessing what to think about the particular weighting system used by a particular pollster for a particular election is very hard. There is no simple pattern of what works best.

The Magic of 1,000 Samples

Whatever sampling and weighting methods a poll uses, a typical sample size these days is around 1,000 for a national poll. This is often a reason for the scepticism and confusion about polling. How can just 1,000 people accurately tell us the views of tens of millions of voters in the UK, or hundreds of millions in countries like the USA?[32]

The mathematical magic of sampling is doubly wonderful. Not only can a sample as apparently absurdly small as 1,000 do the business, but what matters in deciding whether the sample is large enough is much more its absolute size (500? 800? 1,000? 1,200?) than the size of the population being sampled. That the USA has an electorate much larger than that of the UK does not require larger poll samples. How can this be?

George Gallup had a simple, powerful analogy. Imagine you have a bowl of soup in front of you. How much of the soup do you need to taste before you are confident what the whole bowl will taste like? Very little. Less than one complete spoonful. Sure, you need to swirl around the soup, especially if it has pieces in it (the soup equivalent of random sampling). But then you can take just a tiny amount of soup and make a confident prediction about the taste of the whole bowl. Adolphe Quetelet, the nineteenth-century inventor of the body mass index (BMI) and the concept of 'the average person', had a more upmarket version of this, although not developed about polling specifically: 'Must I drink the whole bottle in order to judge the quality of the wine?'

Returning to soup, now imagine replacing the soup bowl with a giant vat of soup. Once again, some vigorous swirling may be required. But once again, you will be confident you know what the soup is like from the tiny proportion you eat. Whether it is a bowl or a vat of soup you are testing does not make much difference to how much you need to taste in order to be confident you know what the soup is like. It is the same with medicine. A blood test takes a tiny portion of your blood, yet those few drops are sufficient. Medical staff don't say 'we'll take double the usual amount of blood today so that we can be really sure about the results.'

To understand some of the mathematics that underpin sampling, imagine first a large box of balls, some red and some blue. The box is opaque and sealed, save for a hole at the top through which you can stick your hand to pull out a ball at random. You do not know what the proportions of red and blue balls are in the box. How many times do you need to stick your hand in and take out a ball before you are confident in judging what proportion is red? One ball on its own is clearly not enough. As you draw out more balls, you will become more confident that their mix matches that inside the box. But as with eating the soup, you do not have to draw out every single ball to reach an answer you are pretty confident is right.

Mathematicians have cracked how to put exact numbers on 'pretty confident'. To see how the mathematics works out, imagine your box contains thousands of red and blue balls and you repeatedly pull out a sample of one hundred of them.[33] Each time you do this, you may pull out a slightly different proportion of red balls in your sample. If the box actually contains 40 per cent red balls, then one batch of one hundred balls extracted might have 38 per cent red balls, another might have 41 per cent, one might be on the nose with 40 per cent, one might see a run of bad luck for red and have only 35 per cent red balls, and so on.

Doing the sampling for a political poll is like pulling out a sample of balls once. How large does your sample need to be for you to be pretty confident that the proportion of red balls you pull out and the actual proportion in the box are close to each other? For historical reasons, statisticians have settled on 'pretty confident' meaning 95 per cent sure, and 'close' meaning ±3 per cent.[34] On this basis, they have calculated that for a sample size of 1,000, the margin of error is ±3 per cent. What exactly a 'margin of error' means gets statistical experts tut-tutting at misuses of the phrase as it is often mangled into 'there's a 95 per cent chance this result is within 3 per cent of the truth.' What it actually means is 'if I repeatedly take samples of 1,000, and each time calculate the proportion of red balls in them, then the true proportion in the box will lie within 3 per cent of my calculated value nineteen times out of twenty.' But the mangled version, while wrong, gives you the right rough idea.[35]

To return to politics, replace balls with people and colours with parties. Carrying out a poll is like pulling balls out of the box. Voting intention figures from a poll are like the proportion of balls that are of a particular colour. So with a 1,000-sample opinion poll, if it puts the Pirate Party on 40 per cent, then the margin of error is ±3 per cent. In other words, if you did twenty different polls and got the Pirate Party on 40 per cent, then expect that for nineteen of them, the true Pirate Party support in the electorate as a whole would have been in the 37–43 per cent range.

The exact calculations of these margins of error can be carried out using a relatively simple formula. If we are seeking a margin of error of ±m per cent, which will include the correct level of support for a political party in 95 per cent of our polls, then the formula for calculating this margin is given by

$$m = 1.96 \times \frac{\sqrt{(p(1-p))}}{\sqrt{n}} \times 100 \text{ per cent}$$

In this formula, p is the percentage support for the political party expressed as a decimal, and n is the sample size. For instance, when the Pirate Party has 40 per cent support, we use $p = 0.4$. The value of 1.96 is derived from some rather complex mathematics relating to what is known as 'the normal distribution'. If we were looking at a 90 per cent confidence level, it would change to 1.64, and if we sought 99 per cent confidence, it would become 2.58.

The table here shows the results of this formula for various common combinations of support level and sample size. Note that

		Percentage support							
		20	30	40	50	60	70	80	
Sample size	100	7.8	9.0	9.6	9.8	9.6	9.0	7.8	**Margin of error**
	500	3.5	4.0	4.3	4.4	4.3	4.0	3.5	
	1,000	2.5	2.8	3.0	3.1	3.0	2.8	2.5	
	3,000	1.4	1.6	1.8	1.8	1.8	1.6	1.4	
	10,000	0.8	0.9	1.0	1.0	1.0	0.9	0.8	

once you exceed a sample size of about 1,000, there are limited gains in taking larger samples: treble the sample size to 3,000, and the margin of error only falls from 3 per cent to 2 per cent – a very modest gain for tripling one's sampling costs.

For a convenient rule of thumb, it is useful to know that the expression $\sqrt{(p(1-p))}$ in the above formula is, in fact, pretty close to 0.5 when the level of support for a political party is in the range of about 20 per cent to 80 per cent. So the formula can usefully be approximated by

$$m = {}^{1}\!/\!\sqrt{n} \times 100 \text{ per cent}$$

That may look a daunting 'simplification' but means that the margin of error simplifies to roughly one over the square root of the sample size. For example, given a poll with a sample of 1,000, you can break out your calculator to input 1,000, then take the square root of it, then do one over that sum (usually with the '1/x' button and then multiply by 100). That tells you that the margin of error is, roughly, ±3 per cent. (As an aside, doing these figures for a sample size of one hundred gives an error range of roughly 10 per cent. This is a figure that I always find impressively low. People – including those who understand that 1,000 is a large enough sample for standard polls – will normally recoil from the idea that a mere one hundred people could be enough. Yet if you poll one hundred people and find that 73 per cent of them think full stops should be followed by one space rather than two, that is still a pretty clear verdict, even taking into account that large error band around it.)

Looking back at the values in the table, note also that the margin of error varies a little depending on the level of support. With the Pirate Party on 40 per cent support, the margin of error is ±3 per cent. But if the Pirate Party had been on only 15 per cent, then doing the same calculations as above, with 15 per cent in place of 40 per cent, gets you a margin of error of ±2 per cent. To help understand why this is the case, consider the extreme situation with no blue balls in the box. Then you would always end up with 0 per cent blue in your sample, and this would always be right. If there are just 2 per cent blue balls, then the closeness of 2 per cent to zero means the balls you draw can never be that far out on the low side. You cannot pull out less than 0 per cent blue. You can go wrong on the high side, true, but overall, you can see that the error range is reduced. Likewise, if the truth is 98 per cent, you cannot go out that far wrong on the high side.

Again, the impact on the true error range is not massive, so the above rule of thumb still works. But it is relevant to bear in mind for political polls in which there are some answers down in single digits. In particular, it helps explain why, in voting intention questions, the smaller parties may move around less than the large parties: random error hits them less.

These margin-of-error calculations are all based on the assumption that the poll involves random sampling, and, as we have seen, that is not how polls actually work. It might therefore seem sensible to abandon them for some other sort of calculation based on how they really work. But such calculations would be very hard, at best, and possibly impossible. As one guide for journalists explains,

> [Imagine] an equally divided country. Suppose everyone who holds view A lives in the northern half of the country, while everyone who holds view B lives in the southern half. In that case, if pollsters ensure that half of each survey is conducted in the north, and half the south, then their polls should be exactly accurate. Structuring polls in this kind of way is called 'stratification'. Properly done, stratification can help to increase a poll's accuracy. Now make a different assumption about our mythical, equally divided country. Suppose people who hold

view A are far more likely to express that view to strangers –
such as survey researchers – than people who hold view B.
Unless the polling company is aware of this bias, and knows
how significant it is, it could well produce results showing that
view A is far more popular than view B. This is an example of
a systematic error. To measure the 'true' margin of error, we
would need to take account of random sampling error, and
the effects of stratification, and possible systematic errors. The
trouble is that it is hard, and arguably impossible, to be sure of
the true impact of stratification and systematic errors.[36]

But all is not lost, as the simple margin-of-error calculations do have
value. For one thing, they are a rough-and-ready, useful reminder not
to become excited about small movements in the polls that are within
the 'margin of error'. Such movements may well be noise rather than
signifying any change in reality. Margin-of-error figures remind you
to 'train your brain to see polls as fuzzy estimates, not the word of
God', as G. Elliott Morris of *The Economist* puts it.[37]

The value of margin-of-error calculations, despite their theoretical shakiness, also goes further than this, as another way of looking
at errors shows. Rather than using statistical theory, we can look at
the final pre-election polls and compare them with the actual election
results. That gives us a measure of the true margin of error around
polls – a comprehensive one that takes into account all the ways in
which the polls may go wrong, and not just sampling error.

This is what the British Polling Council (the industry self-
regulation body) did in 2018, coming up with a new margin-of-error
statement:

All polls are subject to a wide range of potential sources of
error. Based on the historical record of the polls at recent

general elections, there is a 9 in 10 chance that the true value of a party's support lies within 4 points of the estimates provided by this poll, and a 2 in 3 chance that it lies within 2 points.[38]

This is not that different from those simple margin-of-error calculations. Globally, the picture is similar to the UK one, with polls in the last few days before an election averaging an error of plus or minus 2.5 per cent.[39] Hence the continuing use of margin-of-error (mis)-calculations when discussing polls. The calculations may be off, but the conclusions drawn from them are not.[40]

Before we move on to how the people in samples are contacted, it is worth noting that the two key concepts we have discussed – about sample sizes and about random variation generating margins of error – are also widely applicable to understanding elements of life devoid of any polling. As an example, one of the teaching incidents that has stuck in my mind from school was my first introduction to the idea of statistical significance. The maths teacher showed us a sports report from *The Times*, discussing changes in rugby union's rules designed to encourage more tries. The report pointed out how more tries had been scored so far that year than in the comparable period the year before, concluding that the changes had worked. Did this make sense, our teacher asked the class? It certainly seemed to, although it was a bit puzzling why such a simple piece of mathematics as adding up the number of tries in two different years and comparing the totals was something to cover in that class. We'd learnt how to do such sums years ago.

Then with the magic of statistical rigour, our teacher showed us how we were all wrong. Just as tossing a coin ten times and getting four heads followed by doing it another ten times and getting six heads does not mean the coin has changed in the interim, so a difference in the number of tries between two sets of matches does not necessarily mean something has changed. Crunching through the numbers, our teacher showed us how the change in the number of tries was not statistically significant, and hence no conclusion about the rule change working could be justified. As with opinion polls, so more generally in life – a variation in the answers you obtain may just be noise, random fluctuations signifying nothing other than that the universe does not merely repeat itself time and time again.

Those two insights: about sample size (no, bigger isn't always better) and that changes between results may still be statistically insignificant, can be applied to numerous other aspects of study and life more generally. If you are, say, looking at qualitative evidence such as diaries of soldiers in the First World War, then you are sampling a selection of data – some diaries out of all the many that were written – and a skewed selection at that, since those are the diaries that survived and have been made available. Knowing how to draw safe conclusions from what you read therefore requires, knowingly or not, an understanding of sampling and statistical significance. Which is why the sub-genre of professors of other disciplines failing to show such understanding when venturing into tweets about political opinion polls and Twitter polls is so depressing. They are not only getting badly wrong something outside their own area of expertise – a failing we are all prone to – but they are getting wrong a fundamental tool of understanding that is applicable across most areas of study.[41]

Survey Mode

There are four basic ways to conduct opinion polls: face-to-face, by post or on the phone and online. Which one is used for a poll is called the 'survey mode'.

Face-to-face came first. Then as postal services spread, their convenience made postal surveys popular. Posting out surveys in batches is easier than having trained interviewers go and speak to people one by one. Moreover, you can target precisely who are sent the surveys.

But postal surveys can be slow – not only do you have to allow for the time for the post out and back, you also have to allow for the time the survey may loiter on people's mantelpieces. Then, as surveys do come back, there is the extra time to process the forms.

The use of phones for polling probably started in Chicago in 1923, to help source extra data from the wealthier parts of the city that were otherwise being under-sampled.[42] Phoning was speedier than face-to-face or the post, with the extra advantage over face-to-face that it did not matter how far apart the people you were phoning were. It took no longer to dial the next person whether they were in the same city or on the other side of the country, in an easy-to-reach location or in the remotest rural corner.

Phoning could attempt a version of randomness too, initially by picking names at random from the phone book. This method rose in usefulness as more people got phones and so phone books became more comprehensive. An alternative was generating phone numbers to call at random, using the known format of valid numbers (RDD, or random digit dialling).[43] This type of polling is random at least as far as people with phones go – and as long as you can match the range of phone numbers to the geographic area the poll is meant to cover. This is usually easier for national surveys than for more focused ones, such as those for states or constituencies, where telephone numbers may not clearly indicate whether or not the person at the end of them is in the right geographic area. Traditionally, phone numbers have indicated the phone's physical location, with the first part of the number varying depending on what part of the country the phone is located in. However, this link between the number and its location has broken down not only with the rise of mobile phone numbers but with the spread of phone number portability. In 2016, one in ten

U.S. adults, for example, had a mobile phone number from a different state from the one in which they were then living.[44]

To make matters harder, some people are more likely to answer the phone and then answer questions than others. In the UK, that often meant samples were skewed towards Labour supporters. As a result, early telephone polling – such as that carried out by Audience Selection Limited (ASL) in the 1980s in the UK – was controversial and often inaccurate. ASL was the first UK market research company totally dedicated to using the telephone for polling and it was the pollster for the SDP, then in electoral alliance with the Liberal Party. Its public polling figures ahead of the 1983 general election being more favourable to that alliance than those from other pollsters added to the controversy.[45]

There was a lot for the phone pollsters to learn along the way about the more subtle ways in which things could go wrong. The time of day and day of the week of calls matter, with polling agency Survation finding that in the 2016 European referendum, 'the later in the evening we spoke with people, the more Remainer the responses.' To give another example, New Zealand polls conducted only on weekdays have put support for right-leaning parties around five percentage points higher than those that poll on both weekdays and weekends[46] – though the 1992 UK polling post-mortem did not find a discernible difference between weekday and weekend voting.[47]

Timing factors can influence non-phone polls too, and the possible impacts of weekends and public holidays are why political polling tends to dry up around major festivals such as Christmas. It is also why polls during the rest of the year rarely do their fieldwork in just the one day. Rather, they usually gather their sample over several days, as crashing everything into the shortest time possible raises the risks of it being skewed.[48]

Even the phone numbers that the calls are made from can influence the sample's balance. Survation found that polling about the

2014 Scottish independence referendum received a larger number of pro-independence answers if the phone numbers the pollsters were calling from were Scottish, and more anti-independence answers if the phone numbers were English.[49]

As pollsters got better at understanding how to weight and adjust their answers to overcome these problems, another challenge came along: the decline of landline phones and the rise of mobiles. Telephone polling generally coped well with this, partly because mobile phone and landline phone users often turned out to be less different than feared, at least in the early stages of the switch, and partly because pollsters started calling mobiles too.

As a result, telephone polling moved on from those controversial early days to being seen as a highly reputable form of polling – with one important exception. Technological developments brought another form of phone polling: automated calling, using voice identification software rather than human interviewers. These are sometimes called IVR polls, for interactive voice-recording. Pre-recorded or computer-generated voices read out the questions, pause to record the answers, and the only human is the one responding.[50] Such automated systems are much cheaper than telephone surveys done by humans, and cheaper still than face-to-face. However, this cost-effectiveness has come with controversy and, outside the phalanx of those marketing such services, a general view that they are of lower reliability – at least for political polling.[51]

However, another type of technology has earned its place at the forefront of political polling, starting with similar controversy before building up a track record that has overcome the reservations. It is online, or Internet, polling. It has followed a similar arc to that of phone polling, with the spread of Internet usage making the technique increasingly accepted as a way of reaching a representative sample of people. But Internet access has still not reached the near-universal coverage phones did. Moreover, with phone polling, the pollsters can 'force' themselves on people by randomly calling them. With Internet polling, people have to be willing to come to an online survey form. The self-selecting nature of Internet polling exacerbates concerns about how representative its samples really are.

Some high-quality social science surveys avoid these problems by selecting their samples first and then providing Internet access to those in their sample who are not online.[52] This is too expensive and cumbersome for regular political polling. Instead, Internet polling firms have built up large panels of people who have agreed to participate in surveys. For each survey, the polling firm selects a group of panellists and contacts them (usually via email), inviting them to participate.

Having such a panel to pick from protects the polling company from the perils of running a simple open-access survey, such as by putting up questions on a publicly accessible website. That would mean anyone can fill the survey in, with the risk that an organized campaign, an army of bots or one group of particularly motivated people, could swamp the result. Such 'voodoo polls', a phrase coined by the veteran pollster Robert Worcester, should be treated with an extremely high degree of caution.[53] Proper online pollsters do not make their surveys open to anyone.[54] Rather, they pick whom to invite from their panel to take part. It is a controlled group, with only those who receive the invite able to take part.

This is still predominantly a self-selecting group – those willing to sign up to be asked to do surveys. It is also a group that may suffer from the panel effects mentioned earlier, so that repeatedly asking questions ends up altering the answers received. However, if you compile a large enough panel to avoid having to ask specific individuals questions on the same topic too frequently, if political polling is only a small part of the overall use of the panel, and if you ask demographic, behavioural and attitudinal questions to check how different your panel is from the population overall (and weight your panel as a result if necessary), then you can obtain good-quality results.

Not only can Internet polling be cheaper than other forms of polling, but as with postal surveying the impersonal nature of online form filling may result in greater honesty than when being asked questions by a person directly or on the phone. How comfortable people feel about giving honest answers is an especial problem for researchers on contentious or sensitive topics, such as sexuality. For politics, this is a much rarer problem, although it helps to explain why exit polls can involve ballot boxes, with those sampled asked to place their answers safely in the box. People may not know for sure that the researcher will not open the box and fish out their papers once their backs are turned, but the theatre of confidentiality and the practical implications of a steady flow of people taking part in the exit poll can give reassurance that encourages honesty.[55]

Aside from the honesty factor, maintaining an Internet survey's quality is much easier than if human interviewers are being used. The pioneering psephologist David Butler was briefly one for Gallup in the 1940s, confessing that, 'The temptation to cheat, to invent the answers or to prompt the respondent is very great, especially when the ballot is long and tedious.'[56] (I was also by no means perfect when I was one.) Whether for phone or in-person polling, these jobs tend to be low-paid and repetitive, dating all the way back to when George Gallup used an illegal sliding scale to try to keep pay down in defiance of federal regulations.[57] Maintaining the quality of interviewers' work is vital. Online surveys sidestep all that, although they open up another problem – bogus responses from people in it for the money. Panels usually pay people a small sum for doing a survey, so there is a risk of incentivizing high-speed junk answers as people seek to earn their money quickly. (Not paying would be worse as people willing to repeatedly give up their time to give their views for free would be even more atypical.) High-quality panels protect against this through measures such as timing responses, looking for obvious patterns (does someone click the first option for every question?) and checking the consistency of answers with previous data about the person. Taking care over such issues is essential because, as a Pew Research Center study found,

> Online polls conducted with widely used opt-in sources contain small but measurable shares of bogus respondents (about 4 per cent to 7 per cent, depending on the source). Critically, these bogus respondents are not just answering at random, but rather they tend to select positive answer choices – introducing a small, systematic bias into estimates like presidential approval . . .
>
> The study also finds that two of the most common checks to detect low-quality online interviews – looking for respondents who answer too fast or fail an attention check (or 'trap') question – are not very effective.[58]

However, the report found that the impact of the bias towards positive answers was small, inflating the results by only 2 or 3 percentage points. An approval score for a policy or politician being, say, 64 per cent in reality but coming out in a poll as 67 per cent is a small error, albeit one that can be psychologically important if the error tips a number from just under 50 per cent to just over 50 per cent or from just above a rival to just below.

Further reassurance comes from the report's comment that

> This study speaks to online polls where the pollster performs little to no data quality checking of their own. To the extent

that public pollsters routinely use sophisticated data quality checks – beyond the speeding and trap questions addressed in this report – the results from this study may be overly pessimistic.

Moreover, online pollsters can – in theory at least – deal better with some of the challenges faced by pollsters using other modes. Over time, online pollsters build up information about the people in their panel, while phone and face-to-face pollsters generally have no previous data about the people they ask. This means online pollsters can not only do more detailed analysis linking together results from different surveys, but they can check whether people's responsiveness is changing and whether they are giving internally consistent answers over time. It is also easier to add precautions, such as tracking how quickly people responded to the survey invitation to help compensate for sudden surges in enthusiasm by supporters of one side – if the Internet panel is carefully run, that is.

Judging from the outside whether an online poll uses a high-quality panel, and uses it well, is challenging. As the Pew report quoted above highlighted, very little information is provided about the quality checks used for polling panels. Even countries such as Britain, where industry standards set an impressive level of transparency, leave outsiders in the dark over quality.

Knowing the basics, such as whether a polling firm is using its own panel or is buying access to the panels run by others, or how members of the panel are recruited, does not get to the heart of the panel's quality. Rather, knowing those factors is like knowing whether a sports team has got a coach, does regular training sessions and has a nutritionist on staff. These factors are only a weak clue as to whether the team is any good or not. You have to dig into the details of how a panel operates to understand its quality and the skill with which it is used. Such details include what mix of questions panellists are asked over time – ask too many questions on one topic, and you will end up with a panel biased towards people interested in it. Exactly how varied the panel's members are is another detail affecting a panel's quality: a sizeable-looking panel may suffer from not having very many people when you venture into critical subgroups, such as young men living in a particular part of the country who are not active followers of the news. What sort of protections are in place to guard against the problems Pew considered is yet another consideration.

'The quality of a panel is almost wholly opaque and, even with more information, almost impossible to judge,' explains Anthony Wells from YouGov.[59] Even if you are a potential commercial client with a large budget asking online polling firms to show you the quality of their panels, only limited information is provided by pollsters about panel quality beyond fairly vague, unverified claims.

The only real test, therefore, is the track record of online pollsters. The record of good Internet pollsters and their final pre-election polls, compared with actual election results, has been such that this is now considered as good as any method of political polling. (Online pollsters were accepted as being among the best in the UK earlier than in the USA, but after the 2020 U.S. election, the influential American polling site FiveThirtyEight acknowledged that online polls could now be among the very best.[60]) Because of the black-box nature of panel quality, though, judge any new entrants warily until they have an election track record.

A final attraction of online polling (and, to a lesser extent, of telephone polling) is speed. This is particularly beneficial when there has been a dramatic event. Internet polling can turn around results within hours and provide hard data that pushes the media towards coverage that runs counter to its usual editorial lines. The first televised debates between party leaders in the British general election in

2010 demonstrated that Nick Clegg, leader of the Liberal Democrats, gave a stunning performance in the first TV debate – so stunning that the following media coverage would have been favourable regardless of polling. But what turned it from favourable into a spurt of wall-to-wall enthusiasm for Clegg, including from newspapers with usually strongly anti-Liberal Democrat editorial lines, was the speed with which online polls appeared after the first debate. YouGov was first to publish figures, a mere eight minutes after the close of the debate. Telephone polls and a text message poll followed, all telling a similar story, and all before the media could otherwise settle on its own line.[61] The rapid appearance of the facts boxed in the media's ability to transmit news through its preferred editorial prisms. This was a win for polling and for the public.

Internet polling has also become increasingly attractive as the downsides of phone polling have increased. The rise of the first answering machines and then caller ID systems, combined with a declining willingness of people to undertake lengthy phone surveys, means that the number of phone calls that have to be tried before you are able to complete a single survey has grown significantly.[62] With a much lower response rate, the pseudo-randomness of phone polling has become even more pseudo, increasing the risk that those who can be reached on the phone and are willing to do a survey are not typical of everyone else.[63]

Most recently, a new form of online polling has been developed, one which can benefit from the principal remaining advantage of phone and face-to-face polling, that being the ability to obtain a representative sample from a small geographic area. Pioneered in the UK by pollster Matt Singh, it is 'river sampling'. This involves placing a survey online in various places to catch people's attention, such as on websites or in apps. These locations can be geographically targeted, through a mix of the places used (for example, a local café website) and through geo-targeting that looks at the location from which someone is accessing the Internet before deciding whether or not to show them the survey.

There is no prior recruitment to an online panel involved, but unlike voodoo polling, the pollster remains in control of who sees the survey. In addition, polling questions are put in front of people in places away from where those most interested in politics spend their time online, and so (hopefully) reach a more diverse sample than one made up of people willing to sign up for a panel in which they are regularly asked about politics.[64]

As Singh himself says,

> It has various advantages even in national polling, because it allows us to reach the sorts of people who, for whatever reason, wouldn't join a panel to take surveys regularly.
>
> But it also allows us to poll locally, including for the [2019] Brecon by-election. This has not been done online before in the UK, because no panel is large enough to have sufficient membership in local areas.
>
> The sampling is typically done through smartphone apps, but can also be applied to other parts of the Internet in order to interview desktop users. Compared with using panels, it requires additional statistical and technological safeguards to catch duplicates and other sample quality issues – indeed several respondents had to be removed in Brecon and Radnorshire for this reason.[65]

In practice, Singh's polls use a mixture of people from panels and river sampling to meld the benefits of both approaches.

With all of these options, is there a best mode for political polls? No. They all have their strengths and weaknesses.[66] Increasingly pollsters mix the methods they use, varying them depending on the needs of the particular poll being done and sometimes running multi-mode polls.

Online surveys require remedial work to make their samples, they hope, representative. Changing circumstances, or taking the eye off the ball on the panel's quality, can break methodologies that used to work well. Telephone surveys with live callers were the suspicious newfangled thing in the past and are still susceptible to that fundamental problem that made them controversial in their early days. Calling a random selection of phone numbers does not end up giving you a truly random sample of the electorate. Postal surveys are slow (and expensive), and very vulnerable to respondents' unwillingness to complete the paperwork. As for door-to-door surveys, they are often called the current gold standard. And yet, as anyone who has done doorstep canvassing for a political party or doorstep sales for someone else will know, who you find at home when you go door knocking has all sorts of biases too.

What makes door-to-door surveys a de facto gold standard is not so much the quality of the method itself, as the fact that pretty much the only people to use them these days are organizations with, by polling standards, huge budgets and a massive focus on the quality of their research. Comparing a face-to-face survey (as long as it is door-to-door and not, say, people stopped in the high street) with a phone or online poll is, in effect, comparing a high-budget poll with a cheap poll. An unfair comparison, perhaps, but one that does mean face-to-face is the best sort of political polling there is.

How Voting Intention Polls Work

Although the details vary between pollsters, there is a basic sequence in which polls go about extracting voting intention answers from participants. It is something like this, based – until close to an actual polling day – on the premise 'if there were an election tomorrow':

1. Find out how likely people are to vote;
2. Ask people whom they are going to vote for;
3. Push the 'undecideds', 'not sures' and similar to give an answer (this is sometimes called the 'squeeze' – that is, pushing people to make a choice),[67] and/or find out how they have voted before;[68]
4. Ask other political questions, such as assessments of party leaders or views on policy proposals;[69] and
5. Ask other questions to help with the weighting (demographic information, level of education and so on).

For the 'headline voting intention' figures, it is common practice in countries such as Britain to exclude from the published calculations of vote share percentages any remaining, recalcitrant, definite 'don't knows'. That is why the voting figures add up to 100 per cent. But in other countries, such as in the United States, it is common for 'don't knows' not to be excluded from headline voting figures.

Whether included in the headlines or not, the number of 'don't knows' can be worth keeping an eye on, especially if it is significantly different from the number in the run-up to a previous election. 'Don't knows' are also worth paying attention to when looking at results split by gender, since men generally are less likely to give a 'don't know' answer in political polling than women. An apparently greater level of support among men for an option can be a misleading impression caused by men simply being less likely to say 'don't' know' in general.

Otherwise, do not get too excited about there being 'don't knows' whom pollsters have squeezed and then excluded from voting-intention totals. They do that because it produces more accurate polling overall – and reflects the absence of a 'don't know' option on ballot papers. Reality in the form of ballot papers forces a squeeze on people. Polls are just replicating this.[70]

Six Ways the Polls Can Go Wrong

There are some clues in the above about how political polls can go wrong, even for good pollsters making diligent and well-informed efforts to get sampling, question wording, survey design and analysis right. One is timing. People's views can change after a poll has been conducted. Usually, that is not a problem in itself for a poll. That changes if the poll is taken as a prediction – such as a poll just before an election or referendum is held. In those cases, ending the sampling too soon can miss last-minute changes in opinion.

A second way in which political polls can go wrong is the random chance of a particular poll having a sample that is very far from being representative. Just as if you toss a coin ten times, you might have the good or bad luck to get ten heads in a row, a pollster may end up with a set of participants for a particular poll who by chance throw up answers that are well off what you would usually expect. Even with weighting, bad luck can give a pollster a result that is off. These are often called 'rogue polls'. Hence, as Will Jennings, professor of political science and public policy, puts it: 'You need to be both a good and a lucky pollster.'[71]

In practice, rogue polls are much rarer than they would be in a world of true random sampling. This is a double-edged sword, for it is both reassuring that polling techniques end up with a reduced risk of a rogue poll, and also a reminder of just how much rests on all the calculations that pollsters do and how far political polls are from being random.

Rogue polls do still happen, and that can provide a convenient excuse when a poll appears whose results someone does not like.[72] This is why when a poll appears suggesting an unexpected or dramatic change, wise polling experts sensibly but boringly respond by telling people to wait for the next one. As Twyman's law puts it, 'any figure that looks interesting or different is usually wrong.'[73]

The third way that polls can go wrong is that the sampling can be flawed in some other – systematic, not random – way. As discussed above, pollsters use weighting to address this. They have the chance at election time to confirm whether their weightings are working properly and, if there is a gap between polling and reality, to adjust their weighting. But something may then change in politics and society to knock their polls off before the next election. Taking a trivial example, pollsters do not weight their polls to ensure they have the correct proportions of bald and non-bald men in them. That has not been a problem for political polling so far. Yet if, say, a new political party, the Bald and Proud Party, were to be founded, that non-problem could become a problem. Changes in society, alternations in the party system or new cleavages in political debate all risk throwing up new sampling challenges that might catch out pollsters, such as the household size issue discussed earlier in the context of YouGov's methodology. In practice, changing contexts is the most significant problem for pollsters: 'context is really important, as every election is different – and that can throw off the polls,' explains Will Jennings.[74]

A fourth way that polls can go wrong is non-response bias. This is a subset of sampling problems but important enough to deserve its own consideration. Supporters of different parties or candidates may have different levels of willingness to take part in polls. Pollsters can usually catch this by seeing how their final pre-election polls performed, and then know in future to take the problem into account. But suppose there is a new party, a new candidate or just a change in circumstances that produces a variation from past willingness to participate in polls (an incumbent regularly trumpeting his disdain for polls and putting his supporters off taking part in them, perhaps). That can knock the polls off. In addition, the changing willingness of supporters to take part in a poll depending on whether or not their side is doing well can cause 'phantom swings' in polling results that exaggerate the actual ups and downs in support. A genuine increase in support for one side is then exaggerated by that side's supporters being more willing to take part in polls as people become excited, and a genuine fall then gets exaggerated too by a declining willingness to take part in polls as people become demotivated. There is some evidence that such exaggerated swings occurred during the 2012 U.S. presidential election.[75]

A variant is that rather than people's willingness to take part in polls being altered, instead people on one side become more likely to answer 'don't know' or refuse to answer a voting intention question in a poll. Such 'shy Conservatives' became a major issue in British polling in the 1990s, as discussed later.

Internet panels should be able to deal well with non-response, as they have the data from previous surveys to use as a benchmark and so are able to spot changes in response rates. I say *should*. People willing to be polled again and again over a long period of time – the sort of data that will protect against non-response bias – are also likely to be atypical of voters in general due to their very tolerance for being surveyed regularly. Changes in non-response bias may be trackable among them, but the very fact that it is trackable among them also means their behaviour may diverge from that of other voters. In the whack-a-mole world of polling methodology, being able to address one risk opens up another.

A fifth way that political polls can go wrong, especially for findings other than vote share, is by getting the question wording wrong. Wrong wording can produce a technically accurate poll that still misleads. There are so many issues over question wording that the next chapter is devoted to them. But for core concepts such as voting intention, issue importance or leader ratings, question wordings have become well established and very rarely cause problems.

Finally, polls can – arguably – go wrong by getting the winner wrong, despite the vote share figures in the final pre-election polls being respectably close to the results. Pollsters and polling pundits are divided on whether picking the winner is the best criterion against which to judge pollsters or whether it is closeness in vote share figures that matters most. If a poll puts the election at 51 per cent for the York Party and 49 per cent for the Lancaster Party, and the final result is 49 per cent York to 51 per cent Lancaster, is that a good result? Both vote shares are only 2 per cent off the result. Or is it a bad result, since Lancaster won, not York?

As an added twist, the way that voting systems sometimes give the party which gets fewer votes the most seats, and therefore victory, can make polls appear to fail (or succeed) when they didn't really. The politician celebrating on election night as the victor may have got fewer votes, and so perhaps polls that showed her behind were right rather than wrong.

The theoretical argument that polls are measuring vote share and that's what you should judge them on is a strong one. However, how interesting really are the vote shares? What we really want to know is who is going to win. Indeed, even those who argue that getting the winner right is not the job of polls are frequently willing to use examples of getting the winner right to defend the accuracy of polling.

Getting the winner consistently wrong would eat away at confidence in polling. As Australian polling expert Murray Goot puts it, 'The job of the election polls is to predict election winners. If they don't, they're in trouble.'[76]

One Way Polls Don't Go Wrong: Herding

On the evening of 3 January 2008, a car pulled into a crammed school car park. Snow surrounded the school. The pavements were full of people – about a thousand – forced to park further away but slipping and sliding on the ice, determined to make it to the school. In the car sat a curious pollster.

It was the night of the Iowa presidential caucus. The pollster, Ann Selzer, had published a poll on New Year's Eve pointing to a significant win for Barack Obama in the Democrat contest. Other pollsters disagreed. The rival Hillary Clinton and John Edwards campaigns most certainly did not agree. A friend, working on the Clinton campaign, rang her up to say, 'I've always trusted your polls – until now.'[77]

Selzer's poll showed a massive surge in turnout from people who had not taken part in a caucus before, propelling Obama into a clear lead. She had spent a chunk of New Year's Day on PBS, getting grilled closely over her findings, the camera zooming in on her face in the way that it usually does when someone is under pressure and facing accusations. Could she really be right and so many others wrong?

Ann Selzer was not new to polling. She had, in fact, been a precocious pollster as young as five, going door to door to survey mothers on whether her family's nickname for her was unflattering.[78] Then, twenty years before that car park visit, she had made her mark as someone special when, working at the *Des Moines Register*, she spotted a problem with a poll from their in-house polling unit on the then-Republican presidential caucus:

They had put in place a technique of trying to save some money by recontacting people from previous polls. And I said, well, let's take a look. We have fresh numbers here, we have recontacts here. We were publishing that George [H. W.] Bush was going to win the Republican caucuses, and I went to the editors and I said, 'I don't think that's true. I think Bob Dole is going to win.' They said, 'What?' So I showed them the data, and they said, 'What would this take to fix?' I said, 'Money.' They said, 'OK.' So I very early had a chance to prove my credibility, because Bob Dole did win the caucuses.[79]

Yet her record was not perfect. In the 2004 presidential election, she had Democratic nominee John Kerry winning the state over incumbent Republican George W. Bush by 3 per cent. The latter won (just, by under 1 per cent). Not a huge vote share error, but the headline was wrong.[80] Moreover, her poll had, along with SurveyUSA, stood out from the crowd in putting Kerry ahead. The other pollsters had it right.

So what was going to happen in 2008? Would being different from the pack of pollsters again be a prelude to error? One way to tell ahead of the official results was to do what Ann Selzer did: head off to a voting location and see if the surge in turnout that her poll predicted, and relied upon for its iconoclastic finding, was happening.

Every person struggling through the winter weather past her into the school was a physical manifestation that she was right. Every extra voter who made it inside the school to play their role in Iowa's contribution to democracy was a sign that the other pollsters were wrong.

'It just honestly – it kind of made my heart melt a little bit because here's democracy, here they come,' she recounted.[81] It was not just democracy. It was the reinforcement of her reputation as one of the very best pollsters.[82] Normally, pollsters or polling firms who receive the accolades for having different results from the crowd and being vindicated by being right have a limited shelf life. Another few elections come along at which they perform, if not poorly, at least no better than their peers, and they no longer seem that special. Ann Selzer has, however, had an unusually long period of having her name graced with gold-standard praise. In 2014 her final Senate poll in the state stood out from the crowd and was right. In 2016 her final Iowa poll for the presidential election had Trump doing better than other pollsters predicted, and she was proved right. Then again in 2020, she repeated the trick.

Yet even for someone as hardened to being the outlier as she was, and as comforted by a record of success as she can be, it is not straightforward being the pollster saying something different from the crowd:

> I call it spending my time in the pot-shot corral . . . Everybody saying this is terrible, she is awful, this is going to be the end of her . . . When we see the data, we know that's going to be the reaction. But it's a few days. A few days of discomfort, and the little talk I have with myself is, 'look, we'll see what happens. I'll either be golden or a goat. Hopefully golden but if I'm a goat, OK I think I can survive it and move forward in some way, lessons learnt'. But it is uncomfortable.[83]

That discomfort is why pollsters may, consciously or otherwise, herd; that is, adjust their figures to put them in line with what everyone else is saying. This can happen because a pollster worries about sticking out from the crowd – better to be wrong in a crowd than risk being wrong on your own. Also, pollsters whose results are out on a limb may be more likely to question whether their methodology is right. There is a very fine line between people seeing that their results are different from others and thinking it wise to double-check they are not wrong, and deciding to find fault in their own figures just because they are different.

These are very human reactions and are why pollster Damian Lyons Lowe says, 'Herding is all about humans and how humans react.'[84] As well as human frailty, there is a potential benign cause of herding – as actual voting nears and voters make up their minds, the differences in how pollsters treat people who say they aren't sure or don't know should matter less. For example, this seems to have been a factor in the variation between pollsters in the ratings for the Liberal Democrats in the 2010–15 parliament. Soon after the 2010 election, a large section of Liberal Democrat voters switched to forms of 'don't know'. How the pollsters treated such people in their calculations, therefore, caused variety in their headline figures, a variety that faded away as time moved on and people's minds firmed up.

Yet for all the possible causes of herding, substantial evidence for the existence of herding as a source of polling error is scarce. Post-mortems after elections often consider herding, yet when they find that it may have occurred, they tend not to highlight it as a significant source of error.[85] That is because herding, when it happens, pulls the polls towards the consensus. If the consensus is right, that makes the polls look better. But if the consensus is wrong – well, it was still the consensus, and good polling advice, repeated in this book, is that one should beware of rogue outliers, the individual poll telling a very different story, and instead pay attention to the pattern across multiple polls. So even without herding, people's attention should mainly have been on the consensus anyway, deprecating those outlying polls.

Herding, therefore, can make polling failures look more spectacular by making more polls wrong, and it can encourage overconfidence in the polls ('look how similar the numbers are from all these different pollsters!'). But it is not a fundamental problem when polls go wrong.

What Should Be Measured?

Let's finish this chapter with an unresolved philosophical question about political polling: quite what is it trying to measure?

A simple answer is that political opinion polls try to reveal the truth of what public opinion is on political choices at the time the poll was conducted. In line with this, political pollsters often like to speak about polls being snapshots and not predictions. To quote Conservative Party politician and pollster Lord Michael Ashcroft, 'A poll is a snapshot not a prediction. A poll is a snapshot not a prediction. A poll is a snapshot not a prediction. A poll is a snapshot . . .'[86] Though pollsters frequently relax that rule for their very last poll before polling day in an election or referendum, conceding that their final poll is a prediction, the essential point is that polls attempt to measure the current views of the public, not to predict the future.

There is a straightforward problem with that. Who is the 'public'? Everyone? All citizens? Adults only? Those who could qualify to be on the electoral register? Just those on the electoral register? Those who are likely to vote in the next election? (And how do you define 'likely' and which election is the one that matters?) Pollsters who repeatedly reaffirm that their polls are not predictions are really in the prediction business because, to decide whom you are trying to measure, you need to venture into predictions – predictions about who might vote and predictions about how people who are uncertain may make up their minds. That is what all the turnout modelling and squeezing of answers discussed earlier in this chapter are about. Even when pollsters say they are not predicting, they are predicting.

Why, though, only those two predictions? In theory, you could add in more predictions, such as digging into how strong people's support is for a party and how likely they are to switch support. Pollsters do not add in more predictions for a pragmatic reason. The two predictions they make are – most of the time – enough to ensure that their final pre-polling day poll, the one they do call a prediction, is a good stab at the final result. Even when the polls are way off, adding in additional predictive criteria doesn't look to be the solution.

But it's not only voting intention questions that raise the question of what is really being measured. As mentioned above, the distinction between 'this is what the people we think are going to vote at the next election say' and 'this is what adults say' can be significant on policy issues such as immigration. Non-voters, whether for legal or voluntary reasons, can have different views from voters. That is an important distinction to remember when looking at political polling questions about topics rather than votes. But that is not the only complication with such polling; the exact wording of questions becomes still more important, as the next chapter shows.

3

THE RIGHTS AND WRONGS OF
POLLING QUESTIONS

'Public opinion polls are rather like
children in a garden,
digging things up all the time
to see how they're growing.'
– J. B. PRIESTLEY[1]

Asking Questions, the classic guide to questionnaire design, uses a story about smoking to show the importance of getting your question wording right:

> Two priests, a Dominican and a Jesuit, are discussing whether it is a sin to smoke and pray at the same time. After failing to reach a conclusion, each goes off to consult his respective superior. The next week they meet again. The Dominican says, 'Well, what did your superior say?'
>
> The Jesuit responds, 'He said it was all right.'
>
> 'That's funny,' the Dominican replies. 'My superior said it was a sin.'
>
> The Jesuit says, 'What did you ask him?'
>
> The Dominican replies, 'I asked him if it was all right to smoke while praying.'
>
> 'Oh,' says the Jesuit. 'I asked my superior if it was all right to pray while smoking.'[2]

It isn't just that different questions obtain different results. Different wording for the same question also gets different results. So let's take a look at what to watch out for with political polling.

The Wording Matters

As pioneering pollster Elmo Roper quipped, 'you can ask a question in such a way as to get any answer you want.'[3] A good example of this comes from the early 1970s, ahead of Britain joining what was then the European Economic Community (EEC), later the European Union (EU). A pollster asked whether people thought such a decision should be up to Parliament or should be made via a referendum. But rather than just come up with one question, the pollster tried out two wordings, each asked to half their sample:

> France, Germany, Italy, Holland, Belgium and Luxembourg approved their membership of the EEC by a vote of their national parliaments. Do you think Britain should do the same?

and

> Ireland, Denmark and Norway are voting in a referendum to decide whether to join the EEC. Do you think Britain should do the same?

Both of those questions were true, accurately reflecting what other countries had done. Both also produced an overwhelming 'yes' verdict from voters even though they were proposing opposite points of view. Such is the power of a leading question.[4]

A much more recent British polling example on the same topic demonstrates this was no one-off. Asked whether 'MPs have spent long enough debating Brexit and now is time to pass the deal,' the public agreed 56 per cent to 25 per cent in October 2019. But asked instead if 'The Brexit legislation is complicated and MPs need more time to scrutinise it,' the public agreed with that too, by 41 per cent to 33 per cent.[5]

Similarly, in early 2018, Lord Ashcroft showed how different wording could produce different results when asking about Britain's membership of the European Union. Asking 'Do you want a second referendum on Europe?' put those in favour behind by a margin of 13 percentage points: 38 per cent to 51 per cent. By contrast, asking 'Once negotiations are complete and the full details of Brexit are known, would you support or oppose holding a referendum on whether to go ahead with Brexit or not?' reduced that to a margin of just two points (40 per cent to 42 per cent). Another form of wording actually flipped the result, putting those in favour of that second referendum ahead. Asked 'Once Brexit negotiations are complete would you support or oppose holding a referendum on whether to accept the terms, or leave without a deal?' people responded in favour by 39 per cent to 31 per cent.[6]

In all of these examples, the variations in wording meant those answering the questions were facing different contexts and being provided with different information. The first question from Ashcroft, for example, did not specify precisely what the referendum would be a choice between, something the third question very much did. This shows how important the choice of wording is – and how difficult it can be to judge which is the best wording to use. Is that extra detail in the third option the better choice because it clarifies the question, or is it obscuring detail that makes the question harder to understand? Plus, of course, the more detail you put in a question, the more people can argue over whether the detail in it is both correct and fair. (Would a second referendum have been between deal or no deal, or between deal or renegotiate, or perhaps a three-way choice between deal, no deal and renegotiate?)

Large variations in results can also be achieved with subtle differences in wording, as demonstrated by an American experiment conducted in 1940 and repeated in 1974. The question options were:

> Do you think the U.S. should allow public speeches against democracy?

and

> Do you think the U.S. should forbid public speeches against democracy?

Despite the questions being nearly identical, the answers were very different. The proportion of people favouring the free speech option nearly doubled thanks to the change in wording. In 1940 only 25 per cent of those asked the first option agreed, but 46 per cent of those asked the second option disagreed. It was a similar picture in 1974, with 52 per cent agreeing with the free-speech option when given the former wording, but rising to 71 per cent when given the latter wording.[7] At least the trend over time was consistent.

As a more recent example, in 2015 Ipsos MORI found that support in Britain for giving sixteen- and seventeen-year-olds the right to vote was much higher if phrased that way than if phrased as reducing the voting age from eighteen to sixteen years (52 per cent support and 41 per cent oppose with the former wording, falling to 37 per cent support and 56 per cent oppose with the latter).[8]

In 1999 the Pew Research Center tested an agree-or-disagree question against a forced-choice question on the American public. The two approaches produced strikingly different results. Asked if they agreed or disagreed that 'the best way to ensure peace is through military strength,' 55 per cent agreed and 42 per cent disagreed. But this apparent support for military strength as a peacemaker disappeared when people were asked instead to choose between the above statement and 'diplomacy is the best way to ensure peace.' Only 33 per cent choose the former, and 55 per cent picked the latter.[9] Part of the difference is likely to have come from how people interpret 'ensure peace'. After all, a country with a strong military that uses it as a threat to back up its diplomacy might manage to keep the peace through diplomacy, while still benefiting from its military strength.

A more peaceful example of how different interpretations of a concept can produce very different results comes with tactical voting, as shown by polling from the run-up to the British 2019 general election. ICM had 35 per cent saying they were likely to vote tactically, when phrased as,

> 'Tactical voting' is when you vote for a candidate/party who is not your first choice because they have a better chance of stopping another candidate/party winning. How likely, if at all, are you to vote tactically in the upcoming general election on December 12?

However, BMG found a much lower figure, with only 24 per cent intending to vote tactically when it was phrased as, 'I am voting for the best-positioned party/candidate to keep out another party/candidate that I dislike.' Ipsos MORI's results were lower still, with only 14 per cent intending to vote tactically on the basis of the phrasing, 'The party you support has little chance of winning in this constituency so you vote . . . to try and keep another party out.' Even that was not the lowest figure, as Deltapoll got only 9 per cent of respondents saying that 'I really prefer another party but it has no chance of winning in this constituency' came 'closest to the main reason you will vote for the party you chose.'[10]

This morass of results is why it is so important to ensure you compare like-with-like question wording when looking at trends. When you do, there is some good news. It is the norm for different sets of wording, asked repeatedly over time, to produce the same trends. So while the different answers that come from different wording may mean we are not able to tell the 'true' level of public support for a position, we can trust the trends to tell us how public opinion is changing.

Why Does the Wording Matter So Much?

That public opinion can be reported as being so different depending on the subtlety of the wording used may seem disturbing, undermining the concept of polling. But the problem here isn't one of political polling. Rather it's the fragility of public opinion in the first place.

That fragility is demonstrated by the ballot paper ordering phenomena: simply changing the order in which the names of candidates appear on a ballot paper changes how many votes each of them gets.[11] Even when a ballot has just two names on it – the simplest, shortest option possible outside of a dictatorship – which name comes first makes a difference (thankfully only 0.6 per cent, yet that is still not zero).[12] This has been such a long-running and pervasive problem, there have been flirtations with and parliamentary questions about circular ballot papers in Australia. Presumably, the professor who suggested printing ballot papers on a single-sided Möbius strip of paper to avoid any top or bottom was joking.[13]

With people swayed in how they cast their votes by such small matters, it is no surprise that the wording of polling questions sways results too.[14] Especially as, when asked a question by political pollsters or completing one of their online surveys, people do not pause for long thought. They answer quickly and without debating the issue with others. This means that their views are more malleable in response to question wording when:

1. The question wording is complicated, rather than simple, such as if there is a double, or triple, negative: 'do you not agree that it would not have been better for Mark to have left this book unwritten?';

2. The issue is one they are not familiar with;

3. The question invites people to agree. People are instinctively more inclined to agree than disagree – hence the impact in the free-speech example above of changing what a 'yes' answer means;

4. Their answer is 'it depends on the full context' and the question only prompts one aspect of the context, such as in the case of the EEC example above, in which the question presents points in favour of only one side of the issue;

5. The question gives a cue, such as associating one option with a particularly popular or unpopular person or party; or

6. One answer is more socially acceptable than another, such as with asking people whether they are going to vote in an election or the consistent finding that people say they consume less alcohol than they really do.[15]

Those problems, you may have spotted, apply more to questions on policy issues than to questions about voting intention. That is why a British parliamentary probe into political polling found that 'some of the key problems we identified for polling, particularly the use of leading questions and misleading presentation of results, were more pronounced for policy issues polls.'[16]

As one of the seminal studies of this topic concluded, 'Large portions of an electorate do not have meaningful beliefs, even on issues that have formed the basis for intense political controversy among elites for substantial periods of time.'[17] Rather, faced with questions on a topic they do not spend much time thinking about, and quite possibly referring to concepts or people they are not particularly familiar with, people construct answers on the fly, susceptible therefore to how the question directed them.[18]

The good news, however, is that not all would-be leading questions succeed, and for those that do succeed, the evidence of their crime is right there in the wording – as long as we think to check. So let us now turn to some of the types of wording problems that repeatedly crop up.

The Horrors of Agree–Disagree Statements

'Do you agree that' may sound an innocent, reasonable start to a polling question. It isn't. It is a booby trap because, as a rule of thumb, between one in ten and one in five people (10–20 per cent) will both agree with a proposition in a question and also agree with its opposite if that is put in a question instead. This is due to 'acquiescence bias' – people's bias towards saying they agree.

This was one of the problems with the Pew question about peace mentioned above, although the other factor was that one option named an alternative to military force and one did not. To give a cleaner example of the acquiescence bias at work, back in May 2009 ComRes asked people in Britain if they agreed or disagreed with the statement that 'Britain should remain a full member of the European Union.' Of those surveyed, 55 per cent agreed. But asked if they agreed or disagreed with the statement 'Britain should leave the European Union but maintain close trading links,' once again 55 per cent agreed. In other words, some people agreed *both* that Britain should remain in the EU *and* that Britain should leave the EU.[19] This is a great example of 'Schrödinger's cat polling', when polls find that an opinion both is and is not there.

As a result, the wise reader of polls treats agree–disagree-type statements with a great deal of caution. As online survey firm SurveyMonkey pleaded with its customers, 'Let's agree NOT to use agree/disagree questions.'[20]

Asking 'do you agree or disagree that' is better than 'do you agree that' but still problematic. At the very least, if you are going to pay attention to agree–disagree answers, the results need to be so lopsided that you can be sure the acquiescence effect has been swamped and/or the topic has been polled with questions put both ways around, such as 'do you agree or disagree that taxes should be raised in order to cut the deficit?' to one-half of the sample and 'do you agree or disagree that the deficit should be allowed to grow in order to keep taxes low?' to the other half. Another option is to present the whole sample with both positions on a topic and ask which their view comes closest to.

One other way of improving such questions is to offer a wider range of answers. In political polls, this usually means giving five answer options – strongly agree, agree, neither agree nor disagree, disagree and strongly disagree, or a version of those options.[21] The two agree and the two disagree categories are often summed together in reporting of such polling questions, but looking at the full answers can identify underlying dynamics, such as opponents of an idea feeling more strongly about their opposition than the supporters feel about their support.

None of this, though, is enough to make agree–disagree questions a good type of question to use. They remain popular because they are a simple, quick and cheap way to *some* insight. Just don't be tempted to rest too much insight on their findings.

More or Less Likely

In 2017 Republican Roy Moore was running for election to the U.S. Senate in a special election (by-election) for what should have been a safe Republican seat. He was already a highly controversial character, having twice lost his job as Chief Justice of the Alabama Supreme Court for misconduct. During his election, something still more serious came to light: multiple allegations of sexual misconduct, including assault of a sixteen-year-old.[22]

Amid heavy coverage of the allegations, and just before the fifth allegation came out, an opinion poll by JMC Analytics and Polling asked,

> *Given the allegations that have come out about Roy Moore's alleged sexual misconduct against four underage women, are you more or less likely to support him as a result of these allegations?*
>
> More likely: 29 per cent
> Less likely: 38 per cent
> No difference: 33 per cent

Were nearly a third of voters (29 per cent) really saying that multiple accusations of sexual misconduct against someone made them *more* likely to vote for them? If so, you may wish to be depressed and perhaps doubt the wisdom of democracy.

That poll, however, contained clues that this answer was not all that it seemed. The special election was for the vacated seat previously held by Republican Jeff Sessions. When he had won in 2008, on the same day that Democrat Barack Obama was getting elected president, Sessions had taken 63 per cent of the vote. Six years later, he soared to 97.3 per cent as the Democrats did not even put up a candidate against him. This should have been a rock-solid Republican seat. Yet this poll found Moore in deep trouble, four points *behind* his Democratic challenger. It also showed his support sinking, as in October a comparable pre-allegations poll from the same pollster had put him eight points ahead.[23]

The explanation for that apparently depressing set of 'more likely' answers, therefore, is that people often use more/less answers to express support for their own side. People often use 'more likely' to mean 'I support' and people use 'less likely' to mean 'I don't support'. They are telling the pollster who they support, not how the intensity of their support has changed. That means you can read something into the answers, just not quite what the question was asking.[24] This problem is greater when, as with this poll, there are no options given such as 'I was previously going to vote for him and still am' or 'I don't believe the allegations.' In both cases, the 'more likely' option is the one that probably best expresses the view of still wanting to back your candidate, even though the allegations have not actually made you more likely to back him. That logic is still stronger if you are also thinking of how the media may report the results. What is the most effective way to obtain the best write-up of the poll? It is to give your side the most positive answers possible, even if they exaggerate your own views. That is a perfectly rational, if calculating, way of answering a poll. Likewise, people are motivated to do just the same to deprecate the other side. It all makes the results from such questions rather misleading, as proved to be the case in this election: Moore went on to lose the election, depriving the Republicans of a safe seat.

Pollster Anthony Wells uses an example from the UK to express similar scepticism about the value of such questions:

In *The Independent* in January 2013 a ComRes poll found
30 per cent of people agreeing they were more likely to vote
Conservative because [Prime Minister] David Cameron
had promised to hold a referendum on Europe. In the
month leading up to Cameron's pledge, the average level
of Conservative support in the polls was 31 per cent. In the
month following, the average was still 31 per cent. Despite
the poll, the pledge had made no difference.[25]

In addition to the factors found in the Moore poll, Wells adds two
other reasons why such questions fail. One is that the act of asking
a question gives artificial attention and focus to its topic. Cameron's
pledge was only one of many possible reasons for supporting or not
supporting his party. Asking about only one of them does not capture
how voters go about making up their minds, free to take into account
other factors. The other reason is that people are not very good judges
of what motivates them to vote (or indeed to do many other things in
life): 'we do not actually understand our decision-making processes
very well; our decisions are based far more upon our own prejudices,
biases and tribal attachments than we would like to imagine.'[26]

That is why when I see a political polling question which asks if
people are more or less likely to support a party or politician because
of something that has happened or might happen, I am always less
likely to pay attention to its results.

Does the Question Only Give One Side of the Story?

Psychologist and pioneering pollster Hadley Cantril is known for his
interest in a fictional alien invasion. In 1938, American radio broadcast
a dramatization by Orson Welles of H. G. Wells's novel *The War of
the Worlds*, allegedly causing widespread public panic. Cantril studied

this in some detail for a book, though both the extent of the panic and the robustness of Cantril's analysis have generated much debate.[27]

During the Second World War Cantril, perhaps uniquely, organized opinion polling to help decide how an amphibious invasion would be conducted. The polling was of Vichy officials in Morocco, revealing strongly anti-British feelings, news that influenced decisions on which nationality of troops to deploy where during the Operation Torch invasion.[28] (Later polling, conducted by the polling institute he co-founded, showing the strength of support in Cuba for Fidel Castro was, however, overlooked during the planning of the failed Bay of Pigs invasion.)[29]

One of the other interests of this multi-talented person was testing different wordings for polling questions. He found that the answers are very susceptible to the context given in questions, such as asking about tax cuts but without mentioning where the money to pay for them might come from. As a result, he warned about the fragility of results from 'questions whose implications are not seen.'[30]

A modern example comes from a YouGov experiment conducted in 2019. Asked if they agreed that 'After Brexit, the UK should maintain workers' rights and regulations, and make sure businesses keep paying the same rates of tax,' a net +68 per cent agreed (71 per cent to 3 per cent). But asked, 'After Brexit, the UK should position itself as the lowest-tax, business-friendliest country in Europe,' a net +23 per cent agreed with that opposite proposition too (39 per cent to 16 per cent).

Likewise, giving only the possible argument favouring a proposition, and no argument against it, tilts the answers, as a 2020 YouGov survey showed. Asked 'Do you think the UK does or does not have a free press?' 43 per cent said it does. But another sample asked at the same time, '3 companies currently own around 80 per cent of the national UK newspaper market (by newspaper readership). Do you think the UK does or does not have a free press?' came back with only 28 per cent saying it does. Those saying it does not went up from 34 per cent to 49 per cent.

Better questions therefore give both sides of the argument, or pair opposite propositions and ask people which most closely reflects their view. There is one exception to this – when asking a slanted question is useful to test a possible campaign message. That second YouGov example comes from a poll commissioned by environmental activists Extinction Rebellion. It gave them some sense of how powerful a campaign message it might be to argue over the freedom of the British press. But by only putting one side of the argument, such polling does not tell you where public opinion will end up after people hear counter-arguments too.

That is why neutral wording of questions is not a simple panacea. As pollster Louis Harris put it, 'The real world is biased.'[31] Political issues usually play out with (at least) two sides making a case and often presenting very different ways of thinking about a topic. The public ends up with its opinion based on partisan takes duking it out. This was the problem that befell the Conservative Party's 'dementia tax' in the 2017 general election. The policy was tested out in market research and came out fine.[32] But in the heat of an election campaign, it was condemned with the nickname of 'the dementia tax'. The debate became all about who would pay and not a debate about the service that would be provided – and that question of who would pay was framed in a very negative way. This gave it a very different appearance to voters than the one it had in the earlier market research. The policy bombed as a result. Neutral wording had not been enough to understand what the public would end up thinking.

The Perils of Combining Two Points into One Question

In May 2019, YouGov asked people in Britain,

> *Do you agree or disagree with the following statement?*
> 'Britain needs a strong leader who is willing to break the rules.'

In response, 45 per cent of those surveyed agreed and 28 per cent disagreed. But at the same time, YouGov asked another batch of people:

> *Do you agree or disagree with the following statement?*
> 'Britain needs a strong leader who plays by the rules.'

To that question, 65 per cent agreed and only 14 per cent disagreed. A sizeable chunk of people therefore *both* wanted a leader who breaks the rules *and* one who plays by the rules. Or rather, they were so keen on a strong leader that the rules part of the question did not matter to them. The moral? Do not combine two questions into one. That way lies muddled answers.

Who to Ask about in Voting Questions

What answer options should pollsters give when asking voters for whom they are going to vote? If there is a small number of parties or candidates in an election, it is easy to decide which answer options to give with a voting intention. List all those on offer to the voters.

Life is not always so simple. Even with small numbers of parties, complications can come from not all the parties standing in all the seats up for election. In the British general election of February 1974, for example, pollsters overestimated the level of support for the Liberal Party. It only stood in 83 per cent of the seats, while pollsters gave them as an answer option to everyone in their samples.[33] Consequently, as election day nears, it is common for pollsters to tailor the answer options to the specific location of each person polled, offering them the exact mix they will find on the ballot paper.

The other complication comes when there is a clutch of minor parties or candidates. Reading out a long list in a phone or face-to-face survey, or presenting a long list on screen in an online survey, comes with practical difficulties. Therefore, it is typical for voting intention questions to have a short list of options followed by 'or another party/candidate', covering the minor runners. In addition, this may more reasonably reflect the reality that some parties or candidates are seen as the main players and receive the bulk of attention. As one pollster explains,

> 'Including smaller parties in the polling question may risk overstating their support. Some of the biggest problems for smaller parties are getting the public to notice them at all, and then being seen as a serious legitimate option on a par with the bigger parties rather than a wasted vote. If a polling company includes them in their question it is, intrinsically, sending a message to respondents that they are a big party, and our job is to measure public opinion, not to lead it.[34]

Political polling, therefore, has its promotion and relegation dramas in which pollsters judge whether to promote or demote a party or candidate, and the supporters of an omitted party or candidate are, of course, frequently convinced the pollster is unfairly doing down their side.

The evidence, however, is that the impact of such judgements by the pollsters is often small. This was shown by an experiment carried out by BMG in Britain in 2019:

Since last month, BMG has reviewed the format of our vote intention question. Running a Random Control Trial (RCT) test, we showed half a representative sample the original version, and half the sample a version where all the parties featured in the initial list. The results showed only marginal differences for the Greens and the Brexit Party in terms of vote share received, all within the margin of error. Thus, including them in the 'another party' list did not appear to be suppressing their support.[35]

The major impact is not on polling results but on the tempers of excitable political activists.

Don't Ask Voters if Something Will Change Their Minds

On 28 April 2010, I published my daftest piece about political polling (so far). It was getting towards the end of a general election campaign which had seen the introduction of televised debates between party leaders in a British general election. Following his breakout performance in the first debate by their leader Nick Clegg, the Liberal Democrats had catapulted into prominence and popularity. The rest of the election was a struggle to ensure that the bubble of support did not disappear before polling day. It was a mostly failed struggle, as the party's vote share only went up by 1 per cent in the event, and it lost seats.[36]

I was then, as now, an active member of the Liberal Democrats and at the time was part of the editorial team running the Liberal Democrat Voice blog. Here is how my piece started:

A poll carried out exclusively for Lib Dem Voice shows that opposition from the *Daily Mail*, *The Sun* and *Daily Telegraph* to the Liberal Democrats actually makes people more likely to vote for the party.

Asked the impact on their voting intention of those papers opposing Nick Clegg becoming prime minister, 15 per cent said it made them more likely to vote Liberal Democrat and only 4 per cent said it made them less likely, making for a net +11 per cent saying they are more likely to vote Liberal Democrat.

Of the rest, 19 per cent would vote Liberal Democrat regardless, 35 per cent would not vote Liberal Democrat anyway and 27 per cent said it wouldn't alter their vote but they weren't yet sure which way to vote.[37]

The piece went on to give the full wording of the question used, the details of the pollster who conducted the research, the dates on which the research was done and information on how the data was weighted. A data file was included for anyone to download. The pollster was a respectable firm, a member of the industry self-regulatory body the British Polling Council.

That was all good, but all daft, because the question was horribly flawed. It read:

The newspapers in this country tend to take a position and support different parties at election time. It has been suggested that *The Sun*, *Daily Mail* and *Daily Telegraph* do not want Nick Clegg to be prime minister. If those newspapers were to take this stance would that make you more or less likely to vote Liberal Democrat?

Part of the problem is the 'more or less likely' wording, as discussed above. Another is that the question in this case tried to isolate one issue, as if it could be measured sensibly on its own. It couldn't be. When newspaper editors and owners take a dislike to a politician, they do not just mention it quietly once and leave it at that. They run repeated negative stories. Those stories become amplified on social media. Newspaper reviews from the TV stations repeat the stories. And so on. The impact is much more significant than my question could hope to capture.

Asking about one factor in isolation is, however, a common feature of political polling. Such polling is often commissioned by pressure groups with a particular policy to promote or oppose. Imagine that the Potato Society wants to obtain a government tax break for potato producers. It commissions a poll that asks if people will be more or less likely to support the government if the price of potatoes is cut. The polling finds a significant lead for those saying that they will be more likely to support the government if such a policy is implemented. That makes it into a media story. In reality, of course, any such tax break will be parsed through all sorts of political debate and media coverage. A corporate handout for Big Potato, letting them gorge on higher profits as public services suffer cuts, sounds rather less attractive – especially if a government minister is revealed to get free crisps every week. It's also all rather less important for most voters than the future of health services or whether you are about to lose your job.

To add to the woes for my choice of question, there was another major problem. As pollster Anthony Wells puts it, 'people are, as a rule, pretty rubbish at predicting how we will respond to hypothetical events. The more unpredictable the consequences of those events are, the worse we are at predicting how we will respond.'[38]

Take as an example an experiment conducted in Pennsylvania in 1996:

The first survey elicited respondents' positions on two political issues (welfare reform and the environment) and on the two major candidates, and also asked them to estimate the likelihood that each of these positions would change during the next 2 months. The second survey elicited positions at that time and also asked voters to recall their prior positions. Measured both by expectations and recall, respondents tended to underestimate the degree to which their own positions would change or had changed over time.[39]

As this and other evidence shows, people are lousy at answering questions about how their political views may change.[40]

To make matters worse, such questions also suffer from our limitations in understanding, or at least being willing to admit, why we are taking particular political viewpoints. An example from political science research illustrates this: candidates who look more attractive do better (though being bald, at least for male candidates, does not count against you):[41] 'Studies document a relationship between perceptions of attractiveness and electoral success in Australia, Brazil, Canada, Finland, Germany, Mexico and Switzerland. British elections are no exception.'[42]

Yet you will have to hunt very hard to find voters who are willing to admit to a pollster (or even to themselves) that such factors influence their votes. Although the likely effect is in the low single digits, that is still enough to swing many close elections. The unconscious mind – along with the too-embarrassed-to-admit-it mind – matters. That is a reason, perhaps, to remember Winston Churchill's quip, 'it has been said that democracy is the worst form of government except all those other forms that have been tried.'[43] (Although it is often conveniently forgotten that this quote was made in defence of an unelected House of Lords.)

For the more prosaic matter of political polling, the lesson is to treat with great suspicion the answers voters give when asked if something would make them more or less likely to support a party or a candidate.

Indirect Questions Reveal Uncomfortable Truths

As attractive candidates do better in elections, so too do taller candidates.[44] Factors like this, that voters may be unaware of or are unwilling to admit to, alter election results yet pass benignly through standard polling questions without registering.

This is why a useful, and underused, alternative to asking questions directly is to run mini-experiments. In its simplest form, a pair of descriptions is written about candidates, both true and with only one difference between them – such as one calling a candidate a millionaire and another calling the candidate a successful business owner. Half of the sample is then given the first description and the other half the second; the results of questions about favourability or voting intention can then be compared. As each person polled does not know that others are getting a different description, the guiltily self-aware cannot hide their embarrassing views on what matters by giving fake answers. Raw discrimination can be exposed as well as more subtle and surprising factors.

These experiments need not be restricted to the descriptions of candidates. Ways of presenting policies can be tested, as can clips of politicians speaking, different possible political adverts and more. This approach has also been used to test variations between fictitious candidates to help political scientists draw more general conclusions about what motivates voters.[45]

Such experiments are an underused form of political polling research, as often the contest in politics is over conflicting ways of describing the same thing. Using polling to understand how much it matters who wins out in such a conflict can be much more enlightening than getting excited over yet another movement within the margin of error between yet another pair of voting intention polls.

The Value of Answers Based on Ignorance

Somewhat to my surprise, I discovered a while back that I had been personally responsible for over a quarter (28 per cent) of all the reports of graffiti on bus stops and shelters to Transport for London in the preceding year. As TfL's area of operation covers many millions of people, I am proud, embarrassed and baffled by that. I mean, other Londoners: what were you doing that year? Not surprisingly, I have a view on the budget for graffiti cleaning of bus stops and shelters in London, especially given the significant reductions in the speed of graffiti removal since my miracle year. I am, at the time of writing and most likely still at the time of reading, firmly in favour of upping the spend. But I also have no real idea what the current level of spending is.

Although it is unlikely that you have a similar interest in bus stop graffiti, substitute something more mainstream – such as policing, the ambulance service or road repairs – and there is a good chance you have both a firm view on whether spending should go up or down and simultaneously not that firm a grasp, if any, on how much is currently spent.

For both of us the research shows that, although our grasp of the facts may be limited, our views do move in line with how the facts change in the real world.[46] As graffiti gets worse, people want more spending to tackle it. My answer on the TfL graffiti-cleaning budget is not based on my (quite possibly wrong) guess as to its actual size but rather by my judgement about how often I see graffiti, how bad it is and how long it stays despite reporting it. Unless the truth turns out to be an absurdly large number, whatever the size of the anti-graffiti budget is, I will still want more. Similarly, as job losses rise, people think unemployment is a more significant problem, notwithstanding the fact that they are not able to recite accurately its current level.

As a result, errors over the facts do not necessarily undermine the value of people's views. Consider a sporting example: how far does a typical footballer run during a match? (If you are a diehard football fan, who loves poring over the detailed statistics, you may know this, in which case substitute a different team sport that involves running around.) You can have no idea of what the answer is, and yet still have a view about which of two teams was the most active in chasing down the ball, and which player seemed the most up for it and was always running into the action. Understanding the numbers would likely add to your knowledge and correct the occasional error when your impression turns out to be wrong. But you don't have to be spot on with your numbers to have reasonable views about the broader phenomena. So too with political issues. This is why I'd confidently predict you have a view about the level of spending in your country's healthcare system, despite the fact that you might be guessing wildly to put a number on it.

Knowledge – or not – of numbers also needs to be put in the context of our overall ability with them. Humans are not very good with large numbers. We struggle to estimate them and we struggle to understand them. The errors caused by these struggles are a staple of books that try to popularize the understanding of statistics. In particular, we tend to overestimate small numbers and underestimate large numbers, a point that Bobby Duffy, the former pollster who is now director of King's College London's Policy Institute, has made when contextualizing data showing people's (apparent) ignorance.[47] One reason is that many of us believe that thousand, million, billion and trillion are equally spaced increments in numbers.[48] Another reason is our tendency to regress towards the middle. People are wary about an extreme answer being wrong and so tend to pick a more moderate answer if given a chance.

Therefore, political polling showing 'shocking' levels of ignorance about political facts can simply be telling us how people struggle with numbers in general rather than telling us something specific about the topic in the question. If a poll finds people greatly overestimating the number of Muslims in their country, do not leap to conclusions about religion, bias or fear. Instead, remember first that it is a common feature of how people think about numbers. This also means that for every shocking finding of ignorance, you can find a positive matching one. Yes, the public may horribly overestimate the proportion of a minority community who are criminals. But the public will also overestimate positive attributes too – such as perhaps also thinking that more of them are super-generous donors to charity. The problem is with numbers, not the topic.

It is not only ignorance of numbers we should be generous about. Consider this question: do you think the murder of Louis Rwagasore, prime minister of Burundi, was right or wrong? Most people are happy to use the word 'murder' as a clue to picking the answer 'wrong', although they have no idea what year the murder took place, would struggle to pick which continent Burundi was in and may also have a sneaking suspicion I have made him up.[49] Picking 'wrong' as your answer might be based on poor knowledge, but it is also based on a strong and admirable moral stance.

Cues in such questions – and the use of 'murder' was a strong cue – help explain how people answer them. That is why there is value in what I call 'ignorant answers'. Those answers are still telling us something about those cues and their power. They may be ignorant answers but they can still be logical answers. That ignorance can even be rational. After all, how much time do you really need to spend learning about Louis Rwagasore before coming to a view on his murder? Likewise, how useful is it really to spend time learning the details of the spending totals for different government departments – and how much will your views on whether spending should go up or be cut change once you know all those numbers off by heart? As political scientist Anthony Downs puts it, voters can be rationally ignorant.[50]

As a result, if the public's views on an issue are not to your taste, delving into the level of public knowledge of the issue – and thinking that all you need to do is educate people better about it – may well miss the point. Take the example of foreign-aid spending by governments. It is a repeated finding in the polls that people think their government spends far more on such aid than it really does and want it to be cut. But when they discover the truth of how low spending is compared with what they thought? They frequently stick with wanting it to be cut. The version of the truth that most alters people's opinions, as research in the USA and the UK has found, is one that gives foreign-aid spending as a percentage of all government spending – at or under 1 per cent in both countries. Asked the question without being given any information about the levels of such spending, Britons plumped by 64 per cent to 8 per cent that such spending was too much rather than too little, and Americans by 63 per cent to 8 per cent. Given the information about how small the aid budget is, this switched to 43 per cent to 12 per cent in Britain and 50 per cent to 11 per cent in the USA. These are significant changes, but note that even with the truth, the preferred option in both countries remained to cut international aid.[51]

This illustration shows yet again that the wording of polling questions matters. Questions which give context and detail on the level of aid spending receive answers more favourable to it. But the example also shows that supporters of foreign aid can only gain so much mileage from correcting public misinformation about aid budget totals.

Answers based on ignorance certainly may be more amenable to change in the face of an issue becoming higher-profile and people learning more, and it is a useful part of the picture to know if people's views are based on little knowledge.[52] Which is why the less people know about a topic, the better it is to give a 'don't know' option and to avoid giving a middle option. Otherwise, the pollster risks polluting the real middle-option answers with those from people who are really 'don't knows.'[53]

But the mistake with an ignorant answer is to assume that the ignorance it reveals determined the answer. Or indeed that the ignorance always undermines the answer. Does your lack of knowledge about Louis Rwagasore really mean your aversion to murder in his case is somehow lessened?

For such reasons, I find unconvincing critiques of opinion polling which knock polls for including the views of those who are ignorant about the topics being polled – for example, voters having views on the merits of a balanced budget despite not knowing the current state of the budget.[54] You don't have to know for sure the current state of affairs to have views on what the ideal state of affairs is. Ignorant answers can still reveal people's general outlook.

Moreover, only counting views if they come from people who pass a knowledge test is a rapid road to snobbery – one that would exclude from opinion polls people who are otherwise considered good enough to make life-changing decisions by being members of a jury. Be cautious about answers based on ignorance, but don't be snobbish.

The Value of Fictitious Options

In the spring and summer of 1996, researchers in the German city of Dresden carried out both face-to-face and telephone polling with an unusual twist. They asked people for their views of politicians – fictitious politicians. These were not politicians from fiction, such as *The West Wing*'s President Bartlet or *Yes, Prime Minister*'s Prime Minister Jim Hacker. Rather, they were politicians dreamt up by the researchers.

How did people respond to such requests? They responded with answers. Quite a lot of answers, in fact. Between 7 per cent and 15 per cent of people responded with views on people they, by definition, could not have known anything about.[55]

People similarly express views when asked about fictitious issues or fictitious legislation.[56] A clue as to what is going on came with a YouGov test of opinions in Britain of the non-existent Public Affairs Act (chosen as this was the name also used in u.s. research in 1978 and 2013).[57]

YouGov found in April 2013 nearly one in five of the British public willing to proffer a view on the non-existent legislation:

> *Some people say the Public Affairs Act 1975 should be repealed. Do you agree or disagree?*
>
> Agree: 9 per cent
> Disagree: 9 per cent
> Neither: 82 per cent

The proportion of those sticking with the safety of 'neither' fell a little when a party cue was added:

> *Some Conservative politicians have called for the Public Affairs Act 1975 to be repealed. Do you agree or disagree?*

Agree: 9 per cent
Disagree: 16 per cent
Neither: 75 per cent

*Some Labour politicians have called for the Public Affairs Act
1975 to be repealed. Do you agree or disagree?*
Agree: 9 per cent
Disagree: 10 per cent
Neither: 81 per cent

In addition, the detailed breakdowns showed that in each case naming a party moved its supporters in favour of the proposition and its opponents against it. Although the movements were relatively small, and the samples for the answers from each party were also small, the pattern was consistent and therefore trustworthy. This pattern also matches that 2013 U.S. research, when mentioning either 'President Obama' or 'the Republicans in Congress' similarly moved people's answers in ways compatible with their party preferences.

What fictitious options show us is the extent to which people look for partisan cues in the question as clues to help them work out their answers.[58] Given how rare it is to be polled and still rarer to be polled with a trick question, people should not be derided for failing to spot its trick nature. They are on the receiving end of a deliberate con job, albeit an ethical one in the name of research. Despite the pollster trying to trick them with a deliberately misleading question, people still manage to ferret out enough clues to come up with logically consistent answers. Well done, survey respondents. Or in the words of peer-reviewed research into this,

> Our results support the view that responses to fictitious issue items are not generated at random, via some 'mental coin flip'.

Instead, respondents actively seek out what they consider to be the likely meaning of the question and then respond in their own terms, through the filter of partisan loyalties and current political discourses.[59]

The answers, then, are not worthless, for they tell us about the clues people use and how much those clues matter to them. The answers to such questions (for example, should the Act be repealed?) are really answers to a different question (do you like or dislike Labour politicians?). The answers therefore are useful, as long as you remember that, once again, the question being answered may differ from the question that is asked.

The Value of Multiple-Issue Questions

As we have seen, marriage proposals aside, asking just one question is rarely enough to understand a situation fully. It is, however, unfortunately widespread when it comes to polling on political issues. It does not have to be that way, as serious research projects will often use multiple questions. The British Social Attitudes Survey, for example, typically uses batches of around forty questions to dig into a topic. However, the media, most pressure groups and even the best-resourced political campaigns do not have the budgets for that. Instead, there is a reliance on a much smaller number of questions, which comes with risks.

In 1940 George Gallup and his employee and fellow pioneering pollster, later a Canadian diplomat, Saul Forbes Rae published *The Pulse of Democracy: The Public-Opinion Poll and How It Works.*[60] Tucked away in Appendix i is a series of poll findings from the American public about the war then under way in Europe, which America had not yet joined. On one reading, people were keen to have nothing to do with the war. 'Keeping out of war' was rated 'the most vital issue before the American people today' in May and December 1939. Moreover, 59 per cent in November 1939 thought it was 'a mistake for the United States to have entered the [First] World War' (with 28 per cent disagreeing). Perhaps not surprisingly, therefore, there were only 50 per cent agreeing (and 37 per cent disagreeing) in April 1939, 'the law should be changed so that we could sell war materials to England and France in case of war.'

Germany's invasion of Poland on 1 September 1939 did not see a significant pro-war shift in American opinion. In October of that year, 91 per cent were against the USA declaring war and sending its army and navy to fight against Germany. Only 27 per cent agreed (with 65 per cent disagreeing) that, 'if it appears that Germany is defeating England and France ... the United States [should] declare war on Germany and send our Army and Navy to Europe to fight.'

However, other questions contained hints of how public opinion might shift in favour of intervention. In July 1939, 43 per cent picked England as the European country they liked best, compared with just 3 per cent choosing Germany. Moreover, 59 per cent agreed (and 36 per cent disagreed) in October that 'the United States should do everything possible to help England and France win the war – short of going to war ourselves.' Add to that the considerable confidence that the Allies would win the war (82 per cent thought that in September), and you can see a picture of an American public that did not want to go to war, wanted England and France to win and, because it was expecting events to go well for the two countries, could reconcile wanting them to win with staying out. That left open a plausible route for support for interventionist policies to shift if the war went badly, as it did with France surrendering in June 1940.

The rounded picture secured from multiple answers was much more informative than if just one of those answers had been cherry-picked as the only one to use to illustrate American public opinion at the time. The lesson? Beware the questions on a single, free-standing issue, especially if it appears touted by a group or organization with a vested interest, or a media outlet desiring an audience-grabbing headline. Reports based on multiple questions are better.

List Experiments

Sometimes the problem with a polling question is not the wording but people's willingness to give an honest answer. That may be due to the topic (such as a question about intimate personal behaviour) or due to the circumstances (such as fearing what the government would make of your answer). A smart way around this is to use a 'list test', an approach to identifying the truth while maintaining a degree of anonymity that is particularly used for polling on topics such as racism and drug use. Half of the sample are given a set of questions, all of which come without any hindrance to honest answers. They are not asked to tell the pollster each of their answers in turn, but rather to tell the pollster how many questions in total they answer 'yes' to. The other half of the sample are given the same questions, but with a problematic one added. They too are asked how many they answer 'yes' to. The difference in the aggregate figures between the two groups reveals how many people answer yes to the problematic question, while still preserving each individual's anonymity.[61]

It is a neat technique that should be used more often in political polling for topics with a socially desirable answer, such as attitudes towards voting or relative preference between personal tax cuts and more money for public services.[62]

Question Order

In an episode of the TV comedy series *Yes, Prime Minister*, senior civil servant Humphrey Appleby is faced with a prime minister who wants to reintroduce National Service (mandatory service in the military for all teenagers).[63] The PM, Appleby is told, has seen an opinion poll that shows the idea to be popular with the public. In response, Appleby demonstrates to a junior colleague how to commission another poll that would show the opposite. He does this by getting him to answer the following questions in order:

Are you worried about the number of young people without jobs?

Are you worried about the rise in crime among teenagers?

Do you think there is lack of discipline in our comprehensive schools?

Do you think young people welcome some authority and leadership in their lives?

Do you think they'll respond to a challenge?

Would you be in favour of reintroducing National Service?

By that last question, Appleby's colleague – initially opposed to National Service – stumbles into answering in favour. The final question is itself leading ('would you be in favour of reintroducing . . .') but crucially also comes after a series of questions designed to make you think a particular way.

That set of questions was fictional, but the effect is real, as the evidence shows.[64] One real-life example comes from British political polling in the 1990s. For many years Gallup showed a higher rating for the Liberal Democrats than did other pollsters. Question order was the most likely explanation, for Gallup first asked about people's views on party leaders before then asking about voting intention. Other pollsters did voting intention first. Thanks to the popularity of then-Liberal Democrat leader and former spy Paddy Ashdown, getting voters to think first about leaders made them more likely to say they would vote for his party in a general election. Similarly, polling firm Harris used warm-up questions in previous decades:

> These are designed so as not to precondition respondents, and they are simple and brief. However, one partial effect they may have is to squeeze the Liberals out from equal consideration as most of the preliminary questions relate to the two main parties.[65]

Or, to take an example from American politics, the order of questions influenced how keen people were to see money spent on social security and Medicare in a test carried out by the Pew Research Center:

> We asked three separate, but similarly worded questions of 1,024 respondents: Whether it is more important to take steps to reduce the budget deficit or: 1) to keep spending for programs that help the poor and needy at current levels; 2) to keep military spending at current levels; 3) to keep Social Security and Medicare benefits as they are. The order in which the three were asked was randomized, meaning that different respondents were asked the questions in a different sequence
> . . .
> Among respondents who were asked the Social Security/ Medicare question first – before the questions on military spending and programs to aid the poor – 63 per cent said it was more important to maintain benefits as they are, while 30 per cent placed greater priority on the deficit.

Among those who were asked the same question later, a higher percentage (72 per cent) said it was more important to maintain benefits. We observed a similar pattern for the questions addressing military spending and programs to aid the poor.[66]

It is debatable which is the 'correct' order for questions, even for the simpler situation of voting intention polls. After all, in an election, party leaders receive heightened publicity. Perhaps therefore a prompt about leader's existence is the better way of obtaining an answer, as it builds in a little piece of simulation of what happens before an election? But, of course, an election involves much more than just a heightened focus on party leaders, so is it perhaps better to avoid trying to simulate just one part of an election and steer clear of all simulation? Although there is no conclusively right or wrong approach, generally getting to voting intention as quickly as possible in a survey is seen as best, as it minimizes the risk of inadvertent bias.

The ordering of answers proffered to the interviewee matters too, as we saw when discussing the ordering of names on ballot papers. However, pollsters can usually rotate the order in which different answer options are presented to different people in the sample. As a result, answer ordering is only rarely an issue, usually when inexperienced or naive organizers of a poll are involved.[67]

Ordering of questions is something particularly to beware of when looking at long-term trends across multiple surveys. Even if the question has stayed the same, changing order and surrounding questions may mean the answers are not fully comparable. Such changes may even create an artificial turning point in the data, although public opinion may not have turned in reality.[68]

Not Everything Should Be Asked

We have seen many ways in which questions, both in wording and in sequence, can produce misleading results, either deliberately or inadvertently. It is why it is important to see at the very least the exact questions asked, and preferably the context of other questions that preceded them. Such transparency varies significantly between countries. Even in the UK, with some of the highest transparency standards, the full ordering of questions is often not revealed. That is because those questions are frequently part of 'omnibus' surveys in which multiple different clients buy space in the survey for their own handful of questions. So if someone commissions polling questions on a topic and the full wording of the questions is revealed, quite what preceded them – other questions from other clients, who may not have made their results public – is left unknown. The rest of us simply have to hope we can trust that the pollsters did not misjudge the questionnaire.[69] It is another reason to rest only a small degree of confidence on any one poll about an issue. Multiple questions and multiple polls, tackling the issue from multiple angles and in multiple sequences, are what is required.

But there is one final problem. Some questions, however skilfully crafted, are best left unasked. Famously, President Bill Clinton chose his family holiday location based on what his polling advisor Dick Morris told him would go down best with voters. The results of specially commissioned polling redirected his holidays from his previous choice, the elitist Martha's Vineyard island, to the perceived-to-be-more-populist Rocky Mountains. After he won re-election for his second and final term, Martha's Vineyard returned to his holiday plans. Perhaps visiting the Rocky Mountains had helped his re-election. Whether it did or not, politicians would be better – and politics would be better – if they didn't reach for such research. Polling had merely helped give an accurate answer to an undesirable question.[70]

4

IS IT ALL ABOUT VOTING
INTENTION?

'Authoritative estimates of public opinion on which were
the most important issues ... was more important by far
than the daily estimates of the total final vote.'
– HAROLD WILSON, prime minister[1]

I n a democracy, politics comes down to votes. Being the most popular
party leader does not mean you win an election. Having the most
popular stance on the major issue of the day does not mean you win
an election. It is the votes and, where applicable, the seats (or electoral college votes in u.s. presidential elections) which result from
the votes that win you an election and give you power. In that sense,
when an opinion poll covers anything other than voting intention, it
is a digression – a digression that gives context, but still a digression.
The voting intention question is the main game.

But you may be bridling at that word, 'game'. Is not politics more
important than a mere game? Is not governing more important than
who is currently up and who is down in the popularity stakes? It is
no surprise that the media's preoccupation with the horse-race aspect
of politics – who is ahead and who is behind – aided and abetted by
polling, has been a cause of controversy throughout polling's history.[2]

George Gallup himself used a sporting metaphor to defend polling: 'Imagine how meaningless and uninteresting a football game
would be for the spectator if he could not learn how the teams stood

at half time.'[3] But in football the goals (or in American football, touchdowns) you score in the first half count towards your total at the end of the match. Being ahead in the polls halfway through a term of office gives no bonus on election day.

A better parallel is with share prices. As with political polls, these provide a running scorecard for how those in charge are performing. As with polls, the amount of attention given to the current score can be criticized for prioritizing short-term excitement over a long-term focus on getting the substance right. Yet as with share prices, there is merit in paying attention to the current score. In a rough and imperfect way, it holds those in power to account. Poor poll ratings and poor share price performance put the pressure on those in charge to up their game.

But should it be voting intention that is followed to give the current score? Some experts are attracted to the idea that party leader ratings matter more than party voting intention figures when looking at polling in parliamentary systems. Mike Smithson, founder of the popular Political Betting website, is rare in political punditry in literally, and successfully, putting his money where his mouth is via political betting. He tweeted in 2020 about 'the ludicrous UK fetish with voting intention polling especially when they are showing a different picture than the leader approval ratings.'[4] As polling day nears, Mike Smithson's focus shifts to voting intention questions, but well ahead of polling day, he emphasizes the value of party leader ratings as a foretaste of what is to come at the next election. Writing six months after the 2020 British general election (and in theory four years before the next one), he said,

> At this stage before a general election I take much more
> notice of leadership ratings than voting intention polls.
> With the former those sampled are asked for simply an

opinion whereas with voting questions they are asked to predict what they might or might not do in 3/4 years time when they could not even turn out. When tested in real elections such as 1992 and 2015 the leader ratings have got the outcome right while the voting polls have been wrong.[5]

There are two different reasons why politicians' approval ratings may be a better measure than voting intention. One is that they may be more accurate, the other that they may better foretell future changes.

Approval rating questions are usually asked in the same surveys as voting intention questions. Even when they are asked in separate surveys, they are asked using similar sampling and weighting methodologies. Therefore, if there is a problem with polling methodology, looking at one rather than the other will not help, with one possible exception: voting intention questions are about what people will do while approval questions are just about what people think. The former, therefore, do not take people's answers at face value in the way the latter do. With voting intention questions, pollsters rarely leave untouched answers of the type 'don't know', 'not sure' or 'undecided'. If people answer 'don't know', then the polling methodology might involve prompting them a bit more, perhaps also taking into account how they voted last time. A 'don't know' who voted Nationalist last time might be taken as, say, half a Nationalist this time when adding up the totals. With politician-rating questions, however, this sort of follow-up push is usually not done. The 'don't know' is left as 'don't know'. That is why pairs of politician ratings figures (approve/disapprove, like/don't like, good job/bad job) do not typically add up to 100 per cent or even come that close. 'Don't knows' and 'unsures' are left in. Likewise for turnout – voting intention questions usually get adjusted for how likely people are to vote, while politician approval ratings are often calculated without such adjustments.

The absence of pushing and of turnout adjusting from politician approval ratings means there is less that can go wrong with them. But there is no truth to check them against. With voting intention, there are election results to check the methodologies against. With approval ratings, there is no reality to check against. So the methodology may be simpler – but it is also harder to know if it has gone wrong.

What, then, of the argument that politician's ratings are a better way to foretell the future than voting intention numbers? Do voters perhaps first start going off a leader before taking the extra step of switching their vote? The academic research evidence is limited, in part because the research on the impact of party leader ratings has focused on a subtly different point. That is whether or not the popularity of a party leader has much impact on how popular their party is. As one paper from 2001 put it: 'Are voters really that concerned with the image of leaders? There is certainly no consensus on the matter.'[6] However, though leader ratings may not be drivers of vote share, they could still be a leading indicator of later vote share changes. On that question, another study concluded that 'leader approval ratings are much more volatile than general election vote shares, and that focusing solely on party leader approval leads to overly pessimistic predictions for the largest parties, and particularly for Labour.'[7] From this and other studies, the evidence is limited and unclear.

Moreover, there are many different ways of defining 'leader ratings'. Let's say party leader Dean Keaton has a 45 per cent approval rating, and a 30 per cent disapproval rating, for a net +15 per cent approval rating. Compare that with rival party leader Dave Kujan, with a 40 per cent approval rating, and a 25 per cent disapproval rating, also for a net +15 per cent rating. Now imagine that in a head-to-head choice over preference for next ruler of the country, Keaton leads 51 per cent to 49 per cent for a 2 per cent gap. Which figure or figures from all of the above should we be paying attention to? Keaton's 45 per cent? Or his net 15 per cent? Or the 2 per cent gap? Or perhaps 0 per cent (as both have a net +15 per cent approval rating)? And what is the metric meant to show? Is it a better indicator than voting intention for the here and now, or is it a leading indicator of future voting intention changes? If so, how far in the future?

Put all these options together, and there is such an extensive menu to choose from that there is always a good chance of being able to pick and mix a different one each time and say, 'look, this was more useful than voting intention!' But if you have to keep changing the theory, then it is no use for prediction, as you do not know which one to pick next. No wonder, then, that pollster Matt Singh is sceptical about the value of looking at leader ratings rather than voting intentions for assessing likely vote shares at the next election: 'There are so many possible versions of this idea, I don't know really what I am meant to be evaluating.'[8]

A further complication is that political parties can change their leaders. There may be a perverse tipping point at which the worse a party leader's ratings are, the more likely the party is to change leader before an election, and so the higher the party's support is likely to be at the next election.

Moreover, the meaning of leader ratings can change over time. New events, such as a pandemic or a war, can alter the attributes the public most wants from its leaders, or the importance of leaders compared with their teams. But such changes in the evaluation of what is important then also have an impact on voting, politics and life in general – and so, contrary to what some polling critics say, this alteration is beneficial. It would be like – to return to soup-related metaphors – polling about which kitchen utensil is most of use to you. Faced with soup, you may say spoon. Replace the soup with a steak, and the poll may find you say knife. Changing circumstances produce changing views, and it is better that polling reflects that.[9]

The complications, caveats and maybes of all this are a reason not to junk voting intention questions for approval ratings. But it is worth paying some attention to the latter as a safety net, as an indicator of whether voting intentions might be soft and liable to change, and especially as, in doing so, you are mirroring what those who run campaigns do – giving you a better insight into how those running campaigns are viewing them. As Dan Pfeiffer, senior advisor to President Barack Obama for strategy and communications (2013–15), put it,

> While reporters and political junkies obsess about the horserace numbers, political operatives often focus on other aspects of the polls. Campaign pollsters track how the electorate rates the candidates on a series of character traits and issues. Using data analysis, the campaigns have a sense of which of these measures most closely correlate with eventual support. For example in the 2012 Obama campaign, we were obsessed with the question of 'which candidate fights for someone like you.' We believed if we won that debate, we would win the election.[10]

5

OTHER TYPES OF POLLS

'A presidential administration without a pollster is as
unlikely as one without a national security advisor.'
– SIDNEY VERBA, political scientist[1]

So far, this book has concentrated on public national political polls about voting intention, politician ratings or views on policies and issues. There is, however, a family of other closely related polls, variously seen as supplementary or perhaps superior to them. Let's meet this family.

Private, Internal Polls

As we saw earlier, the polling triumph for Gallup and other pollsters grabbed public attention in 1936 and secured a place in both polling and political history. However, a strong case can be made that it was really 1932 that saw the birth of modern political polling, thanks to the largely forgotten – though acknowledged by Gallup himself – work of Emil Hurja.[2]

Hurja's role advising the 1932 Roosevelt presidential campaign was what we now call being a campaign pollster, and he was the first to have such a role.[3] He inadvertently gave us the word 'pollster' (see Introduction) and his pioneering skill earned him the nickname 'the Wizard of Washington'.[4] It was an impressive ascent into political influence and fame for someone born the second of twelve children of Finnish immigrants. Travelling the country to find work, he tried

many jobs, including working in the oil industry and owning a series
of newspapers.

His interest in using statistical data to understand politics may
well have come from his time studying at the University of Washington,
Seattle, and the professor Frederick Jackson Turner. Best known for
his influential essay 'The Significance of the Frontier in American
History', Turner impressed on Hurja and others the importance of
economic and statistical evidence for understanding the past: 'the
method of the statistician . . . is absolutely essential.'[5] Added to that
was what Hurja learned about the extractive industries. As he later
put it,

> You apply the same test to public opinion that you do to
> ore. In mining you take several samples from the face of
> the ore, pulverize them, and find out what the average pay
> per ton will be. In politics you take sections of voters,
> check new trends against past performances, establishing
> percentage shift among different voting strata, supplement
> this information from competent observers in the field,
> and you can accurately predict an election result.[6]

Hurja had a break into political circles with a job working as
secretary to Charles Sulzer, then Alaska's non-voting representative
in Congress. But his initial attempts to meld his enthusiasm for
statistics, politics and history into helping in contemporary politics
were rebuffed by the Democratic Party, as he was seen as a crank on
such matters.

He overcame this rebuff in early 1932, setting out a plan for the
Roosevelt campaign to use the (flawed) polling of others such as the
Literary Digest polls, promising to use his contacts to source much
data ahead of its official publication.[7] He saw how such data could

also be improved by being combined with historical election data and with information from Democrat campaigners on the ground. His appetite for additional data even took him to analysing patterns in letters from the public and to using the data from private house-to-house surveys carried out by bookmakers.[8] He later added in tracking media coverage in thousands of U.S. newspapers.

In modern terms, his system was a mix of being a polling aggregator, an analyser of canvassing data and a carnivorous data scientist, sucking up everything he could lay his hands on into one model showing how Roosevelt was doing in each of the states.

Hurja understood the power of good sampling and proper weighting better than those whose data he used. He combined and reweighted their skewed data to make it more accurate, including spotting that the *Literary Digest* was under-recording Democrat performance and adjusting its figures accordingly. He also understood the power of trends, with the trend in estimated political support being useful – such as to see that a campaign message was working – even if the actual numbers were skewed.

Getting people interested in this approach to political intelligence was made easier for Hurja by the independent efforts of the president of Macy's department store, Jesse I. Straus. Straus had polled Democratic convention delegates on who their preferred candidates for president were, with the results seen as having helped swing the selection for Roosevelt by revealing the strength of his support.[9] As a result, the idea that polls were useful and could influence an election was in vogue with key Democratic figures, notwithstanding the lack of respect for the rigour of Hurja's analysis, a lack of respect which led to his acquiring a second nickname, 'Weege', as in the mystic Ouija board. Hurja was also helped by having a candidate and then president in Roosevelt who was concerned to keep in touch with public opinion and to assess it via a multitude of sources.

Hurja's analysis was used to allocate campaign activity, and the campaign went as far as to boast in public about his work. The publicity sought credibility for the analysis by emphasizing just how much data was being used, including at one point speaking of '387 different polls taken by newspapers, magazines, volunteers on radio, trains, ships, airplanes'. On the last weekend before the election, a press release bragged that the Republican Party was 'going to sink to the lowest state that it has experienced in two-party contests since the Civil War'.[10] (This itself says something interesting about the political campaign strategy that Hurja thought was best – campaigners normally stay well away from claiming that victory is in the bag, for fear of depressing the turnout of their own supporters.) Hurja and his data were right about Roosevelt scoring a massive win: he was only 300,000 votes out in his prediction of Roosevelt's lead in the popular vote (7.5 million compared with 7.2 million in reality).

Following Roosevelt's victory, Hurja went to work for the administration, applying his love of data and analytical skills to the disbursement of government posts to Roosevelt supporters. He developed a coding system for the begging letters he received, using colours to indicate how strongly he wished someone to be given a job, from buff-coloured for a mere recommendation, through to white for giving someone a position if one was available, and up to blue for top priority in finding someone a role. He was unabashed about his partisan allocation of jobs: 'Patronage is guarding the government against disloyalty. If you place your friends in office, the government benefits. They work out of loyalty and don't do just a routine job.'[11] As a result, it was best for job hunters to be endorsed by a loyal member of Congress from a key swing district – rewarding loyal friends most in need of electoral popularity was Hurja's focus.

Hurja went on to predict – and help bring about – Democrat gains in the 1934 midterms, against the expectations of many political pundits. Being right once again propelled him to the height of his fame. An appearance on the front cover of *Time* magazine came on 2 March 1936, the first pollster to appear there. To give a sense of just what an accolade that was, on the previous week's cover were Emperor Hirohito of Japan, Soviet leader Stalin, Chinese leader Chiang Kai-shek and the last Chinese emperor, Puyi. The following week's cover was adorned by Léon Blum, only two months away from becoming French prime minister. Covers later that year included Hitler, Mussolini, Shirley Temple and Clark Gable.

Hurja had set the template for how the best political campaigns use polling data: combining polling with other sources of information, including canny modelling and tracking of trends to guide campaign decisions. A century on, his approach still looks sophisticated.[12]

However, Hurja quit the Democrat administration in 1937, in part because his hopes of becoming ambassador to Finland had never been met. He was also growing disillusioned with Roosevelt's political direction, such as his increasingly vociferous attacks on business and his plan to pack the Supreme Court with additional appointees to secure rulings he preferred. Hurja even later switched to become a registered Republican and twice ran unsuccessfully in Republican congressional primaries. He was no longer *Time* magazine front-cover material.

Hurja's disappearance from the history of polling and political campaigns was given further impetus by his 1940 prediction failure. Although Roosevelt won a third term, Hurja had predicted a victory for his Republican challenger, Wendell Willkie. What is more, that 1940 election was not close. Hurja was no longer the magic man of numbers. He got it wrong again in 1944, incorrectly predicting that Dewey would beat Roosevelt, and then yet again in 1948 with 'unmistakable' evidence that Dewey would beat Truman.[13] As with many later political pollsters and consultants, iconoclastic success was followed by embarrassing failure. He did, though, make amends by grabbing headlines in 1952 with confident predictions of a Dwight D. Eisenhower landslide victory, while other pollsters, following the 1948 debacle, were more restrained. He was right about both the win and it being a landslide, though even he underestimated the scale of Eisenhower's electoral college win.

Nevertheless, Hurja's subsequent descent into obscurity is curious. Explanations such as his personal political papers being a dispersed mess or the way in which the Democratic National Committee (DNC) chair James A. Farley, perhaps envious of the attention and credit that went to a subordinate, mostly wrote Hurja out of his memoirs do not really suffice given that in his time Hurja was the talk of the town.[14] His lasting fame should not have had to rely on his sometime boss putting him in a book.

More likely, Hurja's descent into obscurity was due to his very innovativeness. He was too far ahead of what others were doing to be properly appreciated. If you did not understand the weaknesses of pre-modern polling, you would not understand the skills with which he compensated for those weaknesses. Moreover, Roosevelt – foreshadowing the Kennedy campaign and Simulmatics Corporation – liked keeping Hurja's research secret so that he was not seen to be pandering to public opinion. And other pollsters came along in 1936 to steal the limelight, especially the skilled publicist Gallup.

During the peak of his career, though, Hurja's internal data for Democrat campaigns had revealed things that external data had not. The breadth of Hurja's sources of information and his skill in turning bad data into good gave his information a deserved special aura. That aura around internal polling has persisted despite the breadth and quality of public data dramatically increasing. To this day, the media often bestows on internal polls a sense of mystique and unique insight, making internal opinion polls sound exciting and especially revelatory. They are not.

Internal political polls are not some magical, superior source of information.[15] Internal political polls generally ask the same or similar questions as public polls. Moreover, the budgets political parties or candidates allocate to such polls are frequently modest, at least outside the USA – and even at many levels of election in the USA. Yet the problems and risks internal political polls have to grapple with are the same as for public polls, and in fact in some ways worse. Being private polls for a particular client, there is a risk that the lack of transparency results in skewed findings that favour the client, deliberately or inadvertently. Likewise, it is much easier for reporting to slip up on what a poll really says if it is a report on a private poll, perhaps only briefly or partially seen by a journalist, and often a general political journalist rather than a polling expert. (The journalistic skills you need to get leaks of internal political information are very different from the skills you need to make sense of a PDF of opinion poll data. One is about charming humans, the other is about analysing data.)

Even at the simplest level of whether some data comes from an opinion poll at all – as opposed to canvassing returns or other data gathered by political campaigns – it is far from rare to see media reports fail to make a clear distinction.[16] You also do not have to be too cynical to wonder if sometimes figures are made up, or at least generously weighted and rounded off.[17] It is smarter to be quizzical than to be excited when hearing of reports of internal polls.

Internal polls, where genuine, can nonetheless be useful, to tease out extra information that those running parties and campaigns need to know, such as tracking voting intention in particular areas of the country or society, adding greater detail than national polls provide or testing out different policy ideas ahead of deciding which to select and campaign on. But if they tell a significantly different story from the public polls, that is almost always because they are wrong.

Take the example of the internal Conservative polls ahead of the 2005 general election, as reported in the *Financial Times*:

> Lord Saatchi this week revealed details of private polling in 130 marginal seats held by Labour constituencies the Conservatives need to win to overturn Labour's majority of 160. The research purported to show that 103 of these seats would fall to the Tories.[18]

When reality, in the form of the general election result, arrived, the Conservatives only gained 31 seats from Labour, not 103. This was not because of some collapse in Conservative support in the interim. Rather, even when that 'private polling' was published, it was well out of kilter with what the public polls were saying. Hence the *Financial Times*'s caution in saying 'purported', followed later in the piece by a wary 'there is some evidence to back Lord Saatchi's bold claim' and rounded off with 'Lord Saatchi's optimistic findings have raised eyebrows.'

Given that pollster ICM had seen its work for the Conservatives cease shortly before this story appeared, you might expect it to have had some acerbic views on this polling. Still, there is wisdom in the words of ICM director Nick Sparrow quoted in that story: 'If an organization doing a private poll is not prepared to release information to allow people to make up their own minds about the validity of the research, you should treat it with caution.' Nor was he the only pollster to cast doubt on the internal Conservative polls. As another polling firm commented, having failed to see any evidence to back up those internal polls in its own data, 'MORI's analysis of voting intentions shows little evidence of a Conservative breakthrough in marginal constituencies.'[19]

None of this means the Conservative data was fabricated. What it does indicate, however, is that the internal polling, with methodology and details kept secret, used an approach that boosted the apparent Conservative chances. It may not quite have been asking, 'is there any chance that you might possibly once before you die decide not always to avoid voting Conservative?' But it perhaps headed a few notches in that direction. This can be quite a rational thing to do. After all, releasing those figures gave the Conservatives positive media coverage and raised the morale of its supporters. Even the sceptical *Financial Times* report at least gave consideration to whether or not the party might be able to win rather than simply writing off its chances. As Lord Ashcroft wrote after deploying his own set of evidence to knock the internal polling, it gave 'the Tory faithful [at their party conference] in Bournemouth some hope (as one senior Tory remarked, "I believe everything Lord Saatchi says because it cheers me up")'.[20]

That reason for cheerfulness is another reason to suspect internal polls. Even when internal polling is done well, there is a bias in which polls are released or leaked. Not surprisingly, good numbers are more likely to make it to the public than bad ones. Good numbers come with reasons to be passed around.[21] Poor numbers are more likely to be buried (unless the infighting within a party is particularly vicious).[22] As polling expert Harry Enten puts it, 'The reason is simple: Partisans don't want to release polls that are bad for their side.'[23]

For all these limitations, however, the secret nature of internal polls gives them an attractive sheen:

> There may well be a feeling, therefore, within the hierarchies of the main parties that something extremely valuable must necessarily be the result of such exercises and that it must be withheld from being disseminated outside a small group of

party officials. Holding that attitude is also vital in order to justify such expenditure to others in the party.[24]

Being secret makes something sound important, whether it is or not. A superb example of the absurd reverence given to 'internal' polling came less than a month before the 2020 U.S. presidential election. The *Sunday Times* reported that in Britain,

> Ministers have been told to forge links with the White House frontrunner Joe Biden after 'writing off' Donald Trump's chances of re-election, amid fears that the UK could be left out in the cold if the former vice-president wins.
>
> Boris Johnson has been warned that Trump is on course for a landslide defeat with his Democratic opponents set to land a historic 'triple whammy' by seizing control of the presidency, the Senate and the House of Representatives.
>
> Private polling and computer models shown to No 10 last month put Biden's chances of victory at more than 70 per cent.[25]

That election was very heavily polled with hundreds of published polls, multiple aggregations and projections made public, and the latest news from the polls and models was a regular feature of news in countries worldwide. In that context, 'private polling' had nothing to add to what you could glean from reading the U.S. polling page on Wikipedia. But 'here are some exclusive private polls, Prime Minister' certainly sounds more impressive than 'here is a page printed from Wikipedia, Prime Minister'.

Sometimes innovative new methodologies pop up in internal polls before they become the norm for public political polls, usually brought in from the commercial sector. Sometimes, too, internal analysis involves smart, experienced people pulling out insights by collating data from multiple sources and digging into public polling data in detail, both things which media coverage of polls can be very light on. The British political scientist Philip Cowley, who has interviewed many politicians and senior staffers, comments that he is 'impressed by the level of sophistication applied to data . . . on the whole they [internal analysts] are quite sophisticated readers of polls'.[26]

Even so, if you see reports of internal polls, and especially if they are giving surprising findings, give the details a hard stare. Do not be fooled by the aura of secrecy. Remember that internal polls suffer from explicit and implicit pressures to make them produce results the boss wants to hear. They lack the pressures to uphold their quality that come with public polling, and they only become public because someone has an agenda that is served by leaking some of their data. You should remain suspicious about their motives and their data.

Tracking Polls

During the weeks immediately before an election, both politicians and the media can be torn between wanting daily updates on how the campaign is going and not being able to afford an entirely new poll every day. Tracking polls are the answer. Possibly first used for the 1976 Republican primary in New Hampshire, they borrow a technique used in the commercial sector to track advertising campaigns: a small sample is polled each day, and then the results from several days are aggregated to produce robust results.[27] Each day in this rolling process the oldest day gets dropped from the sample and a new day of polling is added (with possible breaks in the daily cycle due to the problems with sampling at weekends). A risk with tracking polls is that in return for their more economical use of polling funds, the occasional rogue day with a wayward sample error is more likely – and such a rogue day then pollutes the results for several days before it drops out.

To make matters worse, the pressure-cooker nature of election campaigns means that people cannot resist peeking at the very latest day's sample only. It is the newest and most exciting data. This undermines the whole point of a tracking poll, as its very design is predicated on any one day's sample not being enough to know what is going on. This is why I am not a fan of tracking polls.[28] There are enough ways that polls can mislead without adding in this extra temptation.

Panel Surveys

Usually, the people sampled for each poll are selected afresh. With a phone poll, another set of random phone numbers is used. With an Internet survey, another slice of people from the panel is selected, and so on. Of course, chance sometimes means the same person will come up again, and for Internet panels, people will be returned to after some time, but basically each poll is a fresh sample.

There are some exceptions to this. Sometimes the same people are deliberately contacted again to check if their views have changed or if they have done what they said they would. After a general election, for example, this can help give insight into what happened to a pre-election poll that was wrong.

Another exception is panel surveys, in which one group of people is repeatedly returned to and asked the same questions over an extended period. The attraction of this approach is the ability to track patterns among groups in detail. What has happened to the Southern men who liked the country's leader at the start of the campaign, for example? If you compare different standard polls, the normal sampling variations will produce statistical noise that clouds the picture.

By asking exactly the same people repeatedly, it is possible to zoom in more clearly on what switches are taking place.

However, as we have seen, panels suffer from the 'panel effect'. The very act of repeatedly asking people questions may change their views. In addition, if, by bad luck, a pollster obtains a skewed sample for the panel, then the pollster is stuck with that through all the subsequent re-polling of the panel. With regular polling with fresh samples each time, one rogue does not pollute the other polls. With a panel, if it is a bad one, all your results end up bad.

The risk of panel effects is one reason why Internet pollsters build up very large groups of people they can invite to take part in any one poll. That way, they can avoid going back to the same individuals too often, avoiding creating a panel effect. (Confusingly, although any reputable Internet pollster does their work in a way that avoids the panel effect, their polls are are sometimes called 'online panel surveys' or 'polling of an online panel'. This use of the word is different, however, from a 'true' panel survey.) Panel surveys are interesting, but, as with tracking polls, should be treated cautiously.

Constituency Polls

The smaller the geographic area, the harder it is to poll accurately. States within the USA are comfortably large enough to be fine to poll. Parliamentary constituencies in Britain, however, are trickier, and individual local government wards almost impossible.

That is because with most sampling methods, it is hard to find enough respondents from within the area. With face-to-face polling, going from door to door in a small area is possible. Its slowness and cost, however, mean it is ruled out most of the time. For telephone pollsters, the decline in the number of phone numbers they can access and in people's willingness to answer the phone and do a survey means it can be tough to hit a decent sample size. Online panels suffer from similar problems, as very large panels still break down to quite small numbers when divided up by the 650 constituencies.[29] Even with the innovative river sampling previously discussed, sampling is tough.

As a result, constituency polls often slip into smaller sample sizes, such as around five hundred rather than the typical 1,000 for national samples. In itself, that is not too much of an issue as we have seen when discussing margins of error.

More tricky is the conundrum of what voting intention question should be asked. It is reasonably straightforward for a national voting intention poll that it should include the party names (or presidential candidate names or similar). But constituency polls happen when there are constituency elections, with constituency-specific candidate names. They may be standing under national party labels, but their names are also on the ballot papers. Moreover, some voters may prefer party X but decide to vote for candidate B from a different party. That might be because they particularly like B or they dislike party X's candidate, or for tactical voting considerations. Whatever the reason, simply asking about the national party may give a misleading result.

There are, therefore, three options available when polling constituencies. One is to stick with the national voting intention question. Another is to make sure the poll emphasizes asking people how they will vote in their particular constituency. Or a third option is to name candidates. This may seem the obvious option to pick, especially when candidate names feature on ballot papers. But candidates are chosen at different times, and some candidates – usually for the weaker parties in an area – are not chosen until shortly before an election. As a result, constituency polls often are carried out before all the candidates are known.

To make matters still harder for political pollsters and those wanting to make political campaign decisions – or place bets – on the results of their constituency polls, the evidence of which wording works best is decidedly mixed. A striking example of this came with the 2015 UK general election. The Liberal Democrats, in coalition with the Conservatives since 2010, went into the election facing perilously low national vote share ratings. Having polled 24 per cent in 2010, the polls had the party down in single digits. In the 229 (!) national voting intention polls with fieldwork starting after 1 January 2015 and before the 2015 general election polling day, the party averaged only 8 per cent. In only 23 of them did the party venture into double figures, and the highest was 12 per cent, achieved just once.

Yet the party touted constituency poll results showing that it would do much better at holding on to its MPs than those figures suggested. This was not just bravado for the public. It was believed by the general election campaign chair and former party leader Paddy Ashdown – so much so that when the exit poll came out on the night of the general election, showing his party dropping massively in seats, he refused to believe it was correct and promised live on national TV to eat his hat if this happened. He was wrong. A hat (of sorts) was eaten.[30] He wasn't alone. On polling day, volunteers at one of the party's phone banks spent time calling voters in Maidstone and the Weald – a seat the party did not hold, and which it went on to lose by the massive margin of 10,709 votes. The party's estimation of its chances in that seat, misled by constituency polling, was way off.

Why were the party's constituency polls wrong? Some rushed in the aftermath to blame the wording of the polling questions as being obviously biased, slanted, wrong, stupid or all four for using candidate names and for asking other questions ahead of getting to voting intention. This, so the argument went, tilted the polls in favour of popular incumbent Liberal Democrat MPs, showing them with a chance of winning, when a 'proper' poll would have shown otherwise.

But the case against naming candidates was as faulty as the polls themselves. An extensive set of constituency polls was carried out on behalf of Lord Ashcroft, which did not name the candidates. Those also turned out to be too optimistic for the Liberal Democrats. Moreover, the internal Conservative Party constituency polls, which did turn out to be pretty accurate, named candidates in their voting questions. Indeed, after the election, one of the pollsters working for the Conservative Party explicitly praised the value of naming candidates in constituency polls:

> Published polls kept showing we were losing seats that our polling showed we weren't, because when you don't measure the incumbency factor through a local candidate name in seats where you are spending enormous time and effort and money upping the name identification of a local member then that's a big mistake.[31]

As for asking other questions ahead of the voting intention question, does that prime those being polled to think more in the way they would when voting (an act people do not come to completely cold) or does it slant the way people are thinking in a way that distorts the results? Again, the evidence is mixed. Although the Liberal Democrat polls failed, Labour's internal polls asked other questions ahead of voting intention, and those polls had a respectable level of accuracy.[32] The conclusion from all of this? Constituency polls often feel like they fill a significant gap in information. But they can go badly wrong and in ways that are tricky to spot in advance or diagnose afterwards. Treat with care.

Marginal Seat Polls

Treat with still more care polls of marginal seats. Sitting between a constituency poll and a national poll, the logic for a marginal seat poll sounds sensible and, prior to writing this section, I have often paid close attention to this sort of poll. It sounds reasonable to say that if the election is going to be decided in the marginal seats (or states), don't poll the whole country, just poll those marginal places. It is cheaper than doing individual polls for each seat, and more focused than doing a national poll whose findings will be clouded by what is happening in safe seats.

That, at least, is the pitch. The reality is different. The reality is that marginal seat polls often mislead. They were one of the reasons why the polling in 1987 – the election at which polls of batches of marginal seats took off in Britain – at times looked more promising for Labour than reality turned out. Sampling only in marginal seats in 1992 was also one reason for the mediocre performance of exit polls at that general election. (The highly reliable modern exit polls discussed below are now done as national exercises, covering a full range of seats.)

The problem is that not all marginal seats are the same, and there is no clear definition of one. Is a marginal seat simply one in which the majority last time was within a certain margin? That might seem easy to answer 'yes' to, but would mean therefore excluding from 'marginal seats' anywhere there are other factors known to influence elections at work, such as a seat in which the majority last time was larger than your threshold but a popular incumbent is not re-standing. This makes selecting where to sample for marginal seat polls much riskier than attempting to do a nationally representative sample. Unless the seats you are happy to include in your definition of marginal seats behave very differently from the overall national picture, you stack up the risks with doing a marginal seat poll without getting any extra insight into what is going on.[33]

Moreover, when the national polls do hit trouble, there is no clear pattern of marginal seat polls (or constituency or state polls) doing better. They are often also off, sometimes by more than the national polls, as in the 2016 and 2020 U.S. presidential elections. It is rare for post-election polling post-mortems to find causes of error which would not also apply to marginal seat polls. Therefore, marginal seat polls look attractive but are more likely to be a hindrance than a help to understanding what is going on.

By-Election Polls

Opinion polls for parliamentary by-elections ('special elections' in U.S. parlance) got off to an impressive start in Britain, before even Gallup's 1945 general election triumph. The first in Britain was for the Fulham West Parliamentary by-election in 1938. It was won for Labour by Edith Summerskill, taking the seat from the Conservatives by 52 per cent to 48 per cent, in the face of widespread predictions by pundits that the Conservatives would hold on. As we've seen, Gallup had polled the seat and pointed to her victory, getting within 1 per cent of both her and the Conservative candidate's vote shares. Yet that early success was in a way misleading, for constituency polls carried out ahead of a by-election are tough to get right.

One complication is turnout. Turnout usually drops sharply at by-elections compared with general elections. That makes the sort of adjustments for turnout discussed earlier still more critical, and yet those adjustments are hard to get right. Another complication is the extent to which public support can move dramatically just before polling day. Back when I used to use a multitude of different data sources to closely track the performance of the Liberal Democrats for the party's by-election team, you could often see a party's support moving by ten percentage points or more in just a few days. That is the sort of move that can take a poll from being bang on to apparently embarrassingly awful in the space of a long weekend.[34] Therefore, the exact dates of when the fieldwork was carried out are particularly important for by-election polls, as is the caution to be applied to polls carried out well before polling day.

Television Debate Polls

Debates between party leaders or presidential candidates are now a common feature of campaigns. Common too is snap polling, rapidly carried out after such debates to identify the winner. Such polling has not always been done well. The 1980 U.S. TV debate between incumbent president Jimmy Carter and Republican challenger Ronald Reagan is usually remembered for Reagan's withering put-down, responding to Carter going on the attack with 'there you go again.' Less remembered, thankfully, is how ABC News ran a poll to find out who had won the debate. Viewers were invited to phone one of two special numbers, costing fifty cents a call. ABC then gave heavy coverage to the results. With more than 700,000 calls made, it was a nice money-spinner for the TV station. But such self-selecting voodoo polls are no way to undertake a proper political poll, or, for that matter, for a proper news station to behave.[35] Proper post-debate polling is now, thankfully, widespread instead.

Such polling is not as straightforward as it may appear. As Stephan Shakespeare, co-founder of YouGov, put it at one election: 'There has been great interest not only in the election debates, but in the polling of who "won" or "lost". At first sight, it may seem obvious how pollsters should measure that, but on closer inspection, it isn't obvious at all.'[36]

Whose opinions are such polls trying to measure? Regular voting intention polls have a standard answer. They are trying to measure the views of those who will vote. Not everyone watches a TV debate, however. Should you be polling just those who saw the debate? What about those who watched the debate but aren't going to vote? Or what about likely voters who did not watch the debate but may be influenced by how it went? Or perhaps all those groups are too hard to define tightly, so is it better to revert simply to adults overall?

There is no simple right or wrong answer as to who such polls should try to measure. To make matters worse, knowing for sure the make-up of those who watched a debate is very difficult, making it nearly impossible for pollsters to weight any samples to make them representative of those who watched. As a result, practice varies greatly as to whom pollsters are trying to measure in such polls. This is also why sometimes a different approach is taken, and polling is done of swing voters (again, a concept open to multiple definitions). Or normal polling is abandoned and focus groups of people who watched the debate at the pollster's invitation are used instead.

Then there is the question of how quickly any poll should be conducted. There is an obvious benefit to speed. The sooner the results are available, the sooner they can inform and influence coverage of the debates. Instant responses are often instructive, but they are not always the responses that stick. That is why so many books about marketing reference the New Coke fiasco of the 1980s. Coca-Cola changed the taste of its famous drink, emboldened by research that showed that people's instant reactions to the new formula's taste were very positive. Their longer-term reception was anything but, and the new formula had to be dropped, at enormous expense. There are similar examples from politics about how the instant reaction is not the same as the considered reaction to a televised debate. In an earlier U.S. presidential debate in 1976, Carter, then the challenger, had been up against incumbent Gerald Ford. Ford spoke about how eastern Europe was not under Communist domination, a blunder that regularly features in lists of the worst political debate gaffes. Yet the immediate impact on polling was very slight, if at all. It only became a famous gaffe as time passed.[37] (Ironically, Carter's chief campaign pollster in 1976, Patrick Caddell, had then gone on to work for Coca-Cola on the failed market research that led to the New Coke fiasco.)

There are, therefore, an important set of particular choices that pollsters have to make when polling debates. These choices tend not to receive much attention, and even if you are the sort of person who reads the small print at the end of newspaper articles and then goes hunting for the data tables on a pollster's website, it can be hard to find out what choices have gone into a post-debate poll.

When someone is the runaway winner of a debate, the variations in results produced by the variations in approaches do not matter much as the polls still all score the same person as the winner. When performances are closer, however, the variations can sow confusion, with different pollsters showing different winners. But really, the different polls are measuring different things. Perhaps being all over the place, therefore, is reassuring rather than worrying.

Emotional Intensity

A form of polling that has started to develop in recent years focuses not on what people say but how quickly they say it. The theory is that response speeds give an insight into factors such as the emotional strength of the response. With its origins in psychology experiments, this technique can most easily be applied to opinion polls conducted online, though it can also be applied to telephone surveys. The speed of response has the technical term 'response latency'.

This is still mostly uncharted territory for political polling. Although there is research to suggest a useful link between speed of response and understanding people's political attitudes, there is little published data that can provide benchmarks for comparison, trend tracking or correlation with election outcomes.[38] If a speed-of-response polling analysis shows that people are much quicker to say they like the leader of the opposition than they are to say they like the prime minister, what does that mean in terms of votes impact? There is little public data to extrapolate from what can sound like exciting (and perhaps scary) research findings into voting effects. Therefore, if you chance across such results, take care not to assume that significant differences in speed signify a notable political conclusion. The onus is very much on those touting the research findings to demonstrate that.

MRP

A recent British general election saw the first public outing in the country of a new, highly sophisticated polling methodology. Using advanced statistical techniques, it generates individual constituency results from a national poll sample that would not usually be considered large enough to use to predict an individual seat. Reassuringly for the new methodology, its findings were in line with the conventional national opinion polls. Then came 10 p.m. on election night. The polls closed. The exit poll was published, and the national polls looked wrong. The safe Conservative election win they had foretold instead turned into a hung parliament. And that fancy new methodology? It was not so fancy after all – it was wrong, along with all the rest.

That was, very nearly, the stillbirth of MRP polling.[39] For ahead of the 2017 general election, there were two sets of the newfangled MRP polls. One was for Lord Ashcroft. It wrongly pointed towards a huge Conservative majority of between 162 and 180 seats.[40] The other was by YouGov for *The Times*, which debuted with front-page coverage pointing – correctly – towards a shock result and a hung parliament.[41] It was a lucky break for MRP practitioners that the one that was right was the one that got attention, and the one that was wrong was the one that was mostly ignored.[42]

Not only was the poll that got the attention the one that was right, but, in an echo of George Gallup's triumph over the *Literary Digest*, it was right in a memorable, headline-grabbing way. It was even – extending the parallels with Gallup – less correct than the headlines made it seem. Gallup got the winner right and so the plaudits despite not being that close on the vote shares. Likewise, YouGov's MRP model got the praise for standing out from the crowd and predicting a hung parliament, even though it hadn't really. As Stephan Shakespeare wrote the day before the general election (by which point the poll's figures had moved a little from the original *Times* front page),

> The model, unlike the traditional methodology, makes estimates for every constituency and when we add them up, it doesn't give the Conservatives a majority. But we never predicted 'a hung parliament.' The model says that it's too close to call whether Conservatives will win a majority (326 seats), not that they will definitely be under 326 seats. A Conservative majority is well within the margin of error and, in any event, these are estimates of voting intentions, not predictions of election outcomes.[43]

Such caveats were little noticed. The original *Times* splash was what had been noticed – noticed first for being very different from what other polling reports were saying at the time and then afterwards for being much more accurate than them. The story was all about the brave iconoclasts who got it right.

Even *The Times*, despite having the editorial self-confidence to put the original MRP story on its front page, had called it 'controversial' and warned of the margin of error:

SHOCK POLL PREDICTS TORY LOSSES
Controversial YouGov estimate points to hung parliament with 20 fewer seats for May . . .
The central projection of the model, which allows for a wide margin of error, would be a catastrophic outcome for Theresa May.[44]

Other media followed suit, such as *The Guardian*:

The polling firm is employing a new 'controversial' methodology only 10 days before the general election . . . In language echoing *Yes Minister*'s Sir Humphrey Appleby, leading pollsters have described YouGov's 'shock poll' predicting a hung parliament on 8 June as 'brave' and the decision by *The Times* to splash it on its front page as 'even braver'.[45]

As Martin Boon, a pollster for another firm, and someone who had received industry plaudits for convention-defying methodology that got it right in the past, tweeted, 'Splashing this on the front page is even braver than @YouGov doing it in the first place.'[46] Ben Page, of Ipsos MORI, replied laconically, 'My thoughts too.'[47] Or for a response from academic polling experts, take this from Will Jennings: 'Very brave!'[48] And in a tweet that can console anyone who regrets making a faulty prediction on social media, Jim Messina, hired by the Conservative Party after his role in getting Barack Obama elected U.S. president, tweeted the next day, 'Spent the day laughing at yet another stupid poll from @YouGov.'[49] He, at least, did not go as far as the *Daily Express*, which ran a headline claiming, 'Holes in the Poll EXPOSED: Why the YouGov Panel Predicting Tory Loss Shouldn't Be Believed.'[50]

It was the perfect set-up for MRP to be transformed from un-known methodology to revered newcomer. But what is MRP? The acronym stands for 'multi-level regression and post-stratification'. It is a form of modelling which allows you to use a national sample to work out accurate estimates of support for parties or candidates in small geographic areas. The key to the model is the understanding that although the specific combination of different factors which impact how we vote (our gender, age, past voting record, occupation, whether we live in a marginal constituency and so on) may not be shared with many other people, each individual factor is shared by many.

Doing a poll that has a large enough sample to allow you to directly find out how, say, a male in his forties who used to vote Labour, works in the public sector and lives in a rural, safe Conservative seat is voting, would require a very large sample to reach enough people to meet all those criteria. MRP, therefore, does something different.[51] It instead looks at what men are doing, what people in their forties are doing, what those who used to vote Labour are doing and so on. For each of these criteria on their own, you do not need nearly as large a total sample to obtain enough results from within it. The MRP modelling then combines the answers from each of these different criteria to work out the views of the voter with that particular combination of male in his forties who used to vote Labour, works in the public sector and lives in a rural, safe Conservative seat.

Those example characteristics I have chosen are deliberately a mix of features of the person (male, forties and so on) and the place where that person is (rural and safe Conservative seat) because MRP caters for the characteristics of both person and place in its modelling.

As well as the local political context, the YouGov 2019 MRP model, for example, had variables for the number of Indian takeaways and the number of fish and chip shops in constituencies, using these as a way of capturing different types of constituencies.[52] Place, in this case, meant plaice.

The next step is to take each constituency in turn, do that modelling for all of its voters, and aggregate the outcomes to give a result for the constituency.[53] What MRP calculates is probabilities, such as that a male in his forties who used to vote Labour, works in the public sector and lives in a rural, safe Conservative seat is 35 per cent likely to vote Conservative, 55 per cent likely to vote Labour and so on. Those probabilities are gathered together for all the voters in a constituency, giving each party an overall probability of winning that seat. The headline seat totals are then based on those seat probabilities. For example, if a party is predicted to have a 90 per cent chance of winning in ten seats, that adds nine seats (90 per cent of 10) to its headline total.

All of this requires much larger sample sizes than a regular national poll, usually around 50,000.[54] However, the ability to extract individual constituency figures from a sample of 50,000 still compares very favourably with the sample sizes that would be required to do a poll in each constituency. In the UK, with 650 constituencies, for example, to obtain figures for each constituency through conventional polling, with a typical 1,000 sample in each and every seat, would add up to a mammoth 650,000 sample instead. Even at 500 per constituency, you would still need 325,000. (Smaller constituency samples would be problematic because, as we've seen, the margins of error really depend on the sample size rather than on the size of the population being sampled.[55])

One question that often arises is whether an MRP model is sophisticated enough to pick up on a particular constituency's idiosyncrasies.

As the explanation shows, MRP is designed to put together constituency figures based on each seat's make-up. Therefore, comments such as 'that can't be right for my constituency as we have many more older people than average' misses the point. MRP is designed to cope with just that. What it cannot cope with are very specific individual circumstances, such as if a large manufacturing site with a local workforce has just closed in a seat, putting lots of people out of work and with the government refusing financial support. That is the sort of one-off constituency event too specific even for MRP.

Between the extremes of something that is just about the one constituency (significant job losses at a local site, government to blame) and something easy for MRP to model (variations in average ages of the population in different constituencies), how can you tell if a factor is too specific or not for MRP to cope? My rule of thumb is to look at the average sample size in each seat, see how many multiples you need to reach 1,000 (a standard poll sample with reasonable overall margins of error), and then conclude that if a factor is present in the number of seats equal to or greater than the number of multiples, then MRP should be able to cope. For example, with a national sample of 50,000 and 650 constituencies, that gives an average of 77 from the sample per constituency. That means you need thirteen constituencies to reach 1,000. Hence a major factory closure hitting four constituencies is still too specific for the MRP model to understand. Widespread flooding, causing chaos and homelessness across two dozen constituencies, though – that it should be able to cope with (provided that information about which constituencies were affected by the flooding is included in the model).[56]

Crucially, as the fate of the pair of MRP models in 2017 showed, for all its sophistication, there is no guarantee that it is right. Not only are there the usual risks with a sample being off due to random bad luck or differential response rates, but there is the risk that the list of characteristics chosen to be modelled renders it a bad list. Do they accurately capture the factors at play influencing someone's votes in this particular election? Of course, those configuring the MRP model for an election can experiment with how different factors work out and compare their results with national polls. It is, though, a skilled task to put together an MRP model, and one that can easily be done incorrectly.

Even when successful for one election, an MRP model can fail at the next. The actual factors used in the 2017 YouGov model demonstrate the risk that a previously good model can turn bad. They included how someone had voted in the 2016 European referendum and also what the percentage 'Leave' vote was in that referendum in the constituency they were in. For the 2017, and indeed 2019, general elections, that was relevant. But how important will the 'Leave versus Remain' divide be at future elections? That will require testing and judgements by the team that update the model for the next election, opening up the scope for error despite the model's current good track record.

One thing, in particular, should remain as a worry at the back of the mind of anyone who wishes to place a high degree of faith in MRP polling. A consequence of its statistical approach is that MRP performs better the greater the variations are between constituencies (or states, or other geographic blocks being projected) rather than within them. An election that is geographically polarized, in which different parts of the country move in different directions, makes for better MRP modelling than an election which is, say, polarized by gender (as constituencies do not vary much in their gender breakdown).[57]

A lesser but still potential source of error comes from working out how many people with each combination of those factors are in each constituency. The sorts of sources used, such as the census, are episodic and may be many years out of date. That requires judgements about whether to extrapolate updates to the data and if so, how. (This is harder than it may seem, and so was one of the sources of errors for conventional polls at the 1992 general election.)

Moreover, the details of which factors have been used and the relative importance given to them is, currently at least, treated largely as a secret black box. Even with the YouGov MRP model in 2017 and 2019, for which a large amount of information was published live during the election campaigns, there was little detail on the key calculations at the heart of the model. Yet if there had been, it would still not have been of much use. Due to the novelty and complexity of MRP, one of the experts in this approach says, 'there are maybe ten people in the UK who could realistically have an informed view' of the quality of an MRP model, even if given all its detail.[58]

That difficulty in understanding the quality of MRP models is a problem because there is no magic at the heart of MRP that means we should expect it always to be right. Compared with conventional political polling, MRP is, in some ways, more challenging to get right. As with conventional polling, the overall polling methodology has to be right, including sampling and turnout weighting. Then, in addition, MRP also has to get right the constituency modelling. In return for that added complexity – and so added risk – MRP should give a better idea of seat numbers, which is important in close elections or ones in which the country's political geography is changing. However, there is a delicate balance to be struck when considering political geography and the use of MRP. If no change in political geography is occurring, then simple extrapolations of seat numbers from national poll numbers will work well, and MRP does not add much predictive power. On the other hand, if too much change in political geography is occurring, or it is of the type that MRP struggles with, then it could undo the MRP modelling. Like Goldilocks with her porridge, in order to shine MRP practitioners need change to be neither too little nor too much. The change needs to be just right.

Given the brief track record of MRP so far, even combining the British examples with those in other countries, there is no firm conclusion one can draw about MRP's overall reliability compared with other polls. It is, at the moment, more an aesthetic choice. Do you view a national election as a national event, played out on the national stage? After all, voters generally are better able to name national party leaders than local candidates. If so, a conventional national poll captures the essence of it. Or do you view a national election as the aggregation of each voter's individual voting decisions, added up at constituency level to produce an overall result? After all, that is how the maths of national vote shares and national seat totals work: they are simply the sum of all the local results based on all the individual votes in each seat. If so, MRP's approach of modelling each individual and aggregating up captures the essence of it. Moreover, when MRP gets it right, this approach means you can explain *why* things are happening much better, by breaking them down into the individual voter switches that caused seats to be gained, held or lost. However, elections are, in truth, both an individual and a national event. This is why the future of polling is likely to involve both MRP and traditional polling – and both can, and will, sometimes go wrong.

Exit Polls: The UK

In recent years, there has been a special bank holiday treat on the BBC Parliament channel: re-running, in full, the election night TV coverage from British general elections. You can re-watch everything from the polls closing at 10 p.m. through to the new or returning prime minister heading off to the palace to meet the queen and starting to form a fresh government. It is a treat for election nerds.

The shows start with several hours of speculation to fill the time before enough constituency results have come in for the winner to be clear, or at least for it to be clear that it is going to be a very close result. Exit polls, released after the close of polls, increasingly fill that speculation interregnum with their own predictions. Their data has not always been trusted, and they have not always been right. But in recent years, UK exit polls have been on a roll. In three general elections in a row – 2010, 2015 and 2017 – the exit polls at 10 p.m. on election night painted a rather different result from what experts – and non-experts – had been predicting.[59] There was the poor seat showing from the Liberal Democrats in 2010, a surprise Conservative majority in 2015 and a shock hung parliament in 2017. In all three cases, the exit poll was right, and the doubting pundits and politicians – including, as mentioned, Paddy Ashdown and his hat – were wrong. By 2019, when the exit poll was again correct, the highest-profile member of the team producing these exit polls, political scientist John Curtice, had not only been knighted; he had become a public persona treated with widespread reverence.[60]

The debut British exit poll was conducted in 1970. It was a mere one-constituency affair, carried out in Gravesend by Taylor, Nelson and Associates.[61] That seat had been selected as the most socially typical of the whole country. The figures, released 30 minutes after the polls closed, did well. They showed the Conservatives moving into a lead over Labour, with a 4.4 per cent swing from Labour to the Conservatives. That not only nearly matched the constituency result when it came out, it was also close to the actual 4.9 per cent national swing. The nascent exit poll had performed better than the final pre-election round of regular political polls. It even out-performed the one final pre-election poll, from pollster ORC, that had correctly put the Conservatives ahead.[62]

The exit poll's exact figures were a prediction of Conservative 46.4 per cent, Labour 45.5 per cent and Liberal 8.1 per cent. The result was 46.8 per cent, 45.0 per cent and 8.2 per cent. Note again the value of luck for making a polling reputation: with the result so close, the exit poll could have got the winner wrong by showing a tiny Labour lead and still been very impressively close to the correct vote shares.[63]

Moreover, for all that Gravesend was typical of the country, there was a degree of luck in its election result being quite so typical, helped by the much smaller impact of MP incumbency and constituency campaigning back then and a lesser variation between the politics of England, Scotland and Wales than that seen in other elections. It would be very risky now to take a seat in southern England with a Labour incumbent and assume that it could accurately foretell what would happen in Scottish seats held by other parties.

National exit polls followed at the October 1974 election, and, with some bumps since then, British exit polls have established an excellent track record, especially for the last six general elections.[64] There are three reasons to believe that this is more than just a run of good luck. The first is that the exit poll is well resourced. As *The Economist* wrote in 2019, 'It is perhaps the world's most expensive one-question social survey. Britain's three main broadcasters – BBC, ITV and Sky News – jointly commission the exit poll from Ipsos MORI, a pollster, and a team of academics, at a cost of some £300,000.'[65]

The second is that exit polling is, in some respects, more straightforward than regular polling. Logistically, it has all the challenges of doing a poll in just one day and turning around the results very promptly. Organizing that reliably is impressive. However, what makes things much easier for exit polls is not having to worry about modelling turnout.[66] A lesser additional helpful factor is that exit pollsters do not have to worry about whether or not people to whom they are speaking are on the electoral register.

The final reason to believe that exit polling is genuinely better than regular political polling is the broader international context. As pollster Nick Moon put it in an industry talk, in many countries if you get an exit poll wrong, you can make it look like electoral fraud has taken place and so trigger riots, perhaps deaths and possibly a coup. The pressure is on to get it right. The skills and diligence learned in those high-pressure environments copy over to more sedate democracies too.

British general election exit polling has evolved a distinctive methodology.[67] This is because Britain's first-past-the-post electoral system means knowing how many votes a party has is a guide, but only an approximate guide, to how many seats it has won. As a striking example, in the 1997 general election, the Liberal Democrat vote share fell by 1 per cent, yet the party's number of MPs more than doubled on the previous general election (20 to 46).[68] To tell you the results, an exit poll has to be able to pick up patterns such as this bucking of the national trend by the Liberal Democrats in their target seats.

To make matters more challenging, exit polls are conducted by asking people how they voted as they leave a polling station. There are around 40,000 of these in the country, across 650 constituencies. However, election results are only declared on a constituency basis. The figures for each polling station are not published. So exit pollsters have to choose which polling stations to do their polling at without being able to cross-check the previous election results from those polling stations against the overall results to see if they were a representative mix.

To deal with these obstacles to running an exit poll that measures accurately current levels of support, the British exit poll instead focuses on measuring changes from the previous election. As John Curtice explains,

> The approach nowadays is based on the observation that although the level of support for each political party varies considerably from one constituency to another, the extent to which the *change* in a party's level of support varies from

one seat to another is much less, and is thus more likely to be estimated correctly by any set of polling stations. Thus rather than attempting to estimate each party's share of the vote, the exit poll attempts to estimate how much each party's vote is up or down since the last elections and then applies these estimates to the actual result last time.

But how can that possibly be done if we do not know the result in each polling station last time around? Well, the one set of polling stations for which we do have an estimate of how people voted last time are the stations at which the exit poll was conducted last time around. So if, wherever possible, the exit poll is conducted at exactly the same places as last time, we can derive an estimate of how much each party's vote is up or down.[69]

As well as concentrating on changes, the exit poll also considers any systematic variation between different types of constituencies and produces different estimates of vote share changes in those different types. This methodology explains why the headline results read out just after the polls have closed at 10 p.m. on an election night are all about seat numbers, not national vote shares. The methodology is tuned to produce the former, not the latter. In that respect, the exit poll is the opposite of a regular voting intention poll.

Exit Polls: The USA

American exit polls deserve their own section because, frankly, they are not very good. In other countries where an election count's accuracy or fairness is in doubt, it is common to see and use exit polls as a safeguard, giving numbers to test against the actual result. Yet in the United States, ahead of the 2020 presidential election, the blunt verdict on U.S. exit polls from a question-and-answer piece run by the Princeton Election Consortium was that they are not up to this task:

> M. D. writes: In third world countries, exit polls are compared
> to election results to see if there has been election fraud.
> Is there anything set up this time in America to compare
> results to how people thought they voted?

> Sam replies: Can't exactly do that because exit polls are
> themselves not very well weighted, i.e. they get adjusted
> to reflect the outcome. Better to use opinion polls, though
> I think that is not standard practice.[70]

This is not because exit polls are a new thing in America, without enough experience yet accumulated for them to do well. In fact, America was home to the first exit poll.

There are multiple claims as to when that pioneering effort occurred, due both to the historical record being imperfectly preserved and also to the question of quite what counts as an exit poll. The modern concept of one is straightforward: polling conducted at or outside polling locations just after people have voted, and with the data turned into an election prediction that is published very soon after voting ends.[71] If we take this as the criterion, then the emergence of otherwise regular polling that takes place on polling day – that is, away from polling stations and (possibly) without being restricted to people who said they had already voted – does not count when looking for the first exit poll.

On this basis, credit for the first exit poll should go to the team from the National Opinion Research Center and their experiment in Boulder, Colorado, in 1940.[72] At each of the sixteen official precinct polling stations, voters were asked both about their votes and also about policy issues. This happened after they had voted but before they had left the polling station. Voters were given a polling questionnaire, to be completed secretly as with a normal ballot, and then placed in a special pollster ballot box. The motivation for this experiment was not one of predicting or explaining the election result. Instead, it was to compare the answers given in the comforting anonymity of a polling booth with the answers given to pollsters carrying out a conventional poll, calling on people elsewhere. This was because, as the researchers explained, 'critics have maintained that the results of surveys on social and economic questions do not express the true opinions people would reveal if allowed to vote on them.' Hence the taking of opinion in polling booths on election day to compare with a regular poll.[73]

Due to this niche purpose, the first exit poll did not inspire others to follow suit. Instead, exit polling had to be accidentally reinvented in 1964 by an employee of pollster Louis Harris with an aversion to walking up and down lots of stairs:

> During the 1964 Maryland presidential primary a Louis Harris interviewer in Baltimore, told to talk to voters in their homes to find how they had or would vote, said she got tired of climbing up and down stairs in tall apartment buildings to find her voters, and instead went along to the local school where the voting was taking place. After asking permission from the polling officials, she interviewed voters as they came out of the polling station. When Louis Harris heard what she had done he liked the idea and put it into wide-scale use for the 1964 Californian Republican primary.[74]

Rewatching the live CBS night show from this Californian election gives many pleasures, not only from the reverence given to early computers but from idiosyncrasies such as the live coverage of one election precinct count being carried out in the kitchen of someone's house. The attempts to make numbers comprehensible to the audience also resulted in the floor of a convention centre being cleared out to make way for a huge bar chart made of chairs, showing the relative success of each Republican presidential candidate.

Louis Harris himself features on the show, including the dramatic moment when, only 23 minutes after polls closed and with only 2 per cent of the Republican presidential primary votes counted, CBS called the election for Barry Goldwater.[75] This was well ahead of others in the media, and as Goldwater remained behind for an extended period in the raw vote tallies, it looked like it might be a major embarrassment too. The wire services wrongly called the election for Rockefeller, as did one local CBS station. But in the end, Goldwater won, just, by 1,120,403 votes to 1,052,053. CBS's reputation was saved and even, by being right and early, enhanced.

CBS had been in a heavy rivalry with NBC to be the first to project winners in previous primaries. It ran up a huge phone bill from using a large team of reporters phoning in local results in one previous failed attempt to best NBC.[76] This time, there were two reasons for the successful and extremely early call. First, there was the VPA (Voter Profile Analysis), a refined operation to gather raw vote totals from a carefully chosen sample of precincts selected to be representative of the whole state. A large team of people on the ground gathered the numbers as they were announced on site in each precinct, with IBM computers crunching the numbers.[77] By using a representative sample of precincts, VPA could (it was hoped) draw a more accurate picture than the one seen by simply looking at the raw vote totals from whichever precincts happened to have counted so far.

VPA had been given a high-profile dry run in the 1962 elections, including in the Michigan governor race between incumbent John

Swainson and challenger George Romney. Raw vote totals showed Swainson ahead, but just before CBS switched to put him live on air, CBS called the race for Romney. Not only did Swainson not believe it, neither did Romney when CBS switched over to him. Yet CBS was right, and Romney won. Given how close the result was, there was a degree of luck in CBS having called the winner correctly (a familiar theme).

The second factor feeding into the early call for California was exit polling. The raw vote totals coming in just after 7 p.m. showed Goldwater ahead, but with no data in from the Bay area. Asked about whether the race could therefore be called for Goldwater or whether more data was needed, Harris explained to colleagues, 'Don't worry about that. We interviewed people coming out of polling places in our sample precincts up there and they'll do okay as substitutes.'[78]

That exit polling had taken an unusual form, as people were asked to pick either a black or white bean depending on who they voted for and the beans were counted up. As the bean totals were used to supplement a forecast based on actual vote data, rather than as a freestanding piece of polling, this was exit polling rather than an exit poll per se.

The combination of VPA and bean counting resulted in a notable 'win' for CBS and Harris. Yet again, there was a degree of luck in all this for Harris and his polling colleagues, as their final polling data had Goldwater ahead, but only within their calculated margin of error.

Harris was not alone in pioneering exit polling in the 1964 California primary, as it also saw NBC's first steps in that direction under I. A. 'Bud' Lewis. Before he became director of polling for NBC, he had been a scriptwriter for TV host Dave Garroway, whose co-host was a (real) chimpanzee. Lewis organized university students to sample the votes in a selection of precincts, although the results were not collated into a systematic attempt at a forecast result.[79]

And so, exit polling was on its way.[80] More inspiration for exit polling came from commercial market research techniques, as explained by two veterans of TV channel CBS's election coverage who, notwithstanding CBS/Harris having inaugurated exit polling in 1964, claimed it was introduced at the network three years later:

> In 1967 we introduced exit polls at CBS. We were led to interviewing voters at the polling places because of a story we heard from George Fine . . . Fine told us about how he interviewed moviegoers after they had seen a moving picture. His purpose was to get feedback for a movie company so they could revise the film before distributing it nationally . . . We interviewed voters at the precincts for the first time in Kentucky in 1967 for a lone governor's race. In 1968 we used them for the six primaries CBS covered and in 21 states for the general election.[81]

Despite that head start, exit polls in the United States have not acquired the reputation they have in Britain and elsewhere. To be fair, part of this is due to the muddling of two different sorts of figures on election night: projections and exit polls.

In the United States, unlike in the UK, votes are counted and official figures published on a more local basis than the area up for election. So in, say, a state-wide election for governor, figures will start coming in from the smallest and quickest precinct. By contrast, in the UK, the only official vote total figures declared are those for the overall result in a seat.[82] In the United States, as we have seen, rather than having exit polls that are used to predict results the moment polling stations close, a mix of exit poll data and actual voting returns is used to call who has won in places later on in the evening (and up to days later in the case of very close contests). Such combined projections had a good run for many decades before the year 2000. There had been,

> [A] superb record of success over nearly a third of a century. When CBS News unilaterally used the methodology between 1967 and 1988 it made five mistakes in naming the winners of state elections and primaries. When the CBS system was adopted by VNS [Voter News Service] the same methodology erred just once during the 10 years of pooled election coverage leading up to the 2000 election.[83]

Then, 2000 came around. In a very close presidential election that ended up hinging on the state, Florida was first called by the TV networks for Democrat Al Gore (based on a mix of actual votes and exit polling). Then that call was rescinded and the state was called for Republican George W. Bush (based on projecting from actual votes), before that call too was rescinded. The result ended up being incredibly close and had to be settled via the courts, with Gore conceding when the Supreme Court ruled against a recount continuing.[84]

Nor was 2000 a one-off blemish. It was the start of a run of stumbles.[85] In particular, 2004's exit polls were faulty, leading many on election day to wrongly start speaking about the victory of John Kerry, based on leaks and rumours of the exit poll data. He did not win.[86] By 2007 it was being written that

> There have been so many problems with exit polls in the last four national elections that news organizations approach 2008 election night coverage without a great deal of confidence in what those polls will show. The six news organizations that jointly conduct exit polls, ABC, CBS, CNN, Fox, NBC, and The Associated Press have been on a roller coaster ride

since Election Day 2000, with a great many successes, some spectacular failures, enormous efforts to 'fix' the polls, and millions of dollars spent in the process.[87]

Since then, the accuracy or otherwise of exit polling has continued to be a matter of controversy.[88] It is not clear why U.S. exit polls are not as good as those in the UK. Notwithstanding the mystery surrounding the cause of it, the mere fact of the unreliability of U.S. exit polls means they should be treated with greater caution than those in other countries.

6

POLLING GETS IT RIGHT

'Any poll that shows us gaining or slightly ahead is accurate.'
– RICHARD KUTZLEB, press officer for
Hubert Humphrey presidential campaign, 1968[1]

The second decade of this century was a tough one for the reputation of political polling. It had several high-profile apparent failures, generating headlines that have stuck in people's memories, undermining the reputation of polling for years after. But there's also been a wave of research showing how, even taking into account those contests, political polling continues overall to be pretty good – not perfect, but certainly good enough to be deserving of continued attention.

A Rough Time for Political Polls

At 7.28 p.m. on 8 March 2016, Ritchie King, of the FiveThirtyEight website, posted on the site's liveblog a graph based on the polls showing predictions for the result in that day's Democrat presidential primary in Michigan. Going back as early as February and up until that day, the predicted chances of Hillary Clinton winning over Bernie Sanders were close to 100 per cent. The final data point is labelled '>99 per cent'.

At 9.25 p.m., site founder and mastermind Nate Silver pointed out, 'If Sanders winds up winning in Michigan, in fact, it will count as among the greatest polling errors in primary history.' At 11.37 p.m., Harry Enten reported: 'In what might be one of the greatest shockers in presidential primary history, The Associated Press has called Michigan for Sanders.'[2]

Michigan was but one of a series of high-profile apparent polling failures clustered within a few years of each other that have battered the reputation of political polls. Yet not all the failures are quite what they seem on closer inspection. Take the UK's referendum on membership of the European Union, held in June 2016, which resulted in a vote to leave the EU. It is often given as an example of the polls getting it wrong. That's understandable, as polling averages put the 'Remain' side ahead, and on polling day itself, although there was not a traditional exit poll, there was online polling from YouGov which asked people how they had voted. It put 'Remain' ahead with an increased lead compared with YouGov's previous poll. Add to that widespread expectations that 'Remain' would win, fuelled by other evidence such as the international pattern of a move towards the status quo in the latter stages of referendum campaigns, and it is easy to see why the shock of a 'Leave' win resulted in people thinking the polls were wrong.

But look more closely. Eight different polling firms had a 'final' poll conducted just before polling day, with an average result of 'Remain' at 52 per cent and 'Leave' at 48 per cent.[3] Compared with the actual result of 'Remain' at 48 per cent and 'Leave' at 52 per cent, that wasn't a great polling result. But nor was it an awful one either. The error on vote share was larger than comfortable for the pollsters, but not massive (four points). Indeed, with 'Remain' polling at 52 per cent, we should have expected 'Remain' to lose around one time in six.[4] That's not frequent, but one time in six certainly feels high if you're playing Russian roulette the traditional way – one bullet in six chambers of a gun. Moreover, two of those final polls had put 'Leave' ahead, and those were from two of the polling firms – TNS and Opinium – who, as we'll see in Chapter Eleven, had been among those least wrong in the polling miss at the previous 2015 general election.

Across all the polls which were wholly or partly carried out in that June ahead of the referendum, there was a near-perfect split: 14 put 'Remain' ahead, 16 put 'Leave' ahead, one pointed towards a tie, and one pointed to either result depending on the methodology preferred.[5]

So despite the expectations of the time, there was plenty of data pointing to the possibility of a 'Leave' win. Even one of the pollsters that got its final poll wrong, Ipsos MORI, accompanied those figures with a calculation giving a 26 per cent chance of 'Leave' winning.[6] At least as much of a problem as the polls had been the undue certainty people had taken from them. Paying more attention to the full details of what the pollsters were saying would have made the result less of a surprise.

Similarly, the national U.S. presidential election polls did seem to get it wrong in 2016, pointing to a win for Hillary Clinton. But they were right to put her ahead in the popular vote because she did win more votes than Trump. In fact, if you judge the 2016 U.S. polls by how close they were to the actual vote shares won by the candidates, they were *more* accurate than those in the previous presidential contest. But in 2012 both the polls and the final result predicted Barack Obama as the winner. Even in the swing states in 2016, the U.S. polls were not badly off.[7] Of course, this factor sometimes breaks the other way too, such as in the second round of the 2017 French presidential election, in which the polls performed poorly when judged by vote share. However, in making that error, the polls pointed to a massive win for Emmanuel Macron, when the actual result was an even more massive win. That is about as boring an error as you can get.

The Evidence

Defending the accuracy of polls, however, is about more than picking a fight over individual examples claimed as evidence of polling failure. It is also about looking at the broader picture – more polls, over more contests, over more years and over more countries. Do that, and you find a solid overall record for political polling. One example comes from Germany and a study conducted by the *Süddeutsche Zeitung* newspaper.[8] It found an impressive level of accuracy, and no decline over time:

> In all surveys on state and federal elections since 2000, which were published within a year before election day, the mean error averaged 2.4 percentage points. Reliability increases significantly in the weeks leading up to election day. 14 days before the election, the mean error drops to 1.6 percentage points . . . No other method can better predict the outcome of elections. And the quality is pretty consistent over the long term.[9]

That finding is backed up by the most comprehensive international study of the reliability of opinion polling, carried out by Will Jennings and Christopher Wlezien. Being academics rather than pollsters or media outlets who commission polls, Jennings and Wlezien went into their research with no preferred outcome. For them, finding polls are accurate or inaccurate would have made for an equally good research finding. What they found was good for pollsters:

> Our analysis draws on more than 30,000 national polls from 351 general elections in 45 countries between 1942 and 2017 . . . We examine errors in polls in the final week of the election

campaign to assess performance across election years . . .
We find that, contrary to conventional wisdom, the recent
performance of polls has not been outside the ordinary.[10]

This is certainly a case in which conventional wisdom and the evidence
are at odds. As Will Jennings explains, 'It is very easy to remember the
high-profile polling misses and blank out all the other polling successes.'[11] Polling failures are more memorable than polling successes
(save for exit polls, in which the surprise correct predictions in the UK
have been memorable, helped by the way that the predictions were
initially met with disbelief by politicians and pundits, as we saw in
the previous chapter).

The average polling error – the gap between the vote share figures in the final pre-election polls and what the parties or candidates
secured – has been just 2.1 per cent across 1942–2017. That is pretty
darn close. Nor has the rate of error been rising, for the average since
the year 2000 is 2.0 per cent. Indeed, there are signs of the error rate
being on a very gently downwards long-term trajectory. Nor does
zooming in to just 2015–17 reveal a spike in the average error levels.[12]

These admirably low error rates come with a catch. According
to Jennings and Wlezien, 'The performance of polls does vary across
political contexts and in understandable ways.' In particular, as with
the other study quoted below, they found that polling error tends to
be largest for the larger parties. These are usually the ones battling for
power and the status of election winner, and so these are the ones for
which polling errors are most eye-catching, especially if they mean
that the party put first in the polls isn't the one that comes out on top
when the votes are tallied.[13]

Another study, also of more than 30,000 polls and over a slightly
longer period – 1936 to 2017 – came to similar conclusions: 'When
examined at a global level polls are generally very accurate[:] the

average error of polls conducted within seven days before an election is ±2.5 per cent.[14] The error rate (calculated in this analysis as the average errors in percentage vote share for the top four parties or candidates) falls the closer to election day polls are carried out:

> 3–6 months out from polling day: 4.4 per cent
> 2–3 months: 4.5 per cent
> 1–2 months: 3.9 per cent
> 3–4 weeks: 3.7 per cent
> 2–3 weeks: 3.6 per cent
> 1–2 weeks: 3.2 per cent
> 1 week: 2.7 per cent
> 2–5 days: 2.5 per cent
> 2 days: 2.5 per cent[15]

This analysis heavily caveats drawing comparisons between countries. There are many factors which make polling easier or harder in particular countries, such as how volatile election results are and how frequently parties come or go. In addition, for many countries, there are not that many elections with which to compare polls. However, if we look at this from the perspective of judging how useful polls are to the public (how close they are to the result) rather than judging how good the pollsters are (which requires allowing for the variations in polling difficulty between countries), then it is worth noting that both the USA and the UK are among the worst for average errors in a sample of eighteen countries – though you should also note that performing worse is not the same as performing badly as the polls still provide a useful guide.[16]

It is bad luck for the reputation of polling that the USA features so highly in the list. It is one of the countries whose elections receive the most international attention, and so its polling struggles receive far more global attention too. (There is an unexplored question about whether the American problem is due to the best pollsters finding it more difficult to obtain good results than in other countries, or whether the commercial dynamics of polling in the USA encourage a greater number of low-quality polls than in other countries, dragging down the overall average polling performance.) For readers in Britain, a country whose media pays heavy attention to American elections, the problem is amplified by the home country being up there too.[17]

Outside of politics, polling that averages an error of just two percentage points or so would nearly always be far more accurate than necessary. If a poll tells you that 65 per cent of people think a mobile phone brand is terrible value for money, even if that number is a long way off and the truth is somewhere between, say, 55 per cent and 75 per cent, that is still really all you need to know. The brand has a problem with perceived value for money. The same also applies to political polling about issues or leaders. Being thought honest by 15 per cent is bad news for any country's leader, whether or not there's a wide margin around that figure. Yet when it comes to voting intention in close contests, especially those run under first past the post, an average error of only two points can be a problem, as two points can be the difference between winning and losing. The problem, though, is not so much the error rate with polling, as with people wanting more certainty than the polls can provide in close contests. Ironically, the closer the contest, the more interesting the details of the polls seem and the more attention they get, despite that very closeness meaning the polls are also more likely to have the winner wrong.

All in all, to have held steady, or to have improved, the accuracy of political polling – with an average error rate down in the low single digits – is quite the achievement for political pollsters, given the trends that have been working against them. As Jennings and Wlezien point out, electorates have become more fluid. Class has declined as a factor in determining voter choice in many countries over several decades, and voter volatility has increased. Response rates to surveys have fallen, including for face-to-face surveys, making good sampling harder.[18] Yet polling has retained its overall accuracy.

As another summary of the evidence says,

> The accuracy of polls conducted within seven days before an election:
> 88 per cent within their own declared margin of error
> 85 per cent correctly predicted the outcome.[19]

Chapeau, pollsters.

7

POLLING GETS IT WRONG

*'I am only completely convinced of the findings of the
Gallup Poll when they confirm my own impression
of what the public is thinking.'*
– RICHARD CROSSMAN MP[1]

For all the evidence that political polling gets it mostly right, it is the the notable failures of political polling that are the punctuation marks in its history.[2] It is failures rather than successes that prompt worrisome headlines, crises of confidence and industry post-mortems.

It is also understanding the failures that best illustrates why political polling is so often right. That understanding comes from borrowing the Swiss cheese model of safety, common in sectors such as aviation and nuclear power – or, more boringly, the 'cumulative-act effect'. One of the pioneers of this way of thinking about safety was the psychologist and expert on human error James Reason, who got interested in safety after putting cat food in his teapot by mistake. It is easier to understand if thinking about cheese than cats. You can imagine the different safety features in a plane as being like a series of slices of cheese. A crash happens if you manage to push your finger through all the slices. Rudimentary safety involves ensuring there are sufficient slices of cheese in the pile for it to be too thick to simply to push your finger through. But these are slices of Swiss cheese, each with some holes in. If the holes are spread around each slice, without many lining up with each other, you still cannot push your finger through. However, when bad luck or circumstances result in a hole in one layer lining up with a hole in the next, and in the next and so on, then suddenly, the nice, reassuringly thick pile of slices is vulnerable to your finger getting through – or your plane crashing. Political polling is similar. As we saw with the 1948 U.S. polling miss, when it goes wrong, it is rarely due to just one thing. Rather, it requires a confluence of problems lining up to cause a polling miss.

1970: The First Great British Polling Disaster

After three Conservative victories in a row in Britain in the 1951, 1955 and 1959 general elections, there had started to be doubts about whether the Labour Party could ever win again. An influential book was even published in 1960, based on detailed survey work (albeit using a small sample), titled *Must Labour Lose?*, by Mark Abrams, Richard Rose and Rita Hinden.

Then under Harold Wilson, the Labour Party seemed to have successfully positioned itself as the party for the future, with the ruling Conservatives stuck in the past and mired in scandal. Wilson became prime minister in 1964 following a wafer-thin victory, turning that into a solid majority at the 1966 election. Ahead of the 1970 general election, he and Labour looked to be headed towards a comfortable re-election. The polls said so. What's more, the polls had done well in both of Wilson's previous victories. In 1964, Gallup, NOP and Research Services Limited all rightly gave Labour a small lead in their final polls, with only the *Daily Express* poll putting the Conservatives slightly ahead. Even that was not such a bad miss, putting the Conservatives 1 per cent ahead, rather than 2 per cent behind. Then in 1966, all of the pollsters had rightly put Wilson's Labour well ahead.[3]

For 1970, the polls looked promising for Labour once more. Four of the five pollsters – Gallup, Harris, Marplan and NOP – had Labour ahead in their final polls with leads of between two and ten points over the Conservatives.[4] Only ORC had the Conservatives ahead, by just one point. Yet ORC's two previous polls had put Labour ahead, as had, in fact, sixteen out of the last seventeen polls (and 25 of the last 27) conducted before polling day. With that backdrop, and with what other pollsters were saying, the final ORC poll putting the Conservatives ahead looked a rogue. Even the *Evening Standard*, which had commissioned the ORC poll, did not fully back its own polling, caveating its coverage on 18 June 1970 with, 'This is one election in which the polls could conceivably get the result wrong, as happened in the Truman–Dewey fight in the USA in 1948.' As it presciently warned, 'The one thing which opinion polls do not like is a close finish.'

Then voters voted, and the Conservatives won by two points. Harold Wilson was out of office and the Conservatives back in power. It was a dramatic and high-profile failure of polling – Britain's answer to 1948. It was made worse by 1970 being the first election campaign in which the British newspapers who commissioned polls did not assert copyright over their polls in order to stop other newspapers reporting the findings. No more holding off polling figures until later editions of a newspaper to stop rivals being able to cover them too, and no more letters threatening action for breach of copyright to others for republishing the numbers. Instead, in 1970 each paper's polls also got coverage elsewhere, and polling coverage dominated media coverage of the campaign, including 8 of the 23 front pages for *The Times* in the run-up to polling day. This made the collective failure of the polls all the more apparent.[5]

What went wrong? The usually authoritative Nuffield study concluded,

> The most plausible explanation for the 1970 failure of the polls (which is also the most convenient for the pollsters) must lie

in a late swing back to the Conservatives. If we take the middle of the interviewing period for each of the final polls we get this picture [for the Labour lead] ...[6]

It gave the following figures to back up that conclusion, with the dates being the middle date of the fieldwork period for each of the polls:

12 June: 9.6 per cent – Marplan

15 June: 7 per cent – Gallup

15 June: 4.1 per cent – NOP

15 June: 2 per cent – Harris

17 June: –1 per cent – ORC

18 June: –2.4 per cent – Actual result

That looks like a clear trend away from Labour, one that seems plausible given what happened late in the campaign. There was a supposed change in national mood caused by a combination of England being knocked out at the quarter-finals stage of the FIFA World Cup on the Sunday before polling day (14 June), followed by a break in the lovely summer weather on the Monday. There was more substantive bad news for the government too with a surprise set of grim balance-of-payments figures also published that Monday.

There are, however, other ways of presenting that data. If you instead sort the table not by the middle day of fieldwork for each poll but by the final day of fieldwork, and when that is the same, putting the poll that started on an earlier date first, the list becomes:

14 June: 9.6 per cent – Marplan

16 June: 2 per cent – Harris

16 June: 4.1 per cent – NOP[7]

16 June: 7 per cent – Gallup

17 June: −1 per cent − ORC

18 June: −2.4 per cent − Actual result

No more neat trend.[8]

The Nuffield study, to be fair, also offered other evidence in favour of the late-swing theory, citing polling carried out shortly after the general election: 'On the weekend of June 20, 6 per cent of those who told ORC interviewers that they voted Conservative said that they had intended to vote Labour at the beginning of the campaign. Only 1 per cent of Labour voters said they had switched from Conservative.'[9] Yet this implies a net rise of only around two percentage points in the Conservative vote share across the campaign from this switching. In fact, ORC had already shown a five-percentage-point rise in Conservative support during the campaign in its polls. Those post-election re-interviews therefore only help explain the movement already captured in the ORC polls, and not the further gap between its final poll and reality. All of that is without getting into the traditional problem that polls taken just after an election often show a victor's bonus − that is, more people saying they had voted for the winner than actually had.

Similar doubts apply to the other polling evidence for a late swing cited in the study: 'Gallup, going back to 700 of its final sample, found something like a 3 per cent net swing to Conservative amongst those who did not vote as they had said they would.' Note that, at least if the reports were accurate, that was only a 3 per cent swing among those who had changed their minds during the election, not 3 per cent overall. Again, a small effect. Moreover, the late re-interviewing from Harris just before polling day showed an *increase*, not a decrease, in Labour's lead compared with the earlier Harris fieldwork.[10]

Stronger, but still limited, evidence comes from two other pollsters:

Marplan, in a similar exercise with 664 of its final sample, found 4 per cent switching to Conservative from Labour and between 1 per cent and 2 per cent from Liberal; the reverse movements were much smaller. (However, even with allowance for such late switches, the Marplan figures would still have left Labour in the lead.) NOP in the most elaborate of the re-interviewing exercises found a net gain in the lead to the Conservatives of 4.3 per cent.[11]

So, the ORC, Gallup and Marplan figures are too small to explain away the pollsters' blushes, and Harris's figures showed movement in the wrong direction. Only NOP's figures venture into the right territory by being noticeably larger, but they are the outlier – and still susceptible to that victor's-bonus problem.

Moreover, other evidence cited by the Nuffield study shows that an increase in the Conservative vote had already been priced into some of the final polls, with pollsters picking up in their campaign polling a rise in Conservative support among people they spoke to compared with earlier in the campaign.[12] All this tentative evidence at least consistently points towards the Conservatives having had a good campaign overall, with rising support, notwithstanding the fact that some of that rise was already captured in the final polls and so cannot explain the polling error.[13]

So what does explain it? Our knowledge is hindered by how much more secretive public polling was back in 1970. Partly this was a matter of practicality. There were no websites on which polling companies could post their data tables. Partly this was a matter of the media and the limited details given in poll reports. The year 1970 did see some moves towards responsible self-regulation by pollsters, with a four-point code of practice introduced.[14] Nevertheless, reports were often sparse on details that we are now used to knowing and which are crucial to polling post-mortems, such as the exact dates on which fieldwork took place.

What we do know is that the closest poll – and the one that symbolically had the Conservatives ahead – used polling up until the eve of the election, saw a trend in their favour and projected that trend further in its final calculations. That ORC poll also made an adjustment for differential turnout – that is, a greater willingness on the part of the supporters of one party to actually go and vote than on the part of supporters of another party. If on polling day morning a higher proportion of Conservatives woke up and decided to vote than Labour supporters did on waking up, then that would have increased the Conservative vote share. Differential turnout is also attractive as a possible explanation, as turnout in 1970 was then the lowest in a general election since the Second World War, and turnout did not fall as low again until the 1997 election.[15] That gives space for a decline in Labour turnout boosting the Conservative vote share. However, pollsters had not found a differential-turnout problem when studying previous parliamentary elections, and when other pollsters tried adjusting for differential turnout at later general elections, this had very mixed results on polling accuracy. Moreover, ORC was *not* the only pollster to make differential-turnout adjustments at the 1970 election.[16] So differential turnout is not the magic explanation either – and anyway, for all the things that ORC did, its final poll was also still short of the result.

This leaves the exact cause of the polling miss a mystery, or – more likely, in Swiss cheese fashion – due to a combination of factors, each too small to leave that much evidence behind on its own. What is more, it is likely that what went wrong was not a simple list of causes that were common across the polling sector, as the pollsters had been painting different pictures of what was going on during the campaign. Graphing their polls carried out during the campaign gives a messy pattern: '[It was] a notably wild month when NOP's trend-lines crossed Marplan's, ORC's crossed Harris's, and Gallup trends crossed themselves.'[17] Different pollsters were wrong in different ways, it appears.

The example of 1970 shows that there are often no easy explanations when the polls go wrong. The apparent easy explanations (such as late swing) are themselves frequently also wrong in whole or in part. Even detailed post-mortems often struggle to come up with 'the' factor or factors, instead identifying a range of things that went wrong to differing degrees and which probably between them explain what happened.

Explaining what happens when polling goes wrong, therefore, is more like investigating someone's overall health than it is like investigating a murder. With murder, you can hope to reach one clear explanation. With overall health, the more thorough the investigations, the more things you will find that are not quite perfect. You can find major and minor problems, and perhaps rule out some factors, but you will be left with a mixed picture, not a simple answer.

One piece of clarity did come from the polling failures: the late movements in support towards the Conservatives, although not wholly responsible for the polling errors, did at least show up the risks of finishing fieldwork well in advance of polling day. That was an easy lesson for pollsters to learn and to apply to future British elections. Fieldwork moved up to be closer to polling day itself.

As a footnote to the events of 1970, the headlines also said that the pollsters got it wrong at the next general election, held in February 1974. The headlines were wrong, for the polls were pretty accurate and much improved on 1970. The polls correctly put the Conservatives ahead on votes. The voting system, however, gave Labour the most seats and therefore the label of winner. It was the voting system that got the election wrong, not the pollsters.

1992: The Second Great British Polling Disaster

In many ways, the 1992 election was the mirror image of the 1970 contest. In 1970 the polls seemed to be saying that a Labour prime minister was safely set for re-election, and yet he – Harold Wilson – lost. In 1992 the polls seemed to be saying that a Conservative prime minister was set to lose, and yet he – John Major – won.

In 1992 there were five final pre-election polls, four of which included sampling on the eve of the poll, remembering a lesson from 1970. Three had Labour ahead, one had it tied and one had the Conservatives one-half of 1 per cent ahead. The polls said it was close, with Labour slightly advantaged. And the polls seemed trustworthy, given their strong record at the three previous general elections.

The voters, however, had other ideas. They said something very different with their ballots. They gave the Conservatives a clear victory with a win by just under eight points. The polling industry had got it badly wrong. As the pre-eminent documenter of British general elections, David Butler, put it: 'The failure of the eve-of-election opinion polls to reflect the actual result of the British General Election on 9 April 1992 was the most spectacular in the history of British election surveys.'[18]

Ironically, what might look to be the most accurate polling day newspaper headlines – The Guardian's 'Tory Hopes Rise after Late Surge' and The Times's mini-headline above its main headline of 'Late Surge by Tories Closes Gap on Labour in Final Hours of Campaign' – were not really accurate. Both were turning small movements within the margin of error into a 'surge'. The newspapers were lucky that wrongly reporting faulty polls gave headlines that aged well.

Not only did the polls mess up in 1992. The exit polls did too. They flattered Labour and underestimated the Conservatives. It was a dramatic shock when Basildon, the third seat to declare on the night – and the first Conservative/Labour marginal – produced a Conservative hold rather than the expected Labour gain. The grinning face of winning MP David Amess becomes one of the seminal images of early 1990s British politics as his win was followed by many more for the Conservatives. Prime Minister John Major wasn't defeated. He was back in power – and the pollsters were scrambling to work out what had gone wrong.

The most significant of the polling post-mortems was organized by the Market Research Society (MRS).[19] It found that three main factors contributed roughly equally to the polling miss. One was late swing. The polls themselves picked up a movement towards the Conservatives at the end of the campaign and, although subject to similar interpretative caution as in 1970, post-election re-contacts by pollsters of people also showed a late swing. The pollsters had polled until later than in 1970, but even those pollsters doing fieldwork on the eve of the poll also – with one exception – used fieldwork from earlier days in their final polls. Hence the late swing opened up a gap between reality and what the fieldwork captured. In addition, as with the hint from ORC in 1970, in 1992 differential turnout exacerbated that late swing in preferences. Turnout rose most in the more Conservative-voting parts of the country. This looks to have boosted the Conservatives beyond what the pollsters were picking up despite their efforts to allow for turnout.[20] Altogether these factors were, however, only responsible for between a fifth and a third of the total error.

A second factor was faulty sampling. The 1992 election provided a good example of how size and quality are different things when it comes to polling samples. The poll with the largest sample size in 1992 was much larger than standard polls: a 10,000 sample by ICM for the Press Association. But not only did it have Labour ahead, it had Labour ahead by more than the average of the other polls using fieldwork from around the same time. Bigger was not better.[21]

The faulty sampling problem came from the pollsters aiming for the wrong make-up of the electorate when putting together their methodologies. Normally the once-a-decade census provides authoritative information to help pollsters know what age distributions, for example, to aim for. But the 1992 general election was held too soon after the 1991 census for its data to be usable. The 1981 census was old, and other sources of information were imperfect. To make matters worse, even if the weighting all been done correctly, the variables being weighted for were not correlated closely enough with voting behaviour to make the samples properly representative. Unrepresentative samples are a common finding of polling post-mortems, showing how tricky it is to pick the right set of weights to ensure that a sample is politically representative.

The third main factor was a problem with who was willing to take part in polls. Conservative supporters were disproportionately reluctant to reveal their party preferences, by refusing to take part in a poll or by either responding to the voting intention question with a 'don't know' or declining to answer it. This problem became known as the 'shy Tories' effect. It meant that the standard pollster ways of squeezing and reallocating those who said they were not sure or wouldn't say did not put enough of those people in the Conservative column, even though the methodologies had worked well at previous general elections. Despite exit polls being free of many of the other problems mentioned, this differential reluctance is at the heart of why they were wrong too.[22]

The Market Research Society's post-mortem also found some other, less important, causes of error. One was that some people polled were not on the electoral register, and so were unable to vote, with such people being disproportionately Labour supporters. (This election pre-dated electoral reforms that made registering just before an election significantly easier.) In addition, the selection of constituencies to be used in their sampling by all but one pollster was faulty, resulting in a probable slight Labour lean in the areas polled.[23]

The conclusion that it is a complex mix of factors – rather than one simple 'gotcha' – that explains the polling error is reinforced by the one poll that got it right in 1992. A face-to-face survey conducted by NOP over the course of a week for the Independent Television Commission (ITC) put the Conservatives nine points ahead. But the nature of the survey meant that the results were not collated until after polling day. There is no one simple explanation as to why it was right when the others were wrong, especially as its approach to sampling was the same as for the published voting intention polls from NOP and others. The poll did use a different approach to the ordering of questions from public opinion polls and this likely helps explain its performance. But as Nick Moon concludes,

> Subsequent analysis suggests that if this were the case it was due to factors which were either particular to an election situation as opposed to the gap between elections; or was specific to that particular election, for there is no sign of any consistent pattern of a similar trend in the years after 1992.[24]

The complexity of causes of the 1992 polling mix also helps explain why the polls were not that good at the next general election either. That 1997 election was a Labour landslide, and the polls were wrong in predicting a still more significant landslide. That made for a low-profile sort of error, but still showed how the pollsters had not (yet) fully caught up with what was off with their polling.

Note, therefore, how unlucky the pollsters were in 1992. Their polling miss was, again, redolent of the Swiss cheese safety analogy, down to a series of different problems. These included factors which undid methodologies that had worked before and unluckily lined up this time to depress the Conservative showing in the polls.[25] There was no landslide to hide their errors. As in 1970, a degree of doubt and mystery remains about exactly what did happen and exactly which factors contributed and by how much. Polling misses are much more complicated, messy affairs than the exuberant critical headlines they generate.

2015: The Third Great British Polling Disaster

Founded in 2010, polling firm Survation faced the first significant test of its reputation at the 2015 general election. It did not yet have the established track record that has helped other polling firms weather their own bad elections. As founder Damian Lyons Lowe later explained, 'If Survation was to compete with established players, and gain publicity for our work, we would need a reputation for accuracy.'[26]

In the years between its founding and its first general election, Survation was not infrequently in the pollster wars, generating different results – and receiving criticism – from other pollsters. YouGov's Peter Kellner, in particular, made a number of plausible criticisms of Survation's approach. However, the comparison of polls and results in both the European elections and the Scottish independence referendum suggested there was some merit in the newcomer's approach.[27] For example, Survation put the UK Independence Party (UKIP) five points in the lead over other parties in the European Parliament elections, compared with an actual two-point lead, though it also overestimated UKIP's vote share by four and a half points. YouGov was more accurate, being only a half a point and one point out respectively on those measures.

In the 2014 Scottish referendum, Survation had run two polls right at the end – its regular online poll and a telephone poll, thereby getting a cross-check on its own work. The two polls generated nearly identical results. For its big general election debut in 2015, Survation intended to repeat this. Its paying media client, the *Daily Mirror*, would receive its usual online poll and also knew about the plan to do a telephone cross-check.

With polling day set for Thursday 7 May 2015, the phone calls were made the day before, through until 9 p.m. As the final data came in, Survation's chief statistician grabbed a marker pen as he rushed to join colleagues and wrote out the results: Conservative 37.3 per cent, Labour 30.6 per cent. A significant Conservative lead, way out of line with the rest of the polling industry that had been showing a neck-and-neck race. It was also, however, out of line with Survation's own previous online polling, which had shown a neck-and-neck race too. Its final online poll for the *Mirror*, conducted over the three days leading up to polling day, had put Labour and the Conservatives tied on 31 per cent each.

Although the *Mirror* had only paid for the online poll and not the phone poll, Damian Lyons Lowe rang them anyway. The phone kept on ringing, and when it was eventually answered, the person there said no one was around to publish anything more at that time of night. The duty to his client covered, the question for Lyons Lowe was, publish or not? Was Survation right, and everyone else, including Survation's other polling, wrong? 'How could everybody else be wrong?' he wondered.[28] Being out on a limb and getting it right could make Survation's reputation – but it would still have to explain away why its other polls were wrong. Going out on a limb and getting it wrong, moreover, would make the newcomer look risible.

The fear of the downside won out. That fear is understandable. Even well-established pollsters worry about being an outlier. To recap how highly regarded U.S. pollster Ann Selzer put it when asked how she coped on the several occasions that her polls bucked the trend,

I call it spending my time in the pot-shot corral . . .
Everybody saying this is terrible, she is awful, this is
going to be the end of her . . . When we see the data,
we know that's going to be the reaction. But it's a few
days. A few days of discomfort, and the little talk I have
with myself is, 'look, we'll see what happens. I'll either
be golden or a goat. Hopefully golden but if I'm a goat,
OK I think I can survive it and move forward in some
way, lessons learnt'. But it is uncomfortable.[29]

So Survation's numbers were not published. Survation left the 31 per
cent each draw as its final pre-election poll.

And then the election happened. The result? Conservatives 37.7
per cent, Labour 31.2 per cent. Survation's last-minute decision had
been a mistake. This result did perhaps have one beneficial effect:
Survation was once again an outlier at the next general election, but
this time did not flinch from being so. Instead, thanks to the memory
of 2015, plus the fact that this time *both* its final methodologies gave
similar outlier results, it stuck to its guns, published and got the
deserved accolades.

But the bigger picture was that Survation's error in its final published pre-election poll was an error shared across the industry. The
polls overall got the election wrong. What is more, they not only got
it wrong, they looked to have misled the media and the public. As the
BBC's David Cowling put it, 'Following the outcome of the 2015 general
election, a mixture of anger and contempt was showered on the pollsters who had spent six weeks suggesting a different result.'[30] Repeated
findings of a close race between Labour and the Conservatives, with
both pegged at levels likely to fall short of a majority, had led to media
coverage heavily framed around the likelihood of a hung parliament.
When the result was instead a clear Conservative lead, and an actual

Conservative majority, it was a result the copious media coverage had barely contemplated, let alone scrutinized.

Survation's decision meant it did not receive the applause for standing out from the crowd and getting the election right. Instead, someone else did. Matt Singh, who was later to become a pollster, had started his Number Cruncher Politics website several months before the general election. The day before the general election, he published a piece casting doubt on the accuracy of the polls. He concluded, 'while I would urge caution with respect to this analysis, it looks a lot like the Tories are set to outperform the polls once again.'[31] He was right.

What had he seen that others had missed? Singh's first memory of elections and polls was the 1992 general election, going to bed as a child on election night, with the polls, including the exit poll, pointing towards one result and waking up the next day to a different outcome. So from the start, 'I had a curiosity about the polling failures.'[32]

For Singh's 2015 number crunching, he was in part prompted by analysis from the pollsters YouGov, which pointed out that there had never before been a case of a party behind both on leadership ratings and on economic competence ratings going on to win. Yet that was what the polls were saying for 2015. Singh looked at a range of factors, including the historical accuracy of polls, their record compared with the results in other types of elections since the previous general election, the Conservative lead on both leadership and economic competence in the polls, and how vote shares in local elections are related to subsequent general election results. Any one of these factors on their own was questionable as a warning sign. Indeed, the 2010–15 parliament saw a highly unusual peacetime coalition between two parties, one that started during an economic crisis and then lasted a full parliament. The parliament also saw the collapse in support of one coalition party (the Liberal Democrats) and a surge in support of a previously irrelevant party (UKIP). Such unusual circumstances provided an apparently good reason to believe that past trends would no longer apply and that instead people should trust to the current polls.

Yet Singh found multiple indicators that something could be wrong. As he says, it 'sounds counter-intuitive' that some of those indicators were themselves based on polls which we now know to have been wrong, but 'the point was that all the indicators suggested error, and error in the same direction,' he explains.[33] As a result, he correctly warned about what was coming and got the plaudits.

So what went wrong with the polls in 2015? When required, the British polling industry does a mean post-mortem.[34] This post-mortem operated like the denouement to a Hercule Poirot story, with all the possible suspect causes of error rounded up and then eliminated one by one through the report. In the process of eliminating many possible explanations, the post-mortem, nonetheless, identified many recommendations for improvements to political polling – improvements that wouldn't have avoided the 2015 fiasco but which were worth making nevertheless.

As for what caused the fiasco, having eliminated all the other suspects, the post-mortem concluded the cause was unrepresentative samples.[35] It was the dominant cause of error, with, at most, small contributions from other factors, such as late swing. That problem with unrepresentative samples, however, was not the single cause of failure that it may at first appear to be. Rather, as with the other examples in this chapter, the failure came from a multitude of factors and once again there is a degree of uncertainty over the full details of what went wrong.

The samples were not unrepresentative in a simple way, such as too many public sector workers or not enough Scottish men. But there were three symptoms pointing towards sampling problems. First, when pollsters weight their samples by age, they use age bands to do this. The top band typically used by a pollster was 65+, and although pollsters weighted their figures to achieve the right proportions of 65+, within that top age band, they had too many young older people (those in their late sixties) and not enough old older people (those well beyond that). Their old people were too young. Second, among postal voters, the pollsters also had samples that were off – by having too many middle-aged people (especially 35–44) and under-representing older postal voters. For both of these factors, it is easy to see why pollsters under-sampled these groups – the very old and those who wanted to vote by post can be harder for pollsters to reach. Third, the pollsters had people who were more politically engaged than average in their samples. Again, it is easy to see why this might happen, with such people being more willing to take part in polls. This is a challenging factor to guard against, as there is no clear yardstick of political engagement that can be used to weight samples to ensure they have the right degree of political enthusiasm within them.

None of these problems were, at least in theory, new. The logic behind each of them could plausibly have applied in the past, and yet did not cause the polls at the preceding elections to have anything like the problems of 2015. What also went wrong for pollsters was the additional bad luck that political support moved to be more polarized by age and by level of political engagement than in the past, and both those age and engagement errors pointed in the same direction. If they had pointed in opposite directions, the errors could have mostly cancelled each other out. Instead, they added to each other, knocking the polls off by a wide mark. It was only the lining up of multiple issues, all pointing in the same direction, that betrayed the polls in 2015.

The issue with the politically engaged being over-represented in polling samples was intriguingly echoed in the 2019 Australian polling 'failure'. It was one of those failures that was arguably not a failure – getting the winner wrong but being not that far out on vote shares.[36] Specifically, the final polls from the five active pollsters had the Liberal and National (LNP) coalition on a losing 48–49 per cent, compared with an actual winning result of 51.5 per cent.[37] Labor was pegged on 51–52 per cent, yet came in at 48.5 per cent.

Neither of those vote share misses was that significant compared with typical margins of error. But the win for PM Scott Morrison – who responded by quipping, 'I've always believed in miracles' – was a surprise because of the long and consistent, albeit fading at the last, Labor lead in the polls. Moreover, all the pollsters got it wrong, the first time this had happened since Australian pollsters had all started reporting two-party preferred-vote figures at the 1993 election.[38] Moreover, since the pollsters split 50:50 on getting the winner right or wrong in 1993, the majority of pollsters had been right for all eight intervening elections until 2019.[39]

The inquiry into the 2019 Australian polls found,

> The most likely reason why the polls underestimated the
> first preference vote for the LNP and overestimated it for
> Labor was because the samples were unrepresentative and
> inadequately adjusted. The polls were likely to have been
> skewed towards the more politically engaged and better
> educated voters with this bias not corrected.[40]

One last observation is worth making about the 2015 British polling miss. Remember that Survation poll that was right but was not published? Survation undertook its fieldwork later than any of the other final pre-election polls. Yet the post-mortem found that late swing was not the cause of the polling error, and so the apparent accuracy of the Survation poll cannot be put down to this. Rather, the most plausible explanation is that the very short period of sampling (hours rather than days) and a dose of bad luck meant that Survation's sample was skewed and off – but off in a way that cancelled the errors that were occurring in all the other polling samples. To put it simply, Survation's final poll was wrong, but wrong in a way that made it right. Welcome to the looking-glass world of polling errors.

2016: The U.S. Polling Disaster that Wasn't

If you look down a table of U.S. presidential election vote shares compared with the average across the final pre-polling-day polls, 2016 is unexceptional. The national polls showed Democrat Hillary Clinton up by a few percentage points, and she did indeed outpoll Republican Donald Trump by a few percentage points. The RealClearPolitics website's average of the polls, for example, ended up with Clinton at 46.8 per cent and Trump at 43.6 per cent. The actual vote shares came in at 48.2 per cent (+1.4 per cent) and 46.1 per cent (+2.5 per cent). Clinton's lead in the final polls was 3.2 per cent against an actual lead for her of 2.1 per cent.

That does not look like a story of national polls being badly wrong. Yet that is how the polls were seen. So much so that father of pollster Courtney Kennedy asked, 'tell me again how you and your friends still have jobs?'[41] The reason? Clinton may have won the most votes but she lost. This was seen by many as being at odds with what the polls had been saying. What is more, the one pollster sometimes praised for getting it right in the face of other pollsters supposedly getting it wrong, was, in fact, one of the most inaccurate. The *Los Angeles Times* poll did indeed put Trump ahead. But Trump did not win the popular vote, and by giving Trump a 3 per cent lead, the poll's figures were more off than those of their rivals.[42]

One reason the polls were seen as having failed was political: that it was Trump rather than, say, Mitt Romney who won. That such a convention-defying candidate as Trump, who frequently operated outside the norms of politics, triumphed made the result still more shocking. The polls were an obvious target for some of those shockwaves.

Three other factors contributed to that sense of failure: the voting system, state polls and polling projections. The voting system contributed because it was widely assumed in 2016 that being ahead on vote share was synonymous with being on course to win the election through getting the most electoral college votes. Only once since 1888 had the popular-vote winner not been elected president, and that was the aberration of Al Gore's loss in 2000. That seemed such a special case – a unique outlier that hinged on a highly convoluted and very close recount in Florida and one of the most controversial rulings related to an election ever made by the Supreme Court – that people returned to the pattern of thinking 'most votes equals winner'.

State polls also contributed to the sense of polling failure. In some vital swing states, the polls were off – and so failed to send up the warning flares they should have about national vote share not being the same as electoral college chances. In particular, the trio of Michigan, Pennsylvania and Wisconsin were crucial to Trump's win. With 46 electoral college votes between them, they all had a track record of voting Democrat in recent previous presidential contests. They were more than enough to account for his electoral college win, which was by 77 (that is, if he had won 39 electoral college votes fewer, he would have lost). In all three, Trump came out less than 1 per cent ahead in the popular vote, yet in all three he had been consistently behind in the state polls.

The cause of these polling misses seems to have been a combination of timing, with polls missing a late swing to Trump, and sampling, with too many people who had been to university included.[43] Also, there was an underappreciation that the chances of a surprise result in a state are not independent of the chances of a surprise result in another state. Sometimes the cause of polling in a state being off might be unique to that state, but as the education factor shows, sometimes it means that errors are likely to have occurred in multiple states. Likewise, if there is a very late swing to a candidate, that might be due to factors specific to just one state, but it is more likely to be due to factors that apply to multiple states. All this makes being ahead in multiple states a more brittle lead than it may appear at first glance. (State polling errors are correlated rather than independent of each other.)

The final factor that contributed to the sense that the polls failed in 2016 was not really to do with the polls, but rather with polling projections – statistical models which, based on what the polls were saying at any one point in time, tried to calculate a percentage chance that a candidate would go on to win. In theory – and often in practice – these are a useful tool. U.S. presidential elections have a long run-up, with a series of high-profile dates fixed in the diary – the New Hampshire primary, the party conventions, Labor Day and so on. Therefore, it makes sense to try to work out, for example, what the odds are that a candidate 10 per cent ahead after their own convention will go on to win. In addition, putting together such models provides a yardstick against which to judge poll movements during the campaign. If a candidate won the first TV debate and went up by three points in the polls, would that be a good outcome? It may sound so, but if the model shows that we should expect the winning candidate to go up by six points and that anyway the boost usually fades within a week, then we know going up by three is nothing to become excited by.

In this respect, polling models are very different from the polls they rely on. A poll tries to answer the question, 'if an election were held today or tomorrow, what would the result be?' A model takes that and then tells us how likely it is that someone will win or lose on the election date off in the future. Four weeks out, a poll may put a candidate six points up. A polling model needs to take into account the chance of that poll being wrong and also, whether or not the poll is right, the chance of movements in support between now and the election.

The polling models mostly had a bad 2016. *Huffington Post*'s final projection gave Clinton a 98.2 per cent chance of winning.[44] The Princeton Election Consortium went further and gave her a 99 per cent chance of winning. (The person responsible for this calculation, Sam Wang, said ahead of the election, 'It is totally over. If Trump wins more than 240 electoral votes, I will eat a bug.' He later went on to eat a spoonful of crickets doused in honey on live TV. In a familiar pattern, his dramatic failure came after having won accolades in 2012 for the accuracy of his predictions.[45]) Despite those high-nineties figures, Trump won. Of course, neither the *Huffington Post* nor the Princeton Election Consortium gave Clinton a 100 per cent chance of winning, so strictly speaking, the fact that he won did not necessarily make those percentages wrong. But people did interpret them as meaning it was basically a done deal, when it was not.

Even with no knowledge of polling or modelling, two things should have given cause for pause about those figures. One was the decimal point used by *Huffington Post*. That implied that it was possible to calculate the chances of the election result down to a 1 in 1,000 level of accuracy. That is a remarkably precise level of predictive ability to claim. You only need to have the briefest of knowledge of polling failures to wonder if 1 in 1,000 levels of accuracy can be achieved. For an event that happens every four years, a claimed 1 in 1,000 level of accuracy is like saying it has a 1 in 4,000 years level of accuracy. Not only has the United States only existed for one-eighth of that time, it is the equivalent of going all the way back to Jesus, and then the same again.

The other reason for caution was that even if you put Clinton's chances at the rounded-off 98 or 99 per cent level, those are still implausible numbers. Remembering again that presidential elections are once every four years, saying something has a one in one hundred chance of happening is saying something will, on average, happen once every four hundred years of presidential elections. Yet by 2016 there had been only 226 years of U.S. presidential elections. Four hundred years is a long time. Is it really wise to be so confident that being ahead in the polls before polling day is so certain to result in victory?

There are many ways someone might lose at the last, from the prosaic of a polling error through to the tragedy of war, terrorism or illness. Or even perhaps due to the polls being rigged? It would be beyond ordinary people to rig a country's polls, but what if you had all the resources of the Chinese or Russian state at your disposal? It would not be easy. But some things would make it less hard. For one, behind the scenes, there is a lot of shared infrastructure in the polling industry. Different polling firms use the same telephone call centre operations. Different polling firms use data from the same Internet panels. Different polling firms also use the same software. Different polling data is stored in the same cloud services. There is no one call centre, one Internet panel, one piece of software and one cloud to corrupt. You would need to corrupt multiple things, but not nearly as many as the number of polling firms may make it appear. Could the Chinese bury a hidden back door in a shared piece of code used in multiple polling firms that provides hackers access which is then used to pollute final pre-election polls? You would not even need to hack every poll. Just enough to make the others look like weird outliers. Weird outliers which could also be discredited by a campaign of online disinformation, such as faked leaked documents over who owns certain polling firms. It would be both difficult and perhaps unclear what the point would be, as pollsters find enough regular ways to embarrass themselves anyway. But it is certainly plausible enough to make a Hollywood movie out of the idea, and it is the sort of thing a one-in-four-hundred-years claim needs to consider.[46] Not to mention the possibility of an armed coup. (Which, with the awful events of January 2021 in mind, is not a risk to put at 0 per cent.)

Of course, none of these are that likely. Add them all up, though, and is a candidate being clearly ahead in the polls just before polling day really such a certainty that you should only expect them to lose once every four hundred years?

As we have seen throughout this book, polling is pretty good, and hence there are also well-crafted projections based on polls – just not a once-in-four-hundred-years level of good.[47] Despite all that, 99-per-cent-level certainties occurred again for the 2020 U.S. presidential election, with *The Economist* team finalizing their forecast, putting Biden on a better-than-99-per-cent chance of winning the most votes. However, the team then wrote a blog post which warned of 'Three good reasons not to believe our numbers'.[48] The third of those, rightly, gets into thinking about the sort of things you need to factor in when speaking about a one-in-four-hundred-years event: 'Big things not in the model can happen, whether these be surprises in voter turnout, unexpected polling errors, major vote suppression . . . not to mention bugs in our code and conceptual errors in our model.' Their 99 per cent was a 99 per cent with so many caveats that it was not really 99 per cent.

2020: Two Polling Disasters in a Row?

The Economist's caveats on its 2020 U.S. presidential election poll proved to be wise, as the 2020 election turned out to be much closer than it appeared the polls had said. The immediate, simple story was one of polling failure again, with the polls having underestimated Donald Trump at two presidential elections in a row. The truth, however, is kinder to the polls. The polls got the big picture right: they put Biden ahead in the popular vote, and he did win the popular vote. The state polls did, overall, point to him winning the electoral college, and he did win the electoral college. The polls also rightly identified the states that might be in play. Results and margins certainly varied a lot from those of some state polls, but in general, the political geography of the country that the polls painted was the one that voters then confirmed with their ballots. The polls were also good at the preceding congressional elections in 2018 and at the subsequent elections in 2021, including the Georgia Senate run-off and the November round of elections.[49]

What the polls got wrong at the presidential election, though, was putting Biden in a much more comfortable position than the results justified. Moreover, this made it two elections in a row in which the polls lowballed Donald Trump and highballed the Democratic challenger. So it was not a great pollster performance, but it was not awful either. At four previous presidential elections to 2016 and 2020, the polls averaged a 3.7 percentage point error in vote share. In 2016 it was 4.9 per cent and then in 2020 it was 5.0 per cent. It was worse than typical, but not massively worse. As Nate Silver concluded, looking at the errors across all u.s. election polls (and not only presidential ones),

> While polling accuracy was mediocre in 2020, it also wasn't any sort of historical outlier. The overall average error of 6.3 points in 2019–20 is only slightly worse than the average error across all polls since 1998, which is 6.0 points. There were also presidential years before the period our pollster ratings cover, such as in 1948 and 1980, when the polls exhibited notably larger errors than in 2020. So while the polling industry has major challenges . . . it's also premature to conclude that the sky is falling . . . There isn't any particularly clear statistical trend showing that polls have gotten worse over time. Yes,

both 2016 and 2020 were rather poor years, but sandwiched between them was an excellent year for the polls in 2018. And in their most recent test, the Georgia Senate runoffs, the polls were extremely accurate.

It wasn't just on vote shares that the polls did all right. They were accurate in predicting the winner correctly too: 'In 79 percent of polls across the cycle, the winner was identified correctly, which matches our 79 percent hit rate overall [in all election cycles from 1998].'[50]

Notwithstanding those defences of the polls, there still is something left to be explained about their 2020 performance.[51] Attempts to explain what happened are clouded by the fact that both 2016 and 2020 had the exceptional circumstance of Donald Trump on the ballot paper. He was a unique candidate and a unique president. His derision of news and polls he did not like as 'fake' could have resulted in putting off his supporters from taking part in the polls in a way that no other candidate had done previously. It is suggestive that the polls were fairly accurate in the non-presidential U.S. elections in the Trump era. That indicates a Trump-related problem, perhaps leading to an under-sampling of people with low trust levels of others, a group that appears to have been particularly willing to vote for Trump. That would fit with international trends in polling difficulties.[52]

It is true that polling for the other elections on the same day as the presidential election also over-reported Democrat support in 2020, even though Trump was not running in those.[53] However, if Trump's disdain for polling put his supporters off taking part in them, they are likely to have brushed off pollsters long before pollsters got to the bit in their polls that revealed if it was a presidential survey or not.

Then there is COVID-19. Compliance with coronavirus restrictions was heavily skewed by partisanship, so it is plausible that Democrats were more likely to obey lockdowns, more likely to be at home, more likely to be off work and more likely to respond to pollsters. If true, it would have been a version of the differential response rates difficulty that we have seen causing problems with British polling.

Or perhaps it was the greater willingness of Democrat campaigners to cease campaign activities such as door-to-door canvassing during lockdowns that knocked their campaign much more than Trump's, reducing Democrat turnout relative to that for Republicans. Certainly, the record-setting turnout at the 2020 elections provides a decent reason why polling methodologies forged in lower-turnout contexts could have got it wrong. As a group of Democrat pollsters concluded, 'at least in some places, we again underestimated relative turnout among rural and white non-college voters, who are overrepresented among low propensity Republicans,' although these pollsters emphasized that there was more to the polling problems than this one factor: 'there is not a single, definitive answer – which makes solving the problem especially frustrating.'[54]

It also seems like the polls had a particular problem with tracking what was happening in some very specific Hispanic communities. In other circumstances, this would have been a detail, but in 2020 this was a high-profile failing, as one of those communities was in Florida – one of the first swing states to start reporting voting figures on election night and so also a state that disproportionately had an impact on people's overall impression of how the election was going and how accurate the polls were turning out to be. Perhaps too there was a late swing towards Trump and the Republicans, which, as we have seen with other polling failures, may not have been the whole story but could have been part of the story of polling error.

Some or all of this may be true. The polling industry's main post-mortem cautiously stayed short of a clear conclusion: 'Some explanations of polling error can be ruled out according to the patterns found in the polls, but identifying conclusively why polls overstated the

Democratic–Republican margin relative to the certified vote appears to be impossible with the available data.'[55]

The problems do seem to rest with faulty sampling, as with the British experience in 2015. Techniques previously successful in securing and adjusting samples to make them representative did not work as well in the very challenging circumstances of 2020 – an election with record turnout, held during a pandemic and with an incumbent president openly and brutishly hostile to opinion polls. Changes in sampling and weighting, and even a revival of postal sampling, are where pollsters are headed in the search for improved results.[56] Most likely, there will still be room for doubt until we can see how the polls perform in the first post-Trump presidential election.

Lessons from Polling Going Wrong

Being a good pollster is like being a tightrope walker. Preparation, practice, expertise, fine judgement and good instincts are all required. Those who become good at it can carry out remarkable feats. (Charles Blondin, perhaps the most famous tightrope walker, not only used to cross Niagara Falls on a tightrope, he also completed the feat blindfolded, on stilts and, with a wheelbarrow, once stopped to make an omelette halfway across.) As you head out along the rope, repeated small adjustments are needed to keep upright. For those with skill, most of the time the little gusts of wind or twinges of muscles are coped with. But every now and again, there will be an unexpectedly strong gust of wind, just as a foot is slightly misplaced and a desperate urge to sneeze works its way through the nostrils. When all those factors combine against you at the same moment, disaster results.

Polling is the same. Polling is not a search for the perfect methodology that, once found, will solve everything. Rather, it is a constant battle against circumstances, adjusting as it goes, trying to stay close to the truth. As we have explored, it is rare that just one thing goes wrong for political polling. Instead, when the polls go wrong, it requires the bad luck of multiple events, stacking up to push the polls off in the same direction, and so adding up to a headline-grabbing error. This also means that even when things appear to have gone right, there will be things behind the scenes that have gone wrong: just small in scale and balancing each other out, rather than the unlucky combination that causes a dramatic cumulative effect. That's why, as pollster Joe Twyman explains,

> Reputable pollsters, after every election, go back and do our own internal post-mortems. We do this whether we have got things 'right' or 'wrong'. This is particularly important in the years that appear 'right' – calling the winner correctly – but were actually 'wrong' – a long way out on vote shares.[57]

In this regard, polls are like aeroplane flights, for there is a little secret about both polls and planes that you may wish to forget before you next board a flight. They both have things that often go wrong – far more frequently than you are likely to notice. Because it is only when the errors line up that disaster – metaphorical or all too real – results. You may think everything is fine, even as there is a burst of errors, each quietly cancelling another out behind the scenes.

This picture of multiple contributions explains why polling post-mortems rarely find just the one simple error. Similarly, it is why, when an individual fix is made to improve polling after one failure, it sometimes ends up making things worse next time because the full story of error is more complicated than a single circumstance.[58] However, what usually does happen is that a polling disaster is followed by improvements and better results in the future (the long run of problems with u.s. exit polls aside).[59]

This pattern also gives us a lesson for judging future polls. Claims that polls are about to be wrong due to one simple error are most likely to miss the mark. Post-election explanations that polls were wrong due to one simple error are most likely to miss the mark. Errors are not that simple. But follow the polls, and generally your political expectations will hit the mark.[60] Gallup was fond of saying that he knew only two things for certain about election polls. One was that they are bound to pick the wrong side some time in the future. The other was that they were better than any other method that is available.[61]

Moreover, even when wrong, polls are still interesting. As we have seen, the reasons they go wrong are due to changes in political, social and demographic circumstances. The very act of being wrong reveals that things have unexpectedly changed. In a counter-intuitive way, by going wrong, polls end up shedding *more* light on what has happened because the failure draws attention to those changes. In such cases, polls are revelatory after the event due to their errors rather than predictive before the event due to their accuracy. Gratification delayed, but gratification nevertheless.

8

REGULATING OPINION POLLS

'The effect of the Bill would be rather like banning meteorologists
from forecasting the weather a week before a garden party in
case anyone might be put off from going.'
– CLEMENT FREUD MP, opposing a bill
to ban opinion polls ahead of elections[1]

Even before modern political polling properly got going, it faced the risk of a legislative ban. The proposal came from Congressman Walter M. Pierce of Oregon in 1935 – the year in which Gallup founded his firm and the year before the *Literary Digest* debacle that made modern polling.[2] Congressman Pierce's political outlook was a complicated mix to modern eyes, being both a progressive Democrat and a friend – and possibly member – of the Ku Klux Klan. A keen supporter of the New Deal and living wages for the unemployed, he helped secure the first progressive income tax in Oregon. Yet he was also a supporter of eugenics and backed attacks on the rights of Japanese immigrants.

He was also the first legislator who tried to take on political polls, both traditional straw polls and the new polling approaches that triumphed in 1936. There was, and can still be, a genuine worry that faulty opinion polls mislead the public, influencing their votes with misleading information. Pierce, a populist politician, was sceptical of the idea of 'scientific' polling and feared powerful elites could use it to sway the public and influence members of Congress. For him, polling was 'powerful, subsidized propaganda which is now a controlling factor in [the] election of candidates'. He spoke of 'the possible dangers of an uncontrolled, private manipulation of public opinion, for financial profit'. He also worried about a bandwagon effect, whereby if polls showed a candidate ahead, people would assume they would win and so be put off voting for them. (That made the 1936 election result a problem for him, as he argued that there had been a bandwagon effect from the *Literary Digest* polls in previous presidential elections, but then unconvincingly had to argue there wasn't a similar one in 1936 because Roosevelt was 'just unbeatable'.[3])

Pierce pushed initially for legislation to ban the use of the mail for political polling, something that would have caught postal sampling by both the more traditional straw polls and also the newer polling of Crossley, Gallup, Roper and colleagues.[4] His 1935 bill, H.R. 5728 in the 74th Congress, would have required,

> That every letter, writing, circular, postal card, picture,
> print, engraving, photograph, newspaper, pamphlet, book,
> or other publication, matter, or thing, of every kind,
> containing any matter relating to the conduct or operation
> of straw polls where candidates and issues are different,
> or employing sampling methods for general referendum
> purposes and for measuring the voting intention of the
> people on candidates for public office and issues, is hereby
> declared to be nonmailable matter and shall not be conveyed
> in the mails or delivered from any post office or by any letter
> carrier.[5]

Referred to the House Committee on the Post Office and Post Roads on 14 February 1935, and then to its subcommittee number eight, Offenses against Postal Services, on 21 March, the draft bill stalled after a hearing on 23 April. The committee did, however, seek the views of the Post Office, with the Postmaster General writing to the committee to say, 'This Department has no particular interest in the proposed measure' but crucially adding, 'no objectionable features' had been encountered by the existing arrangements for polling by the post, and that such arrangements 'have been a source of considerable revenue, amounting in some cases to hundreds of thousands of dollars'.[6]

Although Pierce continued to pursue the issue for several years, it never came to anything much.[7] Along the way, the Post Office's opposition hardened, with the Postmaster General warning in 1937 that such a ban 'will result in the loss of a considerable amount of revenue'.[8] Pierce himself later put the estimated loss of revenue in a presidential election year at $2 million.[9] He believed that this risk to the Post Office's revenue was fatal to his efforts, though it is possible that the Post Office's opposition meant that others simply did not get around to, or need to articulate, a defence of polling in principle.[10]

Speaking in Congress on 29 February 1940, Pierce explained his desire for polling regulation. His concern was that:

> Polls are often wrong in theory, in practice, and in fact, and that when interpreted an entirely erroneous conclusion may be drawn. The taking of polls and securing the wide use of the results of polls through syndicated columns in newspapers has become a feature of our elections and legislation which can no longer be ignored by legislative bodies nor by candidates. The matter appears to be wholly commercial. I think it is not scientific, and never can be scientific. It appears to me to be a very successful attempt to make public opinion, rather than a method of measuring public opinion.

This was not just a matter of doubting the methodology of Gallup – repeatedly mentioned in his speech – and that of other pollsters.

Pierce went on in his speech to doubt the right of the public to hold views in the first place: 'I do not believe that a scientific poll can be taken of the city of Washington, or any other city, based upon questions on which very few people are sufficiently informed to entitle them to an opinion.' Pierce worried polls could be deliberately rigged by people with money and influence. But – as with his claims about the polls being hopelessly inaccurate – what was missing was good evidence to substantiate his claims (although his claims about how easy it was to manipulate the results of straw polls did sometimes highlight genuine weaknesses in their methodology, such as with the lack of control over who really filled in forms that were posted back).

Pierce's regulatory efforts were followed up by others in the USA and around the world. Often, it is a question of power that motivates actual or attempted polling bans. In semi-democracies, and especially in non-democracies, political opinion polling is often restricted by authoritarians not wishing the public to know what the public thinks. Even in fully functioning democracies, political pollsters have come under regulatory pressure, most commonly to ban polls in the run-up to polling day.

Two fears have primarily driven such pressure. The first is a fear that polling is wrong, and hence pollutes election debates and coverage. This is why talk of regulation often spikes after an election in which pollsters are perceived to have done a bad job. It is also why regulation often features banning polls for a specific period ahead of polling day.[11]

The second fear is that polling influences the results, and that such influence is bad. Perhaps people like to back the winner and switch to whoever is ahead in the polls. Or see who is out of the running and abandon them for someone else. Clearly, if the polls are wrong, then this is bad as such changes are happening based on wrong information. However, a more contentious view is that even if the polls are right, people having such knowledge is wrong, as it would lead them to decide how to vote based on factors that – in the view of those promoting regulation – they should not be allowed to consider. For such regulators, accurate polling is a forbidden fruit. This was the argument used by Pierce and is a rather patrician attitude towards democracy: you are free to vote, but can only think about the things that *I* decide are important. It means arguing that, for example, thinking in 2020 that Donald Trump was an awful president and wanting to vote for whoever was best placed to defeat him was somehow an illegitimate train of thought for a voter, and therefore that it is right to deprive people of information to help make such a choices.

Critics of polling bans have several counter-arguments. One is that it is wrong to say the polls are wrong – they are pretty good in practice, as we have seen. What is more, banning good information leaves the field open to bad information. Rather, the more good-quality information voters have, the better. If voters want to use good information on the relative support for parties or candidates to help decide how to vote, who are you or I to tell them they should not?

Then there is the argument that overall, the polls do not make a significant difference to how people vote. They are useful for helping frame elections properly (who is really in with a chance of winning and so should receive media coverage, for example). They can be useful in very specific places for mobilizing tactical voting – and if a voting system gives opportunities for tactical voting, why shouldn't voters be able to make such decisions with the most information possible?[12] But overall, the polls do not cause major problems such as bandwagon effects for whoever is in the lead or depressing the turnout of supporters for whoever the polls show is going to lose. As a review of the research into this says,

The results of numerous studies on the topic can be summarized as follows:

a) The results are inconclusive and depend to a great degree upon the method used and the particular circumstances at the time.

b) In general, we can say that the more natural the test situation, the smaller the influence which is measured, or the lack of an influence at all. Experiments and self-reports give the strongest indications, and natural experiments provide the least indication of an effect of poll results.

c) If there were any influence at all, then it would be upon voting intention in the sense of a bandwagon effect.

d) Under the prerequisite of certain electoral systems (five per cent margin [thresholds for winning seats]), supporters of the smaller party, or the party which requires the smaller party for a coalition, can be convinced by opinion polls to vote for their party of second choice.

As a whole, the effects remain, first of all, minimal, and secondly, they can be seen as completely harmless.[13]

Another argument is one of practicality. Banning public polls does not stop polling happening, and often leaking via the Internet. All bans do is restrict polling to those who can afford it, such as hedge funds who can make large sums of money by predicting election results accurately. The rich are able to circumvent polling bans while ordinary people are left with inferior information.

Polls – especially, but not only, exit polls – also safeguard against fraud, giving a public yardstick against which to judge election results.

A final argument against polling bans is that being able to conduct a poll just before polling day is crucial for the health of political polling overall. It is those late polls which can be most usefully compared against actual election results and so can show up problems in polling methodology. Without such checks, political polling is working blind.[14]

A subset of polling bans applies specifically to (not) publishing the results from exit polls before the polls close. These are based on a different, and more defensible, fear that knowing how the actual voting is going in a contest is much more likely to risk putting people off voting (because their side is winning easily or doomed). Moreover, with exit polls much smaller in number and constrained to a short period of time, there is a greater risk of a wayward individual poll being unduly misleading without a chance for other or subsequent polls to clarify matters. Whether legislative or self-regulatory, exit poll bans are not perfect – as the early leaking of exit poll data on the day of voting in u.s. presidential elections shows. But such leaks are generally restricted to the most politically engaged and have a record of inaccuracy, further reducing their impact.

For all the power of the arguments against banning polls, legislation restricting political polls is widespread, with just under two-thirds of countries having some sort of polling embargo according to a global survey carried out for two of the international trade bodies for survey research, ESOMAR (originally the European Society for Opinion and Marketing Research) and WAPOR (World Association for Public Opinion Research). The survey found restrictions of some sort on the freedom to publish election polls in most countries, and in only a third of countries where the survey got data is polling information known to be available immediately before an election.[15]

Exit polls are outright banned in one in ten countries and have been conducted freely in only about one in three countries. In most countries in which exit polling has occurred, it has taken place with limitations on both where interviewers can stand and when exit poll results can be reported.[16] There are ten countries where exit polls cannot be reported at all by the news media.

For pre-election polling,

> This study finds embargoes on the publication of pre-election poll results lasting 30 days or more beforean election in four countries – Bolivia, Cameroon, Honduras and Tunisia. In another ten (Chile, El Salvador, Guatemala, Italy, Montenegro, Panama, Paraguay, Singapore, Slovakia and Zambia), blackouts last at least two weeks . . . In addition, there are seven countries where polls are not used at all in pre-election periods.[17]

Polling blackouts are universal in Latin America and then second most common in Europe. They are least common in North America and the Caribbean, though the European blackouts are, on average, only two days, much shorter than the global average of five days.[18]

What is relatively rare is industry self-regulation, as the survey also found:

> In only 29 countries is there a professional association or other group responsible for addressing complaints about election polls. In about as many countries (27), a government body controls the conduct of election polls. 12 countries have both. More than half the countries with professional associations that deal with election polls are in Europe.[19]

Curiously, an underexplored avenue of potential regulation is to improve the transparency of political polling. Using regulation to improve transparency and so, hopefully, outcomes is common in other areas. Transparency is relevant to properly understanding polling, as much of this book illustrates. Yet transparency can be lacking in surprising places, such as in the Australian political polling sector resulting in a remarkable unwillingness to cooperate with that polling post-mortem discussed earlier.

Knowing who was asked, what was asked, when it was asked and how the results were weighted are all essential to making proper sense of the polls. Transparency around the quality of Internet panels and MRP models is more challenging, as we have seen that judging quality is complicated in both cases. Here, though, basics could be required by transparency rules, such as whether pollsters use their own internal panels and what variables are used in an MRP model.

Transparency is also a common feature of industry self-regulation, when it exists for the polling industry. The British Polling Council rules say, for example, that

> 2.1. All data and research findings made on the basis of surveys conducted in the United Kingdom by member organizations that enter the public domain, must include reference to the following:
>
> - Client commissioning the survey;
> - Dates of interviewing;
> - Method of obtaining the interviews (e.g. in-person, telephone, Internet)
> - The universe effectively represented (all adults, voters, etc)
> - The percentages upon which conclusions are based;
> - Size of the sample and geographic coverage;

2.2. Whenever it is practical to do so the following information should also be published:

- Complete wording of questions upon which any data that has entered the public domain are based;
- A web address where full computer tables may be viewed.[20]

Despite the importance of transparency, and the example set by people such as the British Polling Council, transparency is underexplored in discussions over polling regulation. Would-be polling regulators would do well to take heed.

9
ALTERNATIVES TO OPINION POLLS

'I don't need any poll. When I want to know what people
are thinking, I go to the toilet during the intermission
at a meeting and listen to what they say.'
– FRANZ XAVER UNERTL, German politician[1]

People have wanted to measure public opinion for far longer than
opinion polls have been around. Judging sizes of riots, listening
to conversations in coffee houses, counting names on petitions,
assessing the numbers on a march, tallying up the scale of boycotts
and more were used to assess – or claim – what 'the people' were
thinking. As public opinion increasingly became something to be
systematically documented and quantified, techniques such as counting protestors or analysing letters to the newspapers were pushed
aside by the development of opinion polls.[2] Yet polls do not reign
unchallenged as the arbiter of public opinion, especially in the immediate aftermath of polling failures. So in this chapter, we assess some
of the alternatives people still occasionally claim are better than
properly conducted polls.[3]

Petitions

Petitioning is so old an activity, it pre-dates the invention of the number
zero by a couple of thousand years. From the likely first petitions –
got up by workers on the Egyptian pyramids – through to modern
times, petitions have provided a way to marshal disparate voices into

one enumerated expression of opinion. Often they have had to substitute for voting power. The huge Chartist petitions of nineteenth-century Britain, for example, provided a way of expressing the scale of public opinion, although most of that public was not allowed to use votes in elections to express its views.

As a way of measuring public opinion, petitions come with two important caveats. One is the practical one of knowing how many signatures are genuine and unique: has the petition been padded out with fake signatures (Queen Victoria didn't really sign the third Chartist petition) or with signatures from people who in some way do not count, such as a petition about introducing parking controls in a village that picks up signatures from people in other continents? Even with online petitions that attempt to restrict multiple signatures by requiring unique email and IP addresses for people signing, protecting against one person faking multiple signatures is not easy.[4]

The other caveat is that petitions do, in full and up front, what bad opinion polls do in the details: they only marshal answers on one side of the question. A petition does not tell you how many are on the other side. If a petition is large enough, taking up a huge proportion of the relevant population (the number in a country petitioning the government over a law, or the number in a village petitioning the council over a pothole), that may not matter.[5] But these are the rare exceptions. Moreover, how many signatures a petition gets is not only a sign of public support. It is also indicates something about the organization behind the petition: is it being promoted by an outfit with an extensive campaign organization to put into getting signatures? Has it been promoted online through advertisements? Sometimes petitions can do surprisingly well despite the absence of such organizing muscle, and that can make their size an interesting indicator. Even at their best, though, petitions only offer a clue – and only a clue – as to what public opinion might be thinking. When up against good polls, it is the polls that should be given your attention.

Letters to Politicians

Mike Kelleher, and then later his successor Fiona Reeves, had a very special task in the Barack Obama White House, one that came with the guaranteed daily attention of the president. As director of the Office of Presidential Correspondence, it was his job to select ten letters, emails or faxes from the public each day for the personal attention of and response from the president himself.[6]

The process started with high-speed, unglamorous sorting by interns, sat around long tables grabbing piles of letters to get through three hundred every day. Another team worked through emails at high speed. All sorts of messages passed through: the strange, the funny, the bizarre, the moving, the enlightening and the disturbing. (So much so that monthly counselling sessions were available to those handling the correspondence.) A filtering system picked out those needing a direct response from a particular federal government agency, those wanting a birthday greeting, those needing an expression of condolence and so on.

Then there was the special category, the one that saw several hundred end up on a round wooden table in Kelleher's office. From there, the final ten were selected each day, put into a purple folder and added to the daily briefing folder for the president. As he explained the task, 'We pick messages that are compelling, things people say that, when you read it, you get a chill. I send him letters that are uncomfortable messages.'[7]

Obama preferred to read the letters after dinner, scribbling notes in their margins for what he wanted done or sent in response. For all their small number and for all the other information that came his way each day, he said they had an impact on him:

> The letters that matter the most to me are the ones that . . .
> make a connection . . . Somebody just recently wrote me a
> letter about when they were growing up – their mom always
> used to use the N word and was derogatory about African-
> Americans, but was also an unbelievably great mom who
> worked three jobs to put the kids through school, and how . . .
> sort of both troubling and proud – how troubling this woman
> saw her mother's prejudice, but how proud she was of her mom
> as a person. And how, toward the end of her life, her attitudes
> changed, and she ended up announcing she was going to vote
> for the black guy. She had now passed away, but she thought
> I should know that. You know, there are those kinds of letters,
> I think, that – shape your attitudes.[8]

There were ten letters a day, not selected at random: not great sampling. Nevertheless, most people understandably have a very positive reaction to stories such as this, about politicians cutting through everything around them to hear directly from members of the public, treating them as individuals, not as data points in an opinion poll cross-tab.

That notion of veracity coming from direct personal contact is a powerful one. Politicians often reference what people have sent to them or said to them. Nor is the idea restricted to politics, for vox pops are prevalent in media stories as a way of supposedly cutting through to what the public is thinking.

Yet these are small, skewed samples. Vox pops are not a good tool for understanding what the public thinks.[9] Not all sides of an issue are equally likely to write or email. Nor are all sides equally likely to contact any one person or organization in particular. For all their other value, there are plenty of examples of correspondence levels not reflecting public opinion.[10]

Counting letters had more value back before opinion polls and before the Internet made it much easier to organize mass letter-writing campaigns to fill mailbags with a very skewed balance of letters.[11] Now? It is far less useful, save for the occasional case in which a *change* in the pattern of letters or emails, unconnected with any pressure group or organized lobby, *might* indicate something is up. As political scientist Philip Cowley wrote,

> A new MP soon learns that their postbag is an imperfect device to measure public opinion. They quickly learn to filter out the coordinated letter-writing or email campaigns. They learn to ignore the correspondent who claims they will never vote for them again, but who has made this threat at least a dozen times before and who anyway never voted for them in the first place.
>
> The sort of issues that can provoke people into writing – or get them steamed up on social media – are not necessarily those that really matter to most of their constituents. As one MP told me: 'God writes an awful lot of letters.' Ditto those who like foxes.[12]

Postbags are only a clue that something might be up, not firm evidence that it is.

Crowd Sizes

The 2012 U.S. presidential election was heavily polled – very heavily polled. And yet the day before the election itself, Peggy Noonan wrote for the *Wall Street Journal*, 'We begin with the three words everyone writing about the election must say: Nobody knows anything.

Everyone's guessing.' The polls overall showed a small but consistent lead for incumbent Barack Obama. But she preferred to look elsewhere for evidence:

> While everyone is looking at the polls and the storm, Romney's slipping into the presidency. He's quietly rising, and he's been rising for a while . . . Romney's crowds are building – 28,000 in Morrisville, Pa., last night; 30,000 in West Chester, Ohio, Friday. It isn't only a triumph of advance planning. People came, they got through security and waited for hours in the cold. His rallies look like rallies now, not enactments. In some new way he's caught his stride. He looks happy and grateful. His closing speech has been positive, future-looking, sweetly patriotic. His closing ads are sharp – the one about what's going on at the rallies is moving . . . And there's the thing about the yard signs. In Florida a few weeks ago I saw Romney signs, not Obama ones. From Ohio I hear the same. From tony [sic] Northwest Washington, DC, I hear the same . . .
> Is it possible this whole thing is playing out before our eyes and we're not really noticing because we're too busy looking at data on paper instead of what's in front of us? Maybe that's the real distortion of the polls this year. They left us discounting the world around us.[13]

Crowds and yard signs. If they, the real world out there rather than the data on a spreadsheet somewhere, were pointing to a Romney win, surely the polls were wrong, and he was set to be president? No he wasn't. Romney lost, Obama won. The polls were right.

In fairness to Peggy Noonan, there is something very human in the desire to trust what seems to be direct experience over the cold stare of a spreadsheet. She is far from alone in making such a mistake, as shown by a curious interlude during election night in the 1997 British general election. The Labour Party was bidding for its first election victory since 1974, and for its first proper working majority since 1966. The polls had pointed consistently towards them achieving this, and the exit poll, released just after polls closed at 10 p.m., said that a Labour landslide was on its way. But before the first results came in, there were doubts as nerves, hopes and fears were fuelled by the knowledge that the polls had been very wrong in 1992 (and the exit polls had been poor in 1987). As a result, the views of a series of Conservatives got airtime on the BBC, casting doubt on the exit poll's prediction of a massive Labour landslide, citing instead that their doorstep canvassing had pointed to somewhat better results for their own party, although defeat was still pretty likely. It is worth noting that, at this point, such politicians had no incentive to mislead. Ahead of voting ending, of course, politicians have an incentive to say something other than, 'you're right, we're about to be smashed.' Once voting has ended, though, and especially when you know you are almost certain to lose and that your leader is going to quit anyway as a result, there is little reason to deviate much from what you really believe. Those Conservatives really did believe their canvassing was telling a different, and likely better, story than the polls. It was not. The polls were right. Labour did win a massive landslide.[14]

Nor is counting the public in the form of attendance at public meetings a sensible alternative to the polls, even if you can count their attendance accurately, as shown by examples from both sides of the Atlantic.[15] During the closing stretch of the 1984 U.S. presidential election, Democratic candidate Walter Mondale, behind in the polls, regularly cited Truman's 1948 win in the face of bad polls. He went as far as to pose with a reproduction of the 'Dewey Defeats Truman' newspaper front page from that election. The crowds, he claimed, were a better sign of what was going to happen:

There's something going on in this country and the pollsters aren't getting it. Nobody who's been with me for the last few days and has seen these crowds, seen their response, seen their enthusiasm, seen the intensity of their response and how they respond to these issues, no-one who's been where I've been, can help but believe that there's something happening.[16]

This wasn't just what he was saying in public:

In the final days of the 1984 presidential campaign, the Democratic candidates were nonplussed by the disparity between their dismal standing in the polls and the applause of the crowds that turned out to hear them. They assured themselves and their followers that the palpable enthusiasm was a better indication of voter intentions.[17]

It was not. The Democrat ticket of Walter Mondale (president) and Geraldine Ferraro (vice president) lost in a landslide, 59 per cent to 41 per cent in the popular vote and a crushing 525–13 in the electoral college.

More recently, it was a similar story in the 2020 contest to be the Democratic candidate for U.S. president:

Sen. Elizabeth Warren's campaign has said she has drawn crowds of up to 15,000. Meanwhile, former Vice President Joe Biden has not exactly been packing them in, even as he continues to lead by a healthy margin in most polls of the Democratic presidential primary.[18]

Biden won, and Warren lost – badly. A similar fate befell Labour Party leader Michael Foot in the 1983 British general election:

As the campaign progressed, the gap between Foot's perception of the campaign, and the public's perception of Foot, grew ever wider. Foot was, indeed, receiving enthusiastic receptions wherever he went; his audiences loved his meetings. But in the final two-and-a-half weeks of the campaign Labour's poll ratings, already well behind the Conservatives, declined almost without break. On the Sunday before the election Foot said, 'There must be two elections going on at the same time. I have been attending a different one from the one reflected in the polls.'[19]

He was right. But it was the polls that were the better measure. Labour crashed not only to defeat but to one of their worst election performances since the party's inception early in the twentieth century.

For politicians like those singled out above, it is not really an option to admit you are behind and on course to a crushing defeat. Saying so in public gets labelled a gaffe rather than being praised for its honesty. There is also a need for politicians to keep themselves and their teams motivated during the closing stages of an election, when they often have to work a hundred hours a week or more. Faced with those pressures, citing the size of crowds is a less embarrassing metric to use than horoscopes or animal entrails, although it is no more accurate.

Election Posters

Another favourite alternative to the polls, supposedly showing the real levels of public enthusiasm for one side in an election, is the prevalence of window posters or lawn signs.

There is a smidgen of evidence that occasionally they have some predictive value. In a limited set of circumstances – including when supporters of rival electoral camps are equally willing to show their support and equally likely to have access to somewhere to display a poster – lawn signs can be predictive. For example, as one study found, 'A pre-election count was made of front yard campaign signs for seven local offices and one local proposition in a small self-contained California city. Candidates with the greatest number of signs received the greatest number of votes in six of the seven races.'[20] That lawn sign effect may have been self-reinforcing. Lawn signs or window posters not only reflect levels of support but then increase that support, as there is some evidence that larger such displays equal more votes, either through raising morale and so turnout of supporters or through winning over new supporters.[21] However, the study went on to add, 'Voting on the proposition was unrelated to the number of signs.'[22]

So the lesson is that there is a clear, better-evidenced alternative: pay attention to the polls, not the poster tallies.

Betting Markets

If you meet me, there is a good chance I will be wearing a suit paid for by the profits from betting.[23] I have a clutch of long-lasting suits from bets placed on elections many years ago, using my political knowledge of specific campaigns. Where my money went reflected what I – an informed expert about those campaigns – really thought was going to happen. More so than what I told the media during those elections as the journalists got the spin while the bookies got the cash.

Former Liberal Democrat leader Charles Kennedy once got into trouble for placing a bet on his own party in a European election, as he put his money on a much more modest election result for his party than it was politic for him or his colleagues to say in public. The bet was an authentic insight into what he thought but, alas for him, did not stay private. If the betting markets are the compilation of all this sort of inside information, then perhaps, in a version of the 'wisdom of crowds' argument, they are the best source of election tracking and predictions.[24] In addition, people placing bets know what the polls say, so the betting markets contain information both from polls and other sources. That sounds like it could make for improved insight over using only the polls. Moreover, people who are polled know that the poll results will be published. So they have a temptation to talk up their own side to give it better coverage from any reports of the poll's results. But offering up your own money? Perhaps that is a more serious matter.

Yet perhaps it is not such a serious matter – because betting money may be placed for fun, to show support or just to take a wild punt rather than simply for careful calculation of optimal returns. (I once completely baffled a group of friends when taking the latter approach to betting during a night at a greyhound track. Apparently, a betting strategy of maximizing cash returns by skipping betting on several races was the act of a killjoy rather than of an astute canine analyst.) Moreover, prices in betting markets are driven by the weight of money. If lots of people want to bet on one candidate winning, that will move the market. This means that if one candidate's supporters are much richer than those of another, that could move the market in a way that reflects relative wealth, not relative chances of success. Worse still for those tracking betting and hoping for insight is the possibility that people might place money in a deliberate attempt to move the markets, and so generate positive coverage for their side. For example, accusations of such self-seeking market-moving betting often pop up during political party leadership contests in Britain.[25] As these are usually lightly polled, if at all, moving the betting market can be a way of securing political momentum. I have certainly seen enough unusual patterns in betting on Liberal Democrat leadership contests over the years to be wary of what those markets are telling us.

If there are theoretical arguments both ways, what does the evidence say? Luckily, betting, and prediction markets based on betting,[26] go back even further than modern political polling, with the first prediction market at least as far back as the 1892 U.S. presidential election.[27] This gives us plenty of evidence.

Headline-grabbing (alleged) opinion poll failures such as the 2016 U.S. presidential election and the 2016 UK European referendum show the limitations of relying on the betting markets. In both cases, and in line with the polls, these showed the surprise loser (Clinton, 'Remain', respectively) very heavily favoured to win.[28] Likewise, a study looking at American elections in 2010 and 2012 found that opinion polls beat betting when it came to predicting winners, as did another looking at U.S. elections between 1988 and 2004.[29] Similarly, betting markets did not have a good record in the 2016 or 2020 U.S. presidential primaries.[30] In addition, a study in the UK found, 'The performance of the seat forecasts that we have produced on the basis of the betting markets did not prove to be very accurate. In fact, the estimates performed less well than those derivable from national-level voting trends using constituency swing projections.'[31]

However, a study of the 2015 British election found it a score draw between polls and bets.[32] Some studies go further still, finding that the polls were worse than betting in both the 2008 and 2012 U.S. elections.[33] A study of elections in several European countries has also rated polls as inferior.[34] Another study has found that,

> Prediction markets are an effective means to forecast elections.
> Evidence to date shows that markets often provide more
> accurate forecasts than established benchmark methods such
> as polls, quantitative models, and expert judgment. With
> data from 43 elections, the evidence is particularly strong for
> the markets' relative accuracy compared to single polls . . .

However ... single polls are a weak benchmark to assess the accuracy of a forecasting method. When comparing the relative accuracy of markets and polls, researchers should thus consider more sophisticated poll-based forecasts such as combined and projected polls. As one study found, the case of the seven U.S. presidential elections – for which comparisons to single polls, combined polls and combined poll projections are available over a 90-day forecast horizon – demonstrates how such approaches increase the relative accuracy of polls compared to prediction markets. Prediction markets out-performed single polls in each of the seven elections, with an average error reduction of 48 per cent. Compared to combined polls, prediction markets were more accurate in six of the seven elections, with an average error reduction of 43 per cent. Compared to combined and projected polls, prediction markets were more accurate in only four of the seven elections, and the average error reduction decreased to 17 per cent.[35]

But before you abandon this book thinking that political polls are not the thing to spend your time on, this study also found,

One concern with prediction markets is that the forecasts are subject to manipulation. Recent experience with two markets in the U.S. and in Germany suggests that certain (groups of) traders were successful in influencing market prices over a longer period. If the media increasingly include market forecasts in their campaign coverage, the potential gains for manipulators – and thus the threat of manipulation attempts – might increase even further.[36]

A version of Goodhart's law likely applies. Named after British economist Charles Goodhart, this states that when a measure becomes a target, it stops being a good measure. When people alight on a metric as the thing to worry about, its value drops. So with betting-based predictions, the more attention they receive as a claimed good predictor, the higher the chance of manipulation and the lower their usefulness.

What is more, the online nature of most such betting makes it vulnerable to manipulation to anyone, anywhere in the world, with a healthy bank balance or a batch of stolen credit cards. A shady foreign state with sufficient resources could easily move the betting prices on an election. It is much easier to rig the markets than to rig polls. The polls still have the edge.

Focus Groups

If this book were an animal, what sort of animal would it be? That is the sort of apparently absurd question beloved of media coverage of focus groups. But there is value in asking what sort of animal a politician would be, because the answers tap into a wide range of characteristics and emotional responses. For example, in the summer of 2020, focus group respondents often picked 'eagle' as the answer when asked about then-leader of the Labour Party in the UK Keir Starmer.[37] An eagle – as in smart, carefully eyeing up opportunities, but detached and elegant rather than cute. An eagle is no panda, nor is it a terrier. There is much meaning bundled up in the choice of eagle. Asking people to pick an animal extracts expressive answers from those less confident with words. It teases out answers that tap into our instincts and subconscious rather than merely prompting people to give a rational, considered answer. A focus group is a more refined version of the Obama letter technique. In both cases, the idea is that hearing in more depth from a selected number of individuals can give greater insight. What is lost from the smallness of the sample (the risk of atypical answers) is compensated for by the depth of what is heard.

A focus group involves inviting a small number of people – often in single figures, very rarely more than twenty – for a discussion lasting over an hour. The participants may all be from a target niche, such as swing voters, older men or students. Often, they are given different stimuli to which to respond, such as being shown a short video clip of a politician, or the design of a poster. And sometimes there will be the seemingly off-the-wall question such as what type of animal a politician would be.

The results of focus groups, when done properly at least, involve very little in the way of numbers. Being told that 25 per cent of a focus group of eight people agree with a particular view gives the finding an undue appearance of precision, given the smallness of the sample. Giving percentages when speaking about a focus group treats it like a poll with a tiny sample – and so a humongous margin of error. (If 50 per cent of a focus group of eight gave the same response to a particular question, this finding comes with a standard margin of error of plus or minus 35 per cent – putting the range of likely truth between 15 per cent and 85 per cent.) Although giving numbers like this is weirdly popular in reporting focus groups in u.s. politics, it is something to avoid, and usually a sign that either someone does not know how focus groups work – or they do but are cynical enough to hope that those hearing their numbers won't know.

A focus group is not a small poll. It is very different. What makes for a great focus group is the incisive quote from a participant that captures the public mood, not the production of detailed statistics. Those quotes are often memorable, and can be highly impactful. 'Get Brexit done' – the election-winning slogan for the Conservatives in the 2019 British general election – came from comments in focus groups. But for understanding the public's views, always check the colour of what focus groups are saying against the numerical context of what public polls are saying.

That is why the best use of focus groups to understand politics is in tandem with polls. Focus groups can help in exploring issues to identify the best questions to put into polls and how to word those questions – and then when you have the poll results, focus groups can help explain the reasons and motivations that lie behind the results. 'If you're only looking at polls, you're missing depth of understanding,' explains Deborah Mattinson, former pollster to British prime minister Gordon Brown. Moreover, using focus groups will 'give you a better-worded questionnaire as well as a better understanding of its results.'[38]

To enjoy these benefits, you need sufficient focus groups to have confidence in their findings, as any single focus group may be off. Unlike with polling and sample sizes, there is no similar rule of thumb for focus groups. But be suspicious of any findings based on just one focus group. That may be driven by understandable time or budget restrictions, such as a media outlet doing one in the aftermath of an election debate, but it is still very brittle information. What becomes trustworthy is a series of focus groups, run alongside polls. This is because focus groups are no more an alternative to opinion polls than vowels are an alternative to consonants. Rather they are both best used in combination with each other. Polls can tell you the what, focus groups the why.

Twitter Polls

Suppose you do not understand sampling and margins of error at all. In that case, it can appear that a Twitter poll completed by 25,000 people must be more accurate than a proper opinion poll with a sample of only 1,000. However, we have already discussed how size isn't everything when it comes to polling, so we both know better. Twitter polls illustrate the perils of the self-selecting sample. A large, self-selecting sample is still a self-selecting sample. If you are standing outside a local McDonald's, asking people about their favourite fast-food chain, whether you ask 100, 1,000 or 10,000, you will still obtain answers skewed towards McDonald's and against Subway.

A striking example of this came with an experiment carried out by Lord Ashcroft. In December 2017 he ran a Twitter poll, asking, 'Please vote and retweet as to whether you want a second referendum on Brexit.' It garnered 180,480 votes, each from a different Twitter account. The result was 67 per cent in favour of a second referendum.[39] However, he followed up with a proper opinion poll, carried out in mid-January. It found only between 38 per cent and 40 per cent favouring a second referendum, depending on the exact question.[40] Although the experiment was not as clear as it could have been – different dates and different question wording – the results were so far apart that it made the point.

This was not just a one-off, as there is solid evidence that, when it comes to politics, people on Twitter are different from people who are not. In 2017, for example, an opinion poll had voting figures of Conservative at 41 per cent and Labour at 28 per cent overall, but this switched to Conservative at 30 per cent and Labour at 39 per cent when restricted to Twitter users. The following year, an online open survey similar to a Twitter poll was compared with a proper poll to judge people's views on immigration. The former produced more extreme views (both pro and anti-immigration) than the latter.[41] The British Election Study has also consistently found a difference in political views between Twitter users and non-users, with Twitter users having voted 'Remain' by 68 per cent to 32 per cent in the European referendum, compared with the actual 48 per cent to 52 per cent result, and Labour leading the Conservatives among Twitter users in all three of the 2015, 2017 and 2019 general elections, although the Conservatives outpolled Labour in all three.[42]

Notwithstanding this evidence, Twitter polls do have a purpose – not as an alternative or improvement on political polls, but to provide a bit of fun or casual insight. Doing a quick poll to find out which password manager service my Twitter followers like using gives me a good clue as to which one to try myself. Twitter polls can also be of some use if you can be confident that the skew in the respondents is not a problem for the particular question being asked, or is consistent over time so you can at least measure trends across Twitter polls. These are pretty niche and risky uses, however. Just as a speaker may take an informal show of hands at a talk, a quick Twitter poll can occasionally shine a ray of light – occasionally.

Counting Tweets

A different use of Twitter as a supposedly superior alternative to political opinion polls involves counting tweets. This approach had an allure in the early days of Twitter. If people were expressing their views on Twitter, perhaps tabulating views for or against a party or candidate could provide solid statistical insight into who was ahead or behind in an election?

Certainly, a whole industry of social media monitoring software and analysts has grown up, claiming that reliable trends and sentiment levels can be derived from looking at what people say on social media. Twitter data is particularly popular for such analysis due to its greater availability to such tools compared with data from other social networks.[43] It is an area I have worked in myself. Done well, such tools and analysis can be valuable for identifying individual messages to which to respond – a version of customer service. They can also act as an early warning: a small number of tweets suddenly appearing about faulty milkshake machines in a restaurant firm's outlets (a real example from my own work) can be a useful clue that something is up that internal management reporting chains may not yet have caught. Social media monitoring can also act as a form of rough-and-ready focus group work – quicker and more flexible than proper focus groups, but with a similar limitation that what you obtain from them are qualitative insights, not percentages.

The subsequent rise of bots, fake profiles and large-scale disinformation on social media has greatly tarnished the allure of social media insight. Social media firms have also reacted to privacy concerns by cutting back the amount of data they make available. But even in the heyday of Twitter, after it stopped being obscure and before it started being so widely gamed, evidence that Twitter analysis (or social media analysis more generally) could replace polling was lacking. In addition to individual studies showing that tweet counting was not a viable alternative to polling from countries such as Chile, Sweden and the United States, more systematic reviews of the research showed the same: Twitter data is not a credible alternative to opinion polls.[44]

Crystal balls

They do not work.[45]

So Remember

Paul the Octopus was briefly famous for his football-predicting 'skills' at the 2010 World Cup. Less well known were Anton the Tamarin, Leon the Porcupine and Petty the Pygmy Hippopotamus. Mani the Parakeet had a good run of predictions initially, but then got it wrong.

Perhaps wisely for protecting his record, Paul died a few months after the World Cup, and so was never put to the test again.

In other words, the contrarian measure that appears to work grabs the headline. All the others sink away. It is that lopsided survivor bias that makes these measures seem much better than they are because it is only the exceptions that hit lucky which grab the headlines. Even when they do, the luck is frequently fleeting, as with the menagerie of animals who are brilliant sports tipsters, until they are not.[46]

So it is with politics and trailers of chickens, as one report recounts:

> Leslie Biffle, Secretary of the Senate in the Eighty-First Congress, after making his own cross-country trek disguised as a poultry dealer with a trailer full of chickens in 1948, accurately divined that the farmers were going to vote for Truman despite a showing of the polls to the contrary.[47]

The chicken trick may have worked in 1948, but the success of such tricks is fleeting. The polls are the better bet, not only in the long run but in the medium and short runs too.

10

EVEN GOOD POLLS MISLEAD

'The same question couched in the same words, even if
in the same language, does not mean the same thing at
any two times or in any two cultures.'

– ITHIEL DE SOLA POOL, ROBERT P. ABELSON
AND SAMUEL POPKIN, Simulmatics Corporation[1]

We have seen many ways to do political polling badly, producing misleading results. However, even done well with impeccable questions, astute sampling and assiduous weighting, polls can still mislead and catch you off guard. Therefore, this chapter equips you with the tools to keep up that guard.

Bad Luck

As discussed earlier, pollsters do not use truly random sampling. But there is enough randomness that it is possible now and again for random bad luck to give a pollster a bad sample. As Nate Cohn, polling expert for the *New York Times*, puts it: 'It's the nature of the game: even a perfectly conducted poll will occasionally yield imperfect results, and sometimes terrible ones.'[2]

It's the same as how tossing a fair coin can, just sometimes, give you ten heads in a row, despite there being tails on one side of the coin. In fact, such bad luck *should* sometimes occur. That is the nature of random chance, which is why you would be wary of a pollster who appears to never have a bad poll. It is like watching someone toss a coin which always gives five heads out of ten. See that often enough, and you should start to become suspicious. So accept that some polls will be wrong due to bad luck – and be reassured rather than worried by the appearance of such polls.

Changes within the Margin of Error

I started collecting opinion poll results after hearing an improbable claim on television. Then-leader of the Social Democratic Party (SDP) David Owen was speaking about the poll ratings for the electoral alliance between his party and the Liberals. He claimed that there was a seasonal pattern, with a drop in the polls for the Alliance each autumn. As excuses for falling poll ratings go, claiming a seasonal effect was both impressive (he sounded really on top of the detail) and baffling (no one seasonally adjusts political poll results). Infuriatingly, if understandably, the interviewer had not anticipated a seasonal-adjustment excuse and was not able to interrogate, substantiate or rubbish the claim.

I sought to remedy that with a spreadsheet, several hours spent with the microfilms at the local library and the start of a dataset that has grown to be the largest collection of national voting intention polls for the UK.[3] Yet to this day, I do not know the truth of the seasonal-trends claim. There are tentative indications of a repeating autumnal pattern in the mid- to late 1980s. But they fall far short of evidence sufficient to be confident of there being anything more than a random collection of noise in the figures.

Despite my failure, my intention was the right one. To understand what is going on in political opinion polls, you not only need to take what protagonists say about them with a pinch of salt, you also need to take each individual poll with a pinch of salt too. You need to look at the bigger picture, collating multiple polls.

A very common mistake flows from this – to look at just two polls and place far too much weight on the changes between them. Even if they are comparable polls, movements in the numbers may be caused by sampling variations rather than by real-world movements in public opinion. If a party or candidate is up two points compared with the last poll, that may be a real move, or it may be just statistical noise. One point here or there means much less than it seems in the excitable reports of polls. As journalist Ariel Edwards-Levy implored, 'How do I hack everybody else's computer to install a macro that replaces the phrase "ahead/behind by 1 point" with "virtually tied"?'[4]

Simply concluding from this that you should only pay attention to changes outside the margin of error is, however, misguided. This puts the bar too high, as change may be real yet also small. That is why you need to look at the bigger picture: more polls, over more time, are your real guide. Yet it is still easy to go wrong, as a simple experiment of mine demonstrates. Consider the polling results for two parties from a series of comparable polls:

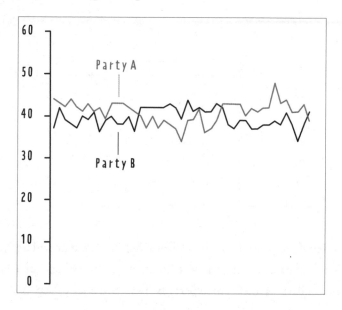

What would you make of these polls if they came out for real? There's an initial period of Party A being ahead, but with several occasions when Party B looks about to catch up. Then Party A seems to hit a slide, slipping to being persistently behind. In fact, it looks like there's a steady, long-term fall from the start through to Party A's low point. Then the trend turns, and there's an upward movement as Party A returns to being in front and builds a consistent lead for a while, before, at the end, there's a sudden, sharp reversal of positions. The graph's turbulence provides many moments to get excited about. It also seems that Party A was on steady slide, hitting a low near the midpoint, then bouncing back and appearing to build a new and increasingly solid lead, before the sudden uncertainty at the end.

Now here's the truth. The above graph was based on giving Party A and Party B pre-allocated levels of support, but then generating noise around the true figures with the sort of random fluctuations you should expect from the polls.[5] Here's what the real position was, minus the noise:

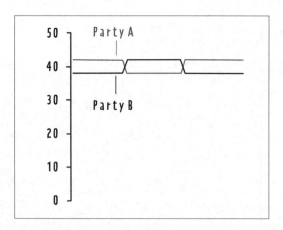

How does the picture drawn from the polls compare with reality? It's not all bad. As you can see, the data with noise still got the basic story of Party A ahead, then party B ahead and finally Party A ahead again. What should we make of the apparent excitements of Party B closing on Party A at times at the start? They are mere phantoms. What about the dramatic surges and dips at the end, with a possible role reversal right at the end? They too are all phantoms. Does that apparently longer-term downward trend in Party A's support, followed then by a trend back up signify anything? It is simply another phantom. Noise turned pan-flat reality into something far more excitable. The mid-graph apparent turnaround in Party A's long-term decline never happened.

So it isn't just that you need to step back from individual polls. You also need to step back from apparently short-term trends, as randomness can serve up imaginary movements that span several polls. You need, rather, to stick with looking at much cruder overall pictures (or stick to very sophisticated modelling of averages of polling which obliterate the phantoms for you with mathematical smoothing).

The Mirage of Momentum

In 1980 George H. W. Bush was running to be the Republican candidate for president of the United States. After winning the Iowa caucuses, he said, 'Now they will be after me, howling and yowling at my heels. What we will have is momentum. We will look forward to Big Mo being on our side, as they say in athletics.' Big Mo didn't see Bush through to victory. Bush went on to lose the New Hampshire primary and the Republican nomination. But he had given modern politics a phrase that stuck. Claims about a party or candidate having momentum in the polls are now common.

However, whatever the merits of believing in momentum in sports or in politics more generally, it does not exist when it comes to polls. Or more specifically, the evidence is that future movements in the polls are not predicted by past movements in the polls. If a party has gone up in the polls, for example, you cannot predict on that basis that it will continue to go up in the polls. *Sometimes* there is a sustained trend. But much more often, a poll showing a movement one way is then followed by a movement back. As Nate Silver puts it, 'It is usually wrong to say that a candidate is gaining ground in the polls – present tense – or that her position is improving. Instead, you should say that the candidate has gained ground or that her position has improved.'[6] Or in the pithier phrase of another polling expert, Leo Barasi, on the myth of momentum in the polls: 'One of the most popular concepts in politics is a figment of the imagination.'[7]

There may be some exceptions (primaries and by-elections are plausible possible exceptions, alas not closely researched). But as a general rule, if someone is speaking about a series of high-quality polls, conclusions are more reliable in the past tense ('X has gone up in the polls') than in the present ('X is rising in the polls').[8]

Opinions Change

People's views can change, as one polling industry tale relates:

> In Tel Aviv a widescale opinion poll was conducted recently. One of the people interviewed was a bright and opinionated housewife who expressed her views in a most convincing manner. When the interviewer finished, he thanked her profusely and walked away. 'Please wait, sir,' the woman called loudly. 'Where can I find you just in case I change my opinion?'[9]

Because views change, even the best of polls age, which is why you should always check the fieldwork dates on a poll. These matter far more than when it was published. With political polls in the news, they are usually pretty fresh. voting intention polls may even be published on the same day that the sampling finished. It is rare these days for there to be a large gap between fieldwork and publication. However, polls on political issues, especially those which come via pressure groups and academics, can be rather old. A news report about a new finding from an academic paper just published may, if you dig into the details, turn out to be based on fieldwork that is years old and has only just emerged from the slow gestation of academic publishing.

Moreover, although ending fieldwork too soon before polling day – and so being caught out by a late swing – is a common contribution to polling disasters (and an even more common contribution to excuses for polling disasters as it is such a convenient cover story), it is still far from rare to find the fieldwork for a final pre-election poll from a particular pollster ending several days before the election.

Timing problems are not just tied to polling day. Take a YouGov poll that asked people in Britain, 'When a leader of a country falls ill, do you think the public have a right to know the leader's full condition?' Conservatives agreed with this 65 per cent to 25 per cent, and Labour supporters agreed by the larger margin of 76 per cent to 14 per cent.[10] But what should one make of that partisan difference? Perhaps there is a genuine left-versus-right difference at work here. But perhaps too it is the timing of the poll that mattered: shortly after a Conservative prime minister in the UK had been ill with COVID-19 (and, perhaps also relevant, at a time when a Republican president in the United States was still ill with COVID-19). In that context, perhaps the survey was telling us something very different from what it would have told us had the prime minister instead been healthy, but the Labour leader had been struck down by COVID-19. We do not know, although there is a clue in the age breakdown of the poll, which shows that older people were more likely to say that the public has a right to know. As older people were more likely to be Conservative, that suggests there was a strong partisan effect at work, but we cannot say for sure.

The context given by the timing matters. So always check the fieldwork dates and think about where they fit in with the flow of events. Do not be afraid to conclude that the dates mean we don't really know what the poll is telling us.

Partisanship Dominates

Tribalism is not unique to politics. Just try asking opposing football fans what they thought of the referee after a heated and contentious football match, especially a derby.[11] It does, however, pose a problem for conducting and understanding political polling, as illustrated by a test carried out in 2005:

> The Conservative label is undermining the party's ability to sell its policies on immigration to swing or floating voters, according to a new Populus poll for *The Times*.
>
> The poll, undertaken last weekend, shows that Conservative policy is more popular than Labour's but the Tory label results in a big drop in support, the implication being that the Tory brand is not appealing.[12]

Poll participants had been read short summaries of the Conservative and Labour Party positions on immigration, and were then asked whether or not they agreed with them.[13] However, half were told which summary applied to which party and the other half were only told that each summary was from 'one of the political parties'. The Labour policy got roughly the same response regardless of whether or not it was associated with the party (net approval was 34 per cent with its name and 32 per cent without). However, the Conservative policy secured very different results – with net agreement dropping from 55 per cent when people did not know they had been read a Conservative policy summary to 43 per cent when they did. The substantial change was in people saying they disagreed with it: up from 18 per cent to 27 per cent when the Conservative label was included. As one analysis of this data concluded,

> The drop in net agreement between the unattributed and attributed descriptions suggested that one voter in eight – and one in six swing voters – had such a negative view of the Conservative Party's brand that they would oppose a policy they actually agreed with rather than support a Tory proposal.[14]

Partisanship is a powerful drug, which is why even an expertly conducted poll will still run into the problem that the answers may be telling you about partisanship rather than about the specific questions posed. As a result, a common mistake is to think that a party or politician is (un)popular because a particular policy or incident is (un)popular. Often the causality runs the other way. It is not that people dislike the government because they do not like its tax policies, but rather that they do not like its tax policies because they do not like the government, and so they automatically give the thumbs down to much of what the government does.

This partisanship can take us to rather risible extremes, as with views of the 10 Downing Street cat. Charged with keeping mice under control at the prime minister's residence, there have been Downing Street cats back to at least the middle of the twentieth century. In more recent years, they have become celebrities, featuring in the media and popular on social media. Views of these cats are filtered by partisanship, as Philip Cowley explained in 2014:

In an experiment run with the survey company YouGov, a
representative sample of voters were shown a picture of the
redoubtable Humphrey [a previous Downing Street cat who
was in place under both Margaret Thatcher and Tony Blair]
randomly varying whether he was described as Margaret
Thatcher's cat or Tony Blair's cat and asked to say whether
they liked or disliked him.[15]

Would people's responses to the photo of the cat be moved by their
political partisanship? Yes, they would: 'The net approval of Humphrey
the cat (the share who like Humphrey minus the share who dislike him)
varied depending on the partisanship of the respondents doing the
rating, and the Prime Minister with whom Humphrey is associated.'[16]
Conservative voters told the photo was of Margaret Thatcher's cat
liked the photo more than Conservative voters who were told it was
Tony Blair's cat. Labour voters were no better in their inconsistency.
And that was just with a photo of a cat, not a question about judging a
policy or the performance of a government department. Partisanship
colours answers heavily, as non-feline research also shows.[17]

In fact, partisanship does more than that. Partisanship also provides a reason to game the answers to questions, as powerfully
illustrated in the summer of 2020. During Britain's exit from the
European Union, a minister in Parliament surprised even many of his
own side by announcing that a proposed piece of legislation related
to this would break international law in a 'very specific and limited
way'. As well as triggering a wave of controversy, Twitter jokes and
legal commentary, this also triggered polling. J.L. Partners asked people
in Britain if they thought this announcement by the government
made it more or less likely that 'The UK can credibly tell countries
like China and Russia not to break international law'. It was no surprise that 57 per cent thought it made this less likely. Another 21 per

cent thought it made no difference, and 16 per cent did not know. That left, however, 5 per cent who said it made it *more* likely.[18] Allowing for the wonders of humanity, which includes people who believe the Earth is flat or that lizard people control the world's governments, that is still an implausible answer.

Two factors explain the results of that poll. One is that all surveys contain weirdness in the small numbers. Online surveys protect against, for example, someone simply rapidly hitting the same answer to every question in order to pass through the survey swiftly (which might be tempting, especially if the panel members are getting a small payment for each survey completion). Nevertheless, whether due to mistakes, laziness, drunkenness, misunderstanding the information or a sense of impish fun, a few seriously weird answers occur. In this case, perhaps some people misread the question and only focused on the part that said, 'The UK can credibly tell countries like China and Russia not to break international law' rather than the preceding wording which said, 'Does the Government's admission that it plans to "break international law in a very specific and limited way" make it more or less likely that'. As a result, perhaps they were wrongly thinking that the question was just about agreeing or disagreeing with that statement rather than about the impact of the government's decision to break the law. But also, partisanship was at work here. Imagine a firmly pro-Brexit, pro-government person being polled for that survey. That person wants to express support for the government's actions as strongly as possible. Faced with that question, saying that the government breaking the law makes it easier to tell off other countries for breaking the law makes sense. It might be technically untrue, but in terms of producing percentage results that make the government look as good as possible, it is the right answer. (Partisanship is one possible cause of people giving answers that are emotionally satisfying although technically not what they believe. There is also some evidence that people sometimes deliberately troll surveys by picking humorous answers, such as claiming to believe in conspiracy theories when they do not.[19])

I once faced a similar dilemma myself when completing a poll that had a question about the performance of the then-leader of my own political party. I did not think that person's performance was brilliant. I also knew the press would love to write up the poll as critically as possible for my party, so an honest answer could also contribute to making the media coverage of the poll more damaging. My memory fails me on whether in the end I plumped for the white lie of the most positive answer available, but whether or not I did on that occasion, it is easy to see why some people will do that.

The answers to a Redfield and Wilton poll conducted on 21 October 2020 demonstrated this factor at work. It asked, 'The next United Kingdom General Election is likely to be held in 2024. Which political party do you think is most likely to win the highest number of seats in the next election?' A total of 4 per cent of people picked the SNP (the Scottish National Party, a party that only stands in 59 out of 650 constituencies – the Scottish ones). This was not a one-off fluke, as the same question was asked in other surveys from this firm, with similar results. It is reasonably safe to say that people taking part in these polls were not expecting a wild multi-party outcome in which the largest party had fewer than one in ten of the MPs. SNP supporters were much more likely to pick this answer, reflecting a desire to big up their own party. (That a few others picked this answer too shows that even partisanship cannot quite explain all the odd results.) Partisanship is a powerful force, and the results from political polls must be interpreted knowing that partisans will have provided many of the answers.

Not All Views Are Equally Held

An experiment by Gallup in 2003 showed how the headline figures about popular backing for President George W. Bush to launch military action in Iraq were not the whole story. Asked, 'Would you favor or oppose sending American ground troops to the Persian Gulf in an attempt to remove Saddam Hussein from power in Iraq?', 59 per cent agreed, and 38 per cent disagreed. However, people were then also asked if they would be upset if the government did the opposite of their preferred choice. Taking into account those results, the apparent strong public support broke down as:

> 29 per cent in favour of sending in troops and upset if troops not sent
>
> 30 per cent in favour of sending in troops but not upset if troops not sent
>
> 30 per cent against sending in troops and upset if troops sent
>
> 8 per cent against sending in troops but not upset if troops sent
>
> 3 per cent don't know if in favour or against sending in troops

These figures can be cut multiple ways, from saying that only 30 per cent were adamantly opposed to the war (against troops and upset if they were sent) through to saying that only 29 per cent were firmly in favour. Overall, the picture was much more one of the public being willing to support troops being sent (29 + 30 + 8 for 67 per cent under this banner) rather than being positively in favour (only 29 per cent under this banner).[20]

Another version of varying intensity is when the strength of feeling differs on either side of an issue. Typically, this applies when people on one side are more numerous but only mildly in favour of a policy, while those on the other side, although smaller in number, feel much more strongly about the issue. In such cases, the majority may be in favour, but the political dynamics are with the minority against. Their fervour gives their views more political bite (they are more likely to lobby, protest and change their vote) and suggests that the switches of opinion are more likely to be towards rather than away from their position.

It is common for polls on issues to give at least some hints of strength of feeling by breaking down answers into categories such as 'strongly agree' and 'agree', though as we have seen, agree/disagree questions comes with a bundle of their own problems. Nonetheless, always keep an eye out for the details when the strength of feelings has been gathered; they can be very revealing.

The Media Can't Help Reporting Polls Badly

Much can be said about how even the reputable corners of the media tend to get some sorts of stories wrong – enough certainly for me to have made a book out of it.[21]

Political polling suffers particularly badly from the media's inaccurate reporting, for two reasons: a commercial one and a chronological one. The commercial problem is that many polls are commissioned by media outlets. If an outlet pays for a poll, it understandably wants value for money from the poll. That pushes the outlet – and especially whoever signed off on the budget for the poll – to make it sound exciting, to want to make it worthy of as high-profile a headline as possible. Who wants to say, 'this poll is a bit boring; let's just bin it and not run any story even though we paid for it'? The financial pressures to find a major headline in the small print of a boring poll are accentuated by the bouts of scepticism in the media that spending money on polls is an effective way to garner an audience.[22]

To make matters worse, not only does the media outlet have an incentive to over-egg its own poll, it also has an incentive to downplay other polls that contradict it. What media outlet would spike its own story by saying, 'our poll turned out to be an outlier and so should be ignored'? Again, the institutional incentive is to double down on your own poll, make it sound as exciting as possible and minimize any context that may undermine its credibility or relevance. Brash self-professed certainty based on a single data point wins out over cautious, nuanced interpretation.

Hence the conclusion from Ivor Crewe, professor of political science and government: 'The more improbable a poll finding, the more likely the media will give it prominence.'[23]

Of course, the better journalists and editors know this. They do not capitulate completely to puffing their own poll. However, the pressures are still there. This is why it is so crushingly rare to find a poll headline that says that nothing much is happening, although when you look at the longer-term polling averages, quite often nothing much is happening. It's also why you find so many pollsters saying most of the time, 'don't pay attention to just one poll, don't pay attention to just one poll, don't pay attention to just one poll'. But then with the publication of their own latest poll, they cannot resist the temptation to switch to 'pay attention to our poll! pay attention to our poll! pay attention to our poll!'

One of the most informative tweeters about British political polls, and a pollster himself, Keiran Pedley, demonstrates this. Pinned at the top of his Twitter profile for a long time was 'I see we're over-reacting to one poll again.'[24] But that doesn't stop him tweeting long threads about individual polls, especially from his polling employer.

This is the frustrating tragedy at the heart of much of public political polling. It has a business model (funding from the media) that both enables it to exist and then distorts the results.

The other problem for polls and the media is chronological. The news, by definition, is about what is new. Focusing on just the latest poll, or the new ones that day, is not the best way to understand what the polls are saying. For that, you want context. You need to see what the longer-term trends are. If you have a 'shock' poll finding that is way out of line with what has come before, the sensible reaction is to say, 'this may be a rogue poll or this may be dramatic; let's see a few more polls before deciding.' The news, however, cannot hang around to do that. Again, the better journalists know this is a problem and caveat their stories somewhat. But it is virtually unheard of to find a story that says, 'new polling shows our story last week should be forgotten as it was wrong.' The other pressures on news production are too great.

Good journalists and good pollsters both understand these problems, but their dependency on each other and the pressures on them pull coverage in the wrong direction:

> The polls and the media, at least at election time, cannot live without the other. The polls depend on the press and broadcasting for payment and publicity. And the media depend on the polls to provide copy ... But as for many couples, living together is almost as difficult as living apart. For what the media and polls most need from each other is what each finds most difficult to provide. The media, as always, demand speed ... simplicity, certainty and brevity; but poll findings are often ambivalent, and their correct interpretation requires balance, qualification and elaboration ... the polls strive after truth, and the truth is not always newsworthy.[25]

Cross-Tabs: A Clever Way to Daft Conclusions

When a political opinion poll is published, it usually comes with tables showing the results broken into categories such as men, women or younger people. These are the 'cross-tabs' (short for 'cross-tabulations'). Cross-tabs contain both wisdom and danger. The wisdom comes from a better understanding of what is causing the headline findings. If a new party is suddenly popular, for example, take a look at the cross-tabs to see if it has particularly drawn support from women, previous supporters of the government or people in the west. Such details help give the story behind the headline.

However, a figure found in a cross-tab is not the whole poll. With a sample of, say, 1,000, then perhaps 550 are women, of whom maybe 235 recall voting for the government party last time, and of them perhaps 75 are in the west. As the sample size shrinks, the margin of error goes up. That means apparently interesting differences, such as between former government supporters in the west who are women and those who are men, is increasingly likely to be just statistical noise rather than revealing a real difference. To make matters worse, the cross-tabs figures are not usually fully weighted in all the ways that pollsters have developed to (attempt to) make their headline voting intention findings accurate. They are a detailed and partial extract taken part way through the statistical production line for the poll.

Teasing out information from the cross-tabs, therefore, requires two techniques. One is to look at the cross-tabs for not just one poll but multiple polls. Suppose that apparent difference between male and female westerners who previously supported the government is repeated across several polls. In that case, the caution about small samples and lack of weighting can be superseded by confidence that there is something there.

The other technique is to look for consistent patterns within a poll. Cross-tabs showing how answers varied by age band are usually a good example. The above warnings may mean you do not want to place weight on an apparent difference in the answers between 18–24-year olds and 25–49-year-olds. But if, say, 25–49-year-olds are a bit more likely to support the new party than their younger compatriots, 50–64-year-olds are a bit more likely again, and those aged 65+ are more likely still, then we have a trend across age.[26] Each difference may be small, but the pattern adds confidence that the differences are real.

Even when both of these techniques are used, however, the cross-tabs can mislead because only some cross-tabs are presented. The choice of which cross-tabs to show (and which to gather in the first place) is not some automatic technical process. Rather, it encodes a way of looking at the world, one selected from multiple options. For example, political scientist Paula Surridge often points out that the cross-tabs on British political polls usually include age and usually do not include level of education. The result is that people see patterns of political views by age and then ascribe them to age, when it may well be that education is really the critical factor.[27] Another example is that ethnicity rarely features in cross-tabs in the UK, which makes it look a less important factor than if it was always present, offering up numbers for tempting conclusions.

An example of how causal factors may be absent from cross-tabs came with polling for CBS News in the USA in 2021. It showed a clear partisan split on how people would use time travel. Liberals were more likely to want to travel to the future rather than the past (61 per cent versus 36 per cent), while conservatives had a greater preference for the past (47 per cent versus 44 per cent).[28] But it's unlikely that these cross-tabs tell the right story. It's most likely not that being conservative means you are more likely to want to travel to the past, but rather that there's a particular set of values that some people have, which make them prefer the past and be less optimistic about the future – and that makes them both conservative and more likely to prefer travelling backwards in time. The cross-tabs often seductively look like they are offering an explanation, but are instead, as in this case, really just giving another symptom of a cause that rests elsewhere. So beware of cross-tabs. They can help explain. But they often mislead, and they are rarely enough on their own to justify a conclusion, let alone a headline.

Don't Always Ignore the 'Don't Knows'

As mentioned earlier, there are traditions about when to include and when to exclude the 'don't know' or 'no opinion' clan from headline figures in a poll. Practice varies according to the type of question and country, which is why 'tradition' is the best descriptor. It is far from clear that there is any careful methodological thought behind why voting figures are presented differently in this respect in the USA and the UK, for example. However, the traditions have evolved and survived because they have a basic utility, providing consistency within a country and type of question, making trends meaningful. Traditions also apply to questions about approval or support for a person or policy. Do you report the percentage agreeing or the net figure (agreeing minus disagreeing)? Tradition usually puts the net figure in the headlines that catch our attention.

Sometimes, however, all such traditions need abandoning, and it is the full context of all the numbers that needs study. This was clearly illustrated by an opinion poll conducted in Britain by Deltapoll in 2020. The younger people were the *more* likely to say yes to 'Do you think you will die from the coronavirus?' At first blush, that was a surprising and counter-intuitive finding. After all, science showed that older people were more likely to be at risk. Likewise, the broader tenor of media coverage was over concerns that younger people were more likely not to be taking the problem seriously enough. Yet instead of showing fear of death being lowest among younger people, the poll showed that it was highest. Moreover, the trend across the different age bands was a consistent trend (so passing the cross-tabs tests mentioned above).

But here are the full figures for the youngest and oldest age bands:

Do you think you will die from the coronavirus?
18–24: 14 per cent 'yes', 70 per cent 'no', 16 per cent 'don't know'
– net minus 56 per cent
65+: 6 per cent 'yes', 50 per cent 'no', 44 per cent 'don't know' –
net minus 46 per cent

The figures for other age bands showed a clear trend between these two endpoints, with both 'yes' and 'no' declining with age, and with 'don't know' rising by age.

You could, therefore, pull two quite different stories from these figures. 'Fear of death greatest among young people' (look at that 14 per cent 'yes'), or 'Fear of death greatest among old people' (look at the 'no' and net figures). Each is true in its own way, and each, therefore, is also unhelpfully misleading in its own way.[29]

The importance of looking at the full numbers, including the 'don't knows', increases if there is a gender divide over a question, because of that consistent pattern, for political polling at least, that men are less likely to answer 'don't know' than women.[30] That can provide a misleading impression if, say, only the percentages agreeing or only the net scores are compared between genders.[31]

So knowing the 'don't knows' can help you understand how firmly held or not people's views are. Knowing that there is a twenty-point lead for a new government tax on belts is rather different if the 'don't knows' are at 5 per cent (sounds like views are quite entrenched and less likely to change) than if they are at 75 per cent (sounds like most people have not yet engaged with the issue and views are liable to change).[32]

Knowing how many people don't know can be rather useful.

The Perils of Comparing Numbers

A frequent problem with the presentation of numbers in the media is the use of proportions without giving the underlying numbers. Consider the news that, say, a particular meat is likely to double your chance of having cancer. That sounds huge. Yet it may be that means your chance of getting cancer has increased from 1 in 10 million to 1 in 5 million. A doubled chance, and yet still exceedingly rare.[33]

A similar problem can happen with the reporting of political polls too. Are Scottish women twice as likely as Scottish men to back relocating the Scottish Parliament to the Western Isles? That sounds much less dramatic, and is much less consequential, if it turns out the numbers are 2 per cent and 1 per cent.

So remember: check the actual numbers.

Beware 'Because'

Finding the word 'because' nestled part way through a media story about a poll usually indicates that a beguiling trap is about to be sprung on you. The trap comes in two versions.

The first version is looking at movements from a previous poll and ascribing the changes to some event that has happened in between polls. Yet the public mostly pays little attention to politics. So although the change in the polls may genuinely be significant and not mere noise, it's unlikely that the change was brought about by something the public mostly ignored. Absent other supporting evidence, ascribing movements in polls to political events should be limited to only the most prominent events, so heavily reported that even children have picked up on them. If children have noticed them, then just perhaps enough voters have noticed them too.

The other version is to assume a causality between different figures in the polls. 'The Greens have moved ahead because of a rise in support among young people' and other such comments rely on picking out different numbers present in the poll's results table and assuming they are telling the story. Yet there is a bundle of possible causal explanations that are not caught on the face of the poll's numbers. Perhaps it is not age that matters, although that is in the poll tables, but instead religion, which might not be.

The temptation always is to give explanations based on the previous poll and on the limited number of possible factors presented in the poll tables. Neither is a solid foundation for anything more than speculation.

The Difference between Intent and Action

Towards the end of the 2015 UK general election, I spent a long stretch of time speaking to postal voters in Cambridge who had previously supported the Liberal Democrats. The conversations were remarkably similar. Respondents were unhappy with what the party had done in coalition government since 2010. But then, when I mentioned the incumbent Liberal Democrat MP Julian Huppert, there were lots of positive words about their MP. I came away thinking that he would just about be all right with this group of voters. When the results came in, it was clear he was not. He lost the seat.

Though his election result was much closer than those of many other defeated Liberal Democrat incumbents, I had made a mistake.

It came from me getting people to consider, 'who do I want as my MP?', to which their answer was 'Julian Huppert'. But when they went to vote, against a backdrop of national media coverage all about how close the general election was looking, many instead were thinking, 'who do I want as prime minister?' Liking Julian Huppert – not in the running to be prime minister himself – was not enough to win their vote when a different question was on people's minds.

What this incident illustrates is the difference that can open up between voter intent and voter action. As the act of voting nears, the question in people's minds can change. Another example of this was in the early stages of the 2017 UK general election. This saw the support for UKIP drop away sharply, to the benefit of the Conservatives. It was not that UKIP supporters had gone off their party. But rather, the question in their minds changed, in this case from 'which party do I like most?' to 'which party is going to best deliver on my views in this specific election?' For these supporters of Brexit, the answer was that they liked UKIP but saw the need to vote Conservative to ensure it happened.

Pollsters were fortunate in 2017, in that the switch in framing happened long enough before polling day that their polls could pick it up and report on it. But it remains an example of how things can change, especially for polling on policy issues when the context switches between asking about an idea in theory and asking about what to make of the current government introducing it now to alter your life. Always watch out for polling answers that are liable to be undermined by this sort of shift. Especially if the polling answers appear at first blush to be cause for depression about the state of humanity.

Take this example from 2016: 'Young Americans are so dissatisfied with their choices in this presidential election that nearly one in four told an opinion poll they would rather have a giant meteor destroy the Earth than see Donald Trump or Hillary Clinton in the White

House.'[34] Young Americans were not really wishing the death of billions on the world. Rather, they were not taking the question literally. They were safely using a theoretical question to express their feelings rather than to make an actual choice. As it turned out, come polling day quite a few young Americans voted, others stayed at home and none, as far as we know, tried to bring about the death of billions in order to avert the election result.[35]

First Impressions Matter

An experiment in which people were asked to guess from which lake a selection of fish had come may not seem immediately relevant to political polling. But it is. The researchers, Jennifer C. Whitman and Todd S. Woodward, studied how we judge evidence that we come across piece by piece, compared with evidence that we come across all in one go.[36] They found that gradual accumulation of evidence leads to us finding the evidence more persuasive than having the same evidence revealed all at once.

For political polling, the implication is that if we come across new political polls one at a time, we will put more weight on any conclusion we draw from them ('look, my party is going up in support!') than if we were to see all those new political polls together in one go. It is common to come across polls one by one, especially if you are on social media. Even if you rely on more traditional media, polls rarely come out together at the same time, except at the busiest of political times. This is all luring us to put more weight on what we think the polls are telling us. So what is the lesson? Try to draw conclusions from looking at a batch of polls in one go, such as looking up a table of the latest voting intention polls all together or employing an Internet search engine to find the latest polls on a topical issue.

The Perils of Comparing Polls

One conclusion you might have drawn from what you have read so far is that comparing the results from lots of different polls will assist in understanding things. That is true, but it comes with some caveats and an odd international distinction. First, as we saw with the impact of question wording on results, it is important to compare like with like. Different wording can produce different results. A good example of this comes with party leader ratings, in which different question wording consistently produces different answers. Take the findings for the Conservative Party leader, Theresa May, in the various leader rating questions used by pollsters in Britain during 2018, a year in which there was no general election and also in which support for all the political parties stayed relatively level throughout.[37] So it makes sense to look at the average answers throughout the year to different question wordings:

Do you think [person] is doing well or badly as [post]? (YouGov)
31 per cent 'doing well' to 58 per cent 'doing badly'

To what extent do you approve or disapprove of the way [person] is handling his/her job as [post]? (Opinium)
31 per cent 'approve' to 46 per cent 'disapprove'

Are you satisfied or dissatisfied with the performance of [person] as [post]? (Sky)
32 per cent 'satisfied' to 63 per cent 'dissatisfied'

Are you satisfied or dissatisfied with the way [person] is doing his/her job as [post]? (BMG)
32 per cent 'satisfied' to 53 per cent 'dissatisfied'

Do you have a favourable or unfavourable opinion of [person]?
(YouGov)

33 per cent 'favourable' to 56 per cent 'unfavourable'

Do you think they are doing very well in their job, quite well,
quite badly or very badly? (Deltapoll)

35 per cent 'very/quite well' to 56 per cent 'very/quite badly'

Are you satisfied or dissatisfied with the way [person] is doing his/
her job as [post]? (Ipsos MORI)

35 per cent 'satisfied' to 58 per cent 'dissatisfied'[38]

All of the different wordings painted a similar, grim picture for Prime Minister May. Similar but with noticeable differences depending on the wording, from an average positive rating through the year of 31 per cent to 35 per cent and, more strikingly, an average negative rating varying from 46 per cent to 63 per cent. This was not merely a case of different pollsters being more or less favourable to the Conservatives with their sampling or weighting. YouGov used two different wording formulations that still threw up a noticeable difference. This therefore illustrates the value of comparing like with like. Otherwise, if you compared, say, a Sky finding from one month that year with an Opinium finding the following month, you might have thought Theresa May's negatives were falling, when really you were just learning about the impact of variations in the phrasing of the pollsters' questions.

More generally, there is the phenomenon of 'house effects', whereby one polling house may consistently find, say, a higher rating for the Green Party than another polling house. It is not necessarily the case that one is right and the other is wrong. Frustratingly, sometimes these house effects close as you get nearer to polling day, and so the election result does not help us distinguish between better and worse house effects. What it does mean, though, is that comparing different pollsters can again give you the impression of a change when there is none.

Lesson one, then, when comparing polls is to compare like with like, ideally complete like with like. In practice, comparing the same question wording from the same pollster combines practicality with sufficient comparability to be meaningful, even if, for example, the question order may not have been the same. One twist, though – watch out for the polling firms that use more than one survey mode, and make sure you compare polls carried out using the same mode.

Comparing polls over time is made more difficult by the fact that pollsters change their methodology, as shown by commentary on the U.S. presidential election during the summer and autumn of 2020. The surprise nature of Republican Donald Trump's victory in 2016 made many people nervous about Democrat candidate Joe Biden's lead in the polls ahead of the 2020 election. After all, his 2016 predecessor as candidate, Hillary Clinton, had been ahead in the polls too. An understandable question to ask, therefore, was how Biden's poll lead – either nationally or in swing states – compared with Clinton's four years ago at the same point in the calendar. That question was, however, easier to ask than to answer because U.S. pollsters had changed their methodologies since 2016. As Robert Ford, a professor of political science, put it,

> Polling methods have changed substantially, particularly in
> state level polls, after 2016 . . . One reason state level polling,
> in particular, looked so favourable for Clinton at this point
> is that pollsters in 2016 did not weight by education. Their
> samples had too many white graduates (who leaned heavily
> Trump) . . . Polls in 2020 nearly always do weight by education,

which *should* make them more accurate (of course other sources of error are possible). But this means comparison with state level polls in 2016 are comparisons of apples with oranges.[39]

(Apples and oranges are, of course, comparable. If I have one apple and you have 72,614 oranges, neither of us would have difficulty concluding who has the most fruit. The Romanian equivalent phrase is much better, involving, as it does, grandmothers and machine guns.)

Ford's point was backed up by analysis reported by the *Financial Times*, which looked at what Biden's lead in the polls in 2020 would have been had there be no weighting by education, as in 2016. Across three swing-state polls, Biden led by between four and six points in 2020. Taking out education weighting, his lead would have been between six and eleven points.[40] Comparing polls in 2020 with 2016 was not comparing like with like.

There is no simple answer to this other than to remember to use your judgement. Even when comparing the most comparable of polls, if the way they are done has changed (or if other circumstances have changed, such as the rise of a new party), wise conclusions may require heavy use of 'maybe' and 'perhaps'.

Lesson two is to remember the discussion about changes within the margins of error, mentioned earlier. Your favoured party going from 40 per cent in one poll to 41 per cent in the next should be met with only muted celebration. You cannot tell if that is noise or a move of substance. If all the pollsters show a small rise in your preferred party's support, however, that is much more likely to be a real move, and if the rise continues over several comparable polls, then it is time to start believing.

Finally, here is a warning about an odd difference between British and American common practice when reporting new polls.[41] Imagine this pair of polling headlines or tweets, reporting two fictitious polls, one from each country:

Generic Congressional Ballot
Democrat 44 per cent (+4)
Republican 40 per cent

New poll
Conservative 44 per cent (+4)
Labour 40 per cent (−4)

That +4 per cent means something different in the USA and the UK. In the USA, it is the lead – Democrats four points ahead of Republicans. In the UK, it is the change from the last comparable poll from that pollster. It tells us that the previous comparable poll showed the Conservatives on 40 per cent.

Both of these approaches have a problem. The American one is bewildering. You can tell there is a four-point Democrat lead with the elementary maths of subtracting 40 from 44, so all the U.S. convention is telling us is something trivially easy to see anyway. It is, though, the clear convention, so watch out if you are used to seeing reports about polls from different countries that the plus and minus signs may mean different things.[42]

Brits reading this should not feel too superior, however. Although the British convention means the plus sign adds extra information, it also strongly emphasizes the change from the last comparable poll as if that is worthy of special attention. It entices you to think that that change is important. What would be much better is a context similar to that often provided in sports. A team might be given a five-match result summary of its wins, losses and draws – WWDLW, perhaps – which gives context for how the team's form is shaping up.

A better, if cumbersome, way of reporting the poll above would be:

New poll
Conservative 44 per cent (40, 43, 41, 44, 42)
Labour 40 per cent (44, 42, 45, 41, 42)

Giving those five previous ratings clarifies that the picture here is one of the parties being neck and neck, rather than one of the Conservatives soaring. In practice, such an approach would, of course, run into issues about how frequent polling has been, whether those five polls stretch back over five days or five months, and so on. This is why, when it comes to comparing polls to figure out what is going on, a nice, large table is almost always much better than a tweet or a headline.

Polling Policies One by One

Tony Blair, winner of three British general elections and the only Labour Party leader born after the First World War who has won at all, speaks of the fallacy of polling individual policies. 'You can take individual policies and each one of them might be popular but you put them all together and it's not popular,' he warns.[43] Prior to his Labour Party winning three general elections in a row (1997–2005), they had lost four in a row (1979–92). During that losing streak, if you looked at polling on individual issues, then for many Labour policies, they came out winners (except for unilateral disarmament), and many of the incumbent Conservative Party's policies came out losers. Yet Labour kept on losing elections. The problem is that people do not vote on individual policies. They vote on the overall package on offer – policies, leaders, values, competence and more.

It was a similar problem for Labour in 2017. As pollster Deborah Mattinson explains, 'While many of [Labour's] policies fared well enough when tested blind and individually, support plummeted when the policy area was associated with Labour. It fell even further when the policies were presented collectively as a package.'[44] It is a lively field of political science research and debate as to quite what determines people's votes. What unifies contrasting theories, however, is that it isn't just about voters scoring each main policy and then picking whoever comes out with the best tally.

Polling individual policies can be useful, as long as the mistakes about giving only one side of the story mentioned earlier are avoided. Yet it's also very limiting if you want to understand what is going to happen to the popularity of parties or politicians. That is a question of politics, not just policies.

Sidenote: When Bad Data Is Still Useful

Karl Marx was a would-be pioneer of bad data. In 1880 he drew up a questionnaire for *La Revue socialiste* about working conditions in France. A large number of copies of the survey were distributed, each prefaced with leading text encouraging workers to complete the survey, as they knew best 'the evils which they endure', and exhorting socialists in particular to complete it. Leading questions such as 'If you are paid piece rates, is the quality of the article made a pretext for fraudulent deductions from your wages?' featured. The only thing that saved this survey from producing biased, bad data was that it produced almost no data. Few completed surveys came back, and the idea was dropped.[45]

Yet as shown by the story of pioneering campaign pollster Emil Hurja and his approach to adjusting bad data, it is possible to make good use of bad data. (That is my defence why, if you were obsessive enough to trawl through my activities over the years, you would find many examples of me using data that is subject to the flaws set out in this book, yet still claiming that you can extract useful insight from them.)

As Hurja found, bad data can be rescued if the problem is a persistent skew in the figures. Identify and measure that and you can adjust the figures to undo that skew. This can be done usefully to tackle those 'house effects' described above. Take, for example, pollster Rasmussen in the United States – it has consistently had figures more favourable to the Republicans than other polls. Rasmussen putting the Republicans three points ahead means something different from, say, Pew Research doing so, given that, on average, Rasmussen was 4.5 points more favourable to the Republicans than Pew Research in a 2012 collation of house effects.[46] When analysing polling data, it is therefore useful to bear such house effects in mind and adjust accordingly.[47] Adjusting for house effects becomes dangerous, however, if you start assuming that the pollster that rates your preferred choice lower is therefore wrong. That does not necessarily mean the pollster is wrong, especially as sometimes it is the outlier polling firm that is the most accurate.

The next use that can be made of bad data comes from the sort of voodoo polls that I have run (see Chapter Two). Their record (originally with the Lib Dem Voice team) in polling Liberal Democrat members on internal party elections is pretty good.[48] I had a mini-Gallup moment with my 2015 party leadership survey that put the contest much closer than many others were expecting, and turned out to be right. I had it as Tim Farron at 58 per cent to Norman Lamb's 42 per cent. The actual result was 56.5 per cent to 43.5 per cent, respectively. There were good reasons to think that, although not 'proper' polls, such surveys had some value, as they often matched up well against either actual results or proper polling. I put quite a lot of effort into trying to expand the reach of the surveys so that they would obtain a good cross-section of party views.

The key question was whether a self-selecting sample of online people doing a survey would be representative of the wider party membership. Sometimes that will be true, and sometimes not. What appeared to be the case at the time in all the elections I covered was that there was not a particularly strong activist-versus-non-activist split in support for different candidates, minimizing the risk that my sample (likely skewed towards party activists) would be misleading. Moreover, questions in the survey such as gender and the length of people's party membership consistently showed that such samples were skewed – but crucially the data also showed that reweighting it made no significant difference to the overall figures. In other words, the samples may not have been typical of the total membership, but the ways in which they were skewed did not seem to have an impact upon the balance of voting preferences. Even in elections that saw a male-versus-female contest, having too many males in the sample did not significantly alter the voting figures. It was, therefore, always a reassurance that faulty data was still insightful data.

In a lesson that is more widely applicable, I had the advantage, when checking and tinkering with the data, that I had no preferred outcome. Not only was I staying neutral in the contests, but I always had mixed feelings about any surprising poll results. They were more likely to be interesting but also more likely to be wrong. On balance, I did not have a particular preference for results to be unexpected or expected. These are the circumstances in which it is much easier to keep bias at bay – an important point to remember when looking at what others are making of tinkering with data.

I may also have been lucky to quit doing the surveys when I did, as I suspect the 2020 party leadership election would have seen the methodology fail.[49] Still, while the run lasted, the surveys showed that flawed data can provide insight when carefully handled.

Another example of bad data being useful comes from surveys that political parties put out. The cross-section of people who decide to do a survey – whether on paper or online – from a political party is very atypical, skewed in particular to that party's supporters. In that sense, this form of research into people's views is inferior to polls. That does not make it without value. Some of the value comes from the individual perspective. It is good to let individuals express their views to politicians, and it is possible for the politicians to follow up on individual answers in return. Additional value comes from the ability to spot unusual patterns. One such survey that I analysed had a few questions about public transport followed by an open-ended question that let people state what improvement to the local bus service they most wished for. What leapt out to me from the answers was that several people mentioned wanting a new bus route between two locations, despite the fact that the idea of this particular link was not one that had surfaced in previous public discussions. That several people independently and spontaneously mentioned the same idea gave a clue that something was up. It was. The survey was being done for a local politician, Lynne Featherstone. She took up the issue; more investigation resulted in a confirmation of the desire and logic of such a new bus route; and after six years of campaigning, the route started in its first trial form. It is still running today.[50]

11
JUDGING POLLING FIRMS

'All of us have doubts about the Gallup Polls from time to time,
especially when they are not favourable to us.'
– HERBERT MORRISON MP[1]

U nder pressure when there are allegations of a polling failure in the
air, political pollsters retreat. They step back from saying political
polling is about predicting the winner or about getting the gap between
the top two parties right. Rather, they say it's all about how close – or
not – they are on the vote share figure for each candidate or party.

We've already discussed whether it is fair to judge political pollsters on their ability to call the winner correctly. But before looking
at how UK polling firms have performed in recent general elections,
let's consider again the merits of judging pollsters on the winner's
lead or on vote share. Pollsters prefer to be judged on the latter because
errors in vote share become magnified when looking at the lead.
Consider a poll that has the contest as 42 per cent to 39 per cent
between the two leading contenders, and a result that is 44 per cent
to 37 per cent. Judged on vote share, the poll did decently – within
two percentage points for both parties – but on lead? The poll had
it close, at a 3 per cent gap, while reality had it at a comfortable 7 per
cent win (and electoral systems can turn 3 per cent into a very close
result as to who wins in terms of seats or electoral college votes, while
7 per cent can become a comfortable win).

But it is the lead, and the winner, that elections are really about.
Clement Attlee in 1945; Jawaharlal Nehru in 1951; Nelson Mandela

in 1994; Donald Trump in 2016: that it was they who won matters far more than the percentage they secured. Get the lead right (and so the winner right too) and being off by a few points for the top two doesn't matter nearly as much as if you get the vote shares right but the winner wrong, or if you get the vote shares right but confuse a landslide with an anaemic win.

So with only a slight apology to pollsters, here is how they have performed in recent British general elections, judged by the lead of Conservative's over Labour.[2] For each election, the Conservative-minus-Labour lead is shown (a negative figure meaning that Labour finished ahead) along the top row, along with, underneath it, the absolute (that is, errors over and under do not cancel out) average error of all the pollsters active in that election. An average absolute error for each pollster in its final pre-election polls is given in a left-hand column, along with how it performed across every election in which it has been active in the body of the table.

The table is full of warnings against misjudging pollsters by using apparently plausible criteria. Take BPIX: active in two elections, it was not a member of the industry self-regulatory body, published only very sparse details of its polling, had a website listed as 'under construction' for years and never replied to any of my emails. Its polls were commissioned by one of the newspapers with a more controversial record for accuracy (the *Mail on Sunday*). All that sounds like a good case to treat its results with a great deal of scepticism, and in 2005, it was the most inaccurate pollster. Yet BPIX still got who was ahead right, and in 2010 BPIX was tied for the most accurate pollster of the lot. A similar thing happened with the Trafalgar Group in the 2020 U.S. elections. There were several run-ins between Five-ThirtyEight and Trafalgar Group over the latter's lack of transparency, and yet Trafalgar Group was one of the best-performing pollsters in that presidential election.[3] Or consider YouGov. In the 2001, 2005

	FIRM'S AVERAGE ERROR	GENERAL ELECTION					
		2019	2017	2015	2010	2005	2001
CON–LAB LEAD		11.8	2.4	6.5	7.2	−3.0	−9.3
INDUSTRY'S AVERAGE ERROR		2.3	5.3	6.4	1.4	2.4	4.1
Angus Reid	4.8				+4.8		
BMG	6.6	−2.8	+10.6	−6.5			
BPIX	2.1				−0.2	−4.0	
ComRes	5.4	−6.8	+7.6	−5.5	+1.8		
Deltapoll	1.8	−1.8					
Gallup	6.7						−6.7
Harris	2.1				−1.2	−3.0	
ICM	4.7	−5.8	+9.6	−7.5	+0.8	−3.0	−1.7
Ipsos MORI	3.1	−0.8	+5.6	−5.5	−0.2	−2.0	−4.2
TNS	2.4	+0.2	+2.6	−5.5	−1.2		
Lord Ashcroft	6.5			−6.5			
NOP	3.9					0.0	−7.7
Number Cruncher Politics	1.8	−1.8					
OnePoll	1.8				+1.8		
Opinium	2.9	−0.5	+4.6	−5.5	+0.8		
Panelbase	5.6	−2.8	+5.6	−8.5			
Populus	3.8			−6.5	+1.8	−3.0	
Qriously	2.8	+1.2	−4.4				
Rasmussen	3.7						−3.7
RNB	1.8				+1.8		
Survation	3.0	−1.0	−1.4	−6.5			
SurveyMonkey	1.6		+1.6				
YouGov	2.6	−1.8	+4.6	−6.5	−0.2	−2.0	−0.7

and 2010 British elections, not only was it pretty accurate, but it was better than the average across all pollsters. Then it gave two poor performances in 2015 and 2017, although not bad compared to the rest of the industry, before returning to a strong result in 2019. As with financial markets, past performance is not a consistent guide to future performance.

Given the very small margins between the best pollster in each election and their closest rivals, being the closest is in part a matter of luck. 'You can have very bad pollsters, but once you reach a certain level, there's going to be pretty much a random distribution in the performance of pollsters,' is how polling post-mortem expert Patrick Sturgis puts it.[4]

The mess of data in the table has only one real conclusion: that there is no simple pattern of who is the best pollster, and therefore no simple pattern of which pollster to whom to pay the most attention ahead of the next general election.

It is, however, worth noting one detail from that table. Of the pollsters who have studied more than two general elections, the one with the lowest average error on the Conservative–Labour gap is, by a small margin, TNS. It has consistently done well. TNS is also one of the lowest-profile pollsters, not being fronted by the sort of media-friendly person who garners coverage for some of the others in the table. It is a reminder, yet again, to look beyond the headlines (especially as it is a similar picture in the case of the 2020 U.S. election, in which the most accurate pollster was also one of the lowest-profile: Atlas Intelligence).[5]

Looking beyond the headlines is also vital when considering the possible institutional reasons for polling firms to be biased. One of the most tedious criticisms of YouGov's polls in British politics is that poll figures unfavourable to Labour should be disregarded because the firm was founded by a Conservative. Such criticisms skip over the key role played in the firm for many years by Labour figure Peter Kellner and the lack of evidence of an anti-Labour bias from comparing final pre-election polls with election results.

Moreover, there is – in the UK – a raw financial self-interest for most polling firms in not being biased. Political polling is a small part of their business, but also one of the highest-profile. Therefore, to run a successful business, pollsters need their political polling to be accurate in order to attract other business. Moreover, even for political polling, it is far from uncommon for the same firm to work for different parties over the years, something they could not do if they were seen as biased. The temptation is still sometimes there to ask poorly phrased questions that are more likely to give clients the sorts of answers they want, which they then try to slip past uncritical journalists. British pollsters square those temptations with their conscience thanks to the industry's transparency rules. If the details of the polls are published, the pollsters can take the cash while also reassuring themselves that the truth is publicly out there in PDFs on their website for anyone to find.

The USA, though, is a more troubled place. Not only are the transparency standards lower, but – perhaps because pollsters can make much more of a business out of being a pollster exclusively for only one side – there are pollsters whose results consistently show a partisan skew. As (UK) pollster Matt Singh puts it, 'There is so much party business (due to huge budgets in the USA) that being biased is in the commercial interest of some (thankfully not many) pollsters.'[6] In fact, the mix of partisan motivations and lack of transparency make some corners of U.S. political polling such a bear pit that fake polls, and even fake polling companies, have been a problem.[7] This fakery keeps polling aggregators and analysts such as FiveThirtyEight busy with their dissections of pollster trends and their scoring of the quality of different polling firms. (None of these fakes are the 'fake polls' Donald Trump attacked. He attacked real polls and left the actual fakes alone.)

But in both the USA and the UK, and indeed in other countries, some basic standards help filter out the questionable polling firms:

1. Does the polling firm publish full data breakdowns of its results?
2. Is the polling firm willing to make public its methodology?
3. How does the polling firm make its money? (You can trust more firms that *either* mostly do non-political polling – the UK model – *and/or* do political polling for clients across the political spectrum, whether that is media outlets, parties, candidates or other organizations.)

As we have seen, track record is a limited guide. Even good firms have bad years. So as well as filtering out the questionable firms, do not go overboard on only believing whoever was best last time. After all, as was first said in the Danish Parliament in the 1930s, 'It is difficult to make predictions, especially about the future.'[8]

Hubris

As well as paying attention to the above questions, there is another rule of thumb the savvy consumer of political polls can use: judge the pollster, not the polling firm. Look at how the leading personality at a polling firm acts when that person's firm has a poll that is out of line with what others say. The best pollsters are humble and cautious; the worst are adamant about their own superiority. Match arrogance with scepticism, and humility with appreciation.

American pollster Warren Mitofsky led the CBS News election and survey team for over twenty years. He had much to be proud of in his career in polling, including his pioneering work on randomized telephone sampling and heading up the first national exit poll in the USA in 1972. But despite being an acerbic character himself, who was happy to tell others how little he thought of them and loved starting sentences with 'Here's why you're wrong,' he advised modesty for pollsters.[9] He warned, 'There's a lot of room for humility in polling. Every time you get cocky, you lose.'[10] Which is why he kept a photo of the 'Dewey wins' *Chicago Tribune* front page on his wall for many years.[11]

Mitofsky's words were wise, but also tricky words for pollsters because those who pay for polls rarely wanted muted, nuanced answers. Media outlets, pressure groups and the rest want headlines. Even the very best polls suffer from the desire to grab attention when reported on or otherwise publicized. But the hubristic over-certainty of those reporting on polls need not fool the wise consumer of news about polls, especially as there is extensive evidence about which sorts of experts best foretell the future. For all types of predictions and forecasts, modesty and doubt are desirable characteristics, not self-certainty and bombast.[12] It is perhaps no coincidence that one of the very best pollsters of the last few decades, Iowa's Ann Selzer, has her corporate offices in a modest, single-storey building in Des Moines, next to a cat café and opposite a quilts shop.

12

MAKING SENSE OF THE POLLS

'Polls can be misused, misinterpreted and misunderstood.
But the basic facts they reveal, carefully studied, are truthful.'
– PETER HITCHENS, journalist[1]

If you follow British political polling on social media, you may be surprised by that Peter Hitchens quote. That is because one of the most popular responses to a piece of political polling that someone, especially on the left, does not like is to repost a different quote of his: 'Opinion polls are a device for influencing public opinion, not a device for measuring it. Crack that, and it all makes sense.' But as Hitchens himself warned, people frequently use those words of his to make a point that he does not actually agree with:

> Please grasp that it is nothing so crude as 'all polls are rigged and they are not telling the truth'. I am absolutely not saying anything so daft. The basic research work in opinion polls conducted by the major organizations is sound. It has to be. Their main work is done not for politicians but for businesses looking to sell their products. They need to be right, or they will be put out of business. Often what you need to watch is not the polls, but how they are presented . . . Polls can be misused, misinterpreted and misunderstood. But the basic facts they reveal, carefully studied, are truthful. If their predictions are wrong it is because opinions change, or because of factors they have

been unaware of. What I said about polls was never intended to be a blanket dismissal of their significance, and people should stop using it as such.

Conducted well, political polls add hugely to our understanding of what is going on and why. They tell us more than election or referendum results tell us on their own. Most people and most issues never make it to a ballot paper. Even for those that do, there are long gaps for polls to fill between the intermittent illuminations of election results.

The rarity of political polls from political history before the early twentieth century and complete absence before the early nineteenth century illustrate this. Imagine how much better we would understand the swings and fortunes in Napoleon's time as leader of France if we had a monthly approval-tracking poll for him. Did military news move his approval ratings more or less than twists and turns in the health of the French economy? Or imagine how polling ahead of the 1832 Great Reform Act could have spotted that, alongside the vibrant enthusiasm for reform that catches the history books, there was a broader apathy which then played out in mediocre and falling turnout in the decade after reform was enacted.[2] Politics would have looked rather different with that extra information.

Polls are useful, as long as you know how to make sense of them.

The Egalitarianism of Polling

Opinion polls are fundamentally democratic: one person, one say. As political scientist Sidney Verba put it: 'Surveys produce just what democracy is supposed to produce – equal representation of all citizens.'[3]

You may have wealth, be the friend of a newspaper owner, go to Royal Ascot with the chief executive of a multinational, spend summer weeks sailing in the Hamptons, be in a WhatsApp group with a senior public official or have been to school with the prime minister, but none of these perks gives you an extra say in a properly conducted political opinion poll. Political polls are to politics what jury selection is to the legal system. When done properly, both are levellers that force fairness past the inequalities of society.

Of course, a plethora of problems lurks within the 'when done properly' caveat. Both juries and polls involve, in the purest and most simplistic descriptions, random selections of the public. Both have a messier reality. But both have a nobility of purpose that shines through. That is why I take the opposite view from French sociologist Pierre Bourdieu, who argued that 'public opinion does not exist.' He viewed it as a weakness that polls treat all opinions as having the same value, regardless of the knowledge or power of the person expressing them. That is true, yet that is the very value of polls – equalizing all such differences, rather than elevating those with multiple degrees or multiple bank accounts. It is a polling feature, not a polling bug. Polls and the concept of a public opinion to be measured are an egalitarian force.[4]

It is debatable to what extent political leaders should follow or lead public opinion. But it is highly desirable that the 'public' in 'public opinion' should be more than just their friends from school or those who choose to riot. Done properly, polls empower the views of the disadvantaged and marginalized. Democratic elections may be the gold-standard measure of public opinion, but polls are the weekly reminders of its existence, importance and stance.

Knowing what other people think also matters because what we think depends on what we think others think. This is illustrated by the disturbing findings from research into the 'live worms' (squiggly lines inching across the screen) that sometimes appear on TV during election debates. These show, in real time, the views of a sample of people on who is performing well or poorly. Sometimes these lines are based on extremely small samples (for example, just thirty people for CNN in the 2008 U.S. presidential election). Yet even when they use more sensible samples, there is a problem with the debate worms. Very simply, if you fake that data and give a politician a better worm track, the audience's estimations of how they do improve:

> Davis and Memon gathered 150 University of London students to watch the third and final 2010 UK election debate. Unbeknownst to the students, the broadcast worms were fake, added by the researchers with live video mixers.
>
> Half the students watched a feed rigged to favor incumbent Prime Minister Gordon Brown. Of them, 47 percent said he won the debate, with challengers Nick Clegg getting 35 percent and David Cameron 13 percent. The other students watched a feed favoring Clegg. Of them, 79 percent said he won, with Brown and Cameron getting, respectively, 9 and 4 percent.[5]

If bad political polling data, or misunderstanding political polling data, warps your view of the world, then there is all the more reason to know how to spot and use good data.

Ten Golden Rules

'I find it surprising how accurate political polls
are given how difficult the job is.'
– PATRICK STURGIS, professor of quantitative social science[6]

The next time you see an opinion poll in the news or on your social media timeline, you are unlikely to pause to reread this book before figuring out what to make of it. I certainly won't. Here, then, is a distilled set of golden rules that you can learn to follow instinctively each time.

1. Do not expect too much of polls. As the historian Arnold Toynbee put it, 'No tool is omnicompetent. There is no such thing as a master key that will unlock all doors.'[7] They are a powerful tool, but they tell you the most when you do not try to get them to tell you too much.

2. Beware going on just how the media has reported a poll. The media is not good at reporting polls. The news requires more drama than is often present in the numbers. So look for what the polling or subject-matter experts, especially academics, are saying about it.

3. Remember that the quality of the sample matters much more than the size of the sample. The only time you should take seriously someone touting the size of that person's sample is when the size is used to justify looking at detailed cross-tabs that would otherwise need to be ignored for being based on too few people. (Other than this, if you *really* want to pay attention to a cross-tab, remember cross-tabs are best viewed in bulk, across multiple polls.)

4. Be mindful of timing. When was the fieldwork for the poll done? Is the poll older than it looks? Might views have changed since then or circumstances altered the meaning of the answers?

5. Trends reveal more than individual polls. Spend more time looking at them than at individual polls. When looking at trends, make sure you compare like with like, especially on question wording.

6. Polls on policy issues have the advantage of not needing to worry about some of the adjustments that most often contribute to voting intention polls going wrong (such as turnout). But they have their own significant risks, especially over getting the question wording right, and they do not have actual election results to check against. That matters because, as John Curtice puts it, 'It is always easier to assess the validity of data that is about behaviour rather than about attitudes.'[8]

7. The more attention-grabbing an individual poll is, the more likely it is to be wrong. Instead, treat polls like a set of ranging shots. You need multiple polls to scope out the truth.

8. Permit yourself only one cheer per piece of polling good news. People love getting overexcited about any one poll, reading far too much into an insignificant change in numbers between polls or assuming that a major change is definitely real rather than a rogue poll. That is a temptation especially perilous when over-reading one poll tells you what you wish to be true. Only go full-on three cheers if you have at least three polls to justify it.

9. Do not idolize any one pollster.[9] Pollsters and their firms are like financial institutions. Some are better than others, but past form is a poor guide to future performance.[10]

10. Finally, remember that the answer to the problems with polls – such as the risks of skewed samples and the limitations of question wording on complicated topics – is not to ignore them, but to seek out more of them.

Follow these rules, and you can make good sense of the polls. They won't always be right. In George Gallup's words, 'With the same certainty that we know we can be right most of the time, we know we will be wrong some of the time. It has to be that way.'[11] But as with weather forecasts, being right most of the time is good enough for it to be far better to pay attention to the details than to ignore them altogether. Especially as polls aren't only about predictions in advance. They are also about explanations afterwards. Polls give you a sense of the landscape, of what is possible, what is likely and why things have happened.

The more polls you pay attention to, the better your understanding.

THANK YOU

'If a polling firm never surprises you, you generally shouldn't trust it.'
– NATE SILVER, U.S. polling pundit[1]

Thank you for reading and making it to the end. I hope you have found it both enjoyable and informative. If you have spotted any errors or been surprised by any omissions, it would be great to hear from you. You can tweet me on @PollingUnPacked or email me at Mark.Pack@LibDemNewswire.com. You might also find my website of interest, as I regularly cover British political opinion polling there: www.MarkPack.org.uk. Or do an Internet search for 'Polling UnPacked' email to sign up to my email newsletter on the same topic.

It would be great if you could help others discover the book too by doing a quick rating or review on your favourite online bookshop website or on Goodreads. Such ratings and reviews help feed the algorithm beasts that get the book in front of other people too. Thank you.

REFERENCES

INTRODUCTION

1 In Arthur Conan Doyle's *The Sign of Four* (London, 1890), Chapter Ten. Holmes says he is citing the views of William Winwood Reade, who was a real person.
2 'Dr George Horace Gallup, punditical pollster of public opinion, last week received at his home in Princeton, NJ, a postcard asking him to choose among the ten leading Presidential candidates. It was from Emil Edward Hurja, the sly, plump ex-newspaperman from Michigan and Alaska, who used to dope expertly for the Democratic National Committee': *Time*, 22 May 1939, quoted in W. Joseph Campbell, *Lost in a Gallup* (Oakland, CA, 2020), p. 215 n. 19. The word's origin is sometimes seen as a deliberate echo of 'huckster' and credited to Lindsay Rogers and his strident critique of polls, *The Pollsters: Public Opinion, Politics, and Democratic Leadership* (New York, 1949). Rogers, however, denied making a deliberate allusion to hucksters.

1 THE FIRST POLITICAL POLLS

1 Robert M. Worcester, 'Political Opinion Polling in Great Britain', in *Political Opinion Polling: An International Review*, ed. Robert M. Worcester (London, 1983), pp. 82–3.
2 Tom W. Smith, 'The First Straw? A Study of the Origins of Election Polls', *Public Opinion Quarterly*, LIV/1 (1990), p. 23.
3 Ibid., p. 26.
4 Credit, though, is due to the *Carolina Observer*, which, on 29 July 1824, stumbled on what we would now see as the benefits of unbiased sampling when it talked up the benefits of straw polls taken at 'promiscuous assemblages of all parties where there is no public electioneering at the time, and the assembly are unexpectedly called upon to make their sentiments known' – quoted ibid., p. 29. The paper, therefore, looked down on straw polls at militia meetings, viewing them as skewed

towards younger people and, given his military record, in favour of
Andrew Jackson.

5 For particular credit to the first two (based, respectively, on tallying a
large number of meetings and looking at more than militia meetings, even
perhaps also setting up some polling sites), see James W. Tankard, 'Public
Opinion Polling by Newspapers in the Presidential Election Campaign
of 1824', *Journalism Quarterly*, LIV/2 (1972). Smith, 'The First Straw?',
p. 27 gives credit to the *Star and North Carolina Gazette* for having
'by early October aggregated results from 155 separate meetings'.

6 24 August 1824. Quoted in Tankard, 'Public Opinion Polling by
Newspapers in the Presidential Election Campaign of 1824'.

7 In dating the birth of political polling to 1824, I follow earlier historians
of polling. However, the idea of asking people what they have done
and counting up the crude totals involves no great insight or ingenuity.
Moreover, the events at which such polls were held – including militia
musters and Fourth of July celebrations – were not new in 1824. So 1824
may only be the first example historians have found, rather than the first
example outright.

8 In 1916 it asked readers across the country to send in news about public
opinion in their area, but only directly polled people in selected places:
George Gallup and Saul Forbes Rae, *The Pulse of Democracy: The Public-
Opinion Poll and How It Works* (New York, 1940), p. 39.

9 See the fascinating pre-1936 analysis of different methods of predicting
election results, including an understanding of sampling error, non-
response bias and other modern concerns, in Claude E. Robinson, *Straw
Votes: A Study of Political Prediction* (New York, 1932), pp. 58–60. It also
discusses how the *Literary Digest* poll appeared to have a built-in pro-
Republican bias (pp. 72–3). It includes this lovely footnote to its final
chapter, on the use of past election results to help predict future election
outcomes: 'This chapter is frankly tentative. A large amount of research
has been required for the present volume and neither time nor resources
have been available for exploring this section of the field in other than a
preliminary way.'

10 Gallup and Rae, *The Pulse of Democracy*, pp. 40–41.

11 *Literary Digest* (31 October 1936).

12 Dominic Lusinchi, 'Straw Poll Journalism and Quantitative Data: The
Case of *The Literary Digest*', *Journalism Studies*, XVI/3 (2014), argues that
the emerging journalistic standards of the day were a particular problem,
with the emphasis on neutrality being interpreted as 'just present the raw
figures'. Adjustments to figures were seen as the equivalent of polluting
the facts with editorializing. For example, 'One of the credos of the

independent press was that the readers should be given the necessary information to allow them to make up their own minds, as opposed to following slavishly the party line.'

13 'What Went Wrong with the Polls? None of Straw Polls Got Exactly the Right Answer – Why?', *Literary Digest* (14 November 1936). In this edition, the magazine defended the accuracy of the vote shares in its earlier polls. However, the criticism of its accuracy in Robinson, *Straw Votes*, pp. 58–60, is more convincing.

14 'The magazine's sample and response were both biased and jointly produced the wildly incorrect estimate of the vote. But, if all of those who were polled had responded, the magazine would have, at least, correctly predicted Roosevelt the winner': Peverill Squire, 'Why the 1936 *Literary Digest* Poll Failed', *Public Opinion Quarterly*, LII/1 (1990), pp. 125–33. Re-analysing the same data, Dominic Lusinchi concludes that non-response bias had around double the impact of biased sampling in producing the wrong result: '"President" Landon and the 1936 *Literary Digest* Poll: Were Automobile and Telephone Owners to Blame?', *Social Science History*, XXXVI/1 (2012), pp. 23–54.

15 For a comparison of the figures, see Gallup and Rae, *The Pulse of Democracy*, pp. 43 and 52–3. Gallup and Rae call the *Fortune* figures, 'amazingly close to the true division of sentiment' (1.1 per cent out once the 'don't knows' are excluded). The *Fortune* survey had the smallest sample size of the three, at around 4,500, further reinforcing the point that sample size is not a guarantee of accuracy, but its remarkably accurate figures were not published until after the election: W. Joseph Campbell, *Lost in a Gallup* (Oakland, CA, 2020), p. 45. Crossley's polling suffered from being commissioned by a news group that was heavily pro-Republican in its editorial line, and so his polling showing Roosevelt ahead was lumbered with headlines such as, 'Landon Needs Only Michigan to Win Election, Poll Shows' and 'Presidential Race Tightens as Election Day Draws Near': ibid., p. 44.

16 George Gallup, 'An Objective Method for Determining Reader Interest in the Content of a Newspaper', PhD dissertation, State University of Iowa, 1928.

17 Henry Durant, William Gregory and Denis Weaver, *Behind the Gallup Poll* (London, 1951), p. 2, claims that 'when the official returns were published, they matched his predictions within 1 per cent'. This polling was based on dividing the country up into six sections. The error rates within each taken separately were much higher, but averaged out across them to give that very low national average figure. See the critique in Abe Blanar, 'How Accurate Are Public-Opinion Polls?', *Appendix to the Congressional Record*, LXXXVI/15 (1940), pp. 3012–13.

18 Squire, 'Why the 1936 *Literary Digest* Poll Failed', p. 126. As he also cites, Hearst Publications did something similar: paying for its own, and as it turned out much better, polls and yet burying the results of those, while featuring the *Literary Digest* results.

19 Gallup and Rae, *The Pulse of Democracy*, p. 47.

20 See, for example, *Pittsburgh Press* (2 November 1936): 'Straw vote fight arouses interest: *Literary Digest* and American Institute Are Far Apart in Pre-election Forecast . . . the battle of the pre-election polls commands almost as much public interest as the election itself'.

21 Gallup was incredibly lucky: either politics didn't move over several weeks or there were counter-balancing errors, with his predicted figures for the *Literary Digest* being wrong one way and movement the other way then cancelling that out. Gallup was also skilful at talking up the apparent accuracy of his polling, including exaggerating how well his 1936 polling did at predicting the result in individual states by claiming he had correctly predicted the results in several states that he had, in fact, put as too close to call, albeit with the eventual winner just ahead. See Blanar, 'How Accurate Are Public-Opinion Polls?', pp. 3012–13.

22 The extent to which Gallup and his peers were an evolution rather than a revolution is emphasized by Claude E. Robinson, 'Recent Developments in the Straw-Poll Field', *Public Opinion Quarterly*, 1/3 (1937). In this account, the rise of Gallup and rigorous scientific sampling is but the fourth of five steps in the development of what we now call polling.

23 Bob Carlson interview with Elmo Roper, 14 August 1968, AAPOR/Roper Center interviews.

24 For example, Nate Silver wrote in 2020, 'And in 1948, it wasn't "the polling" that was off since there was just one polling firm, Gallup': 'Trump Can Still Win, but the Polls Would Have to Be Off by Way More than in 2016', FiveThirtyEight, www.fivethirtyeight.com, 31 October 2020.

25 *Detroit Free Press* (4 November 1948). When it came to the formal electoral college vote, one of the 304, Preston Parks from Tennessee, was a 'faithless elector' and voted for Strom Thurmond instead of Truman.

26 David W. Moore, *The Superpollsters: How They Measure and Manipulate Public Opinion*, 2nd edn (New York, 1995), p. 70.

27 Hans L. Zetterberg, 'U.S. Election 1948: The First Great Controversy about Polls, Media, and Social Science', paper presented at the WAPOR regional conference on 'Elections, News Media and Public Opinion' in Pamplona, Spain, 24–6 November 2004. See also Susan Rosegrant, 'ISR and the Truman/Dewey upset', *ISR Sampler* (Spring 2012) pp. 8–9.

28 'Dewey Defeats Truman', Wikipedia, https://en.wikipedia.org, accessed 15 July 2021.

29 See Amy Fried, *Pathways to Polling: Crisis, Cooperation, and the Making of Public Opinion Professions* (New York, 2012), Chapter Five, for other examples of the widespread confident expectation of a Dewey win.

30 'Oral History Interview with Willard A. Edwards', Harry S. Truman Library, 17 September 1988; and Todd Andrlik, 'Dewey Defeats Truman: The Rarely Told Story of *Chicago Tribune*'s Most Famous Issue', *HuffPost*, www.huffpost.com, 6 December 2017.

31 'Healthy Principles', *Der Spiegel* (11 June 1948).

32 Daniel J. Robinson, *The Measure of Democracy: Polling, Market Research and Public Life, 1930–1945* (Toronto, 1999), p. 15.

33 Nick Moon, *Opinion Polls: History, Theory and Practice* (Manchester, 1999), pp. 12–13.

34 'In the wake of the 1948 polling fiasco, many newspapers canceled their subscriptions to the Gallup Poll, and a number of clients of Gallup's then thriving movie research business canceled or refused to renew contracts ... Roper's commercial marketing research business suffered a contraction, temporary but sharp' – Irving Crespi, *Public Opinion, Polls, and Democracy* (Boulder, CO, 1988), p. 15.

35 This sentence glides over many bumps along the way in the development of political polling. For a beautifully named and well-executed study of those bumps, see Joseph Campbell, *Lost in a Gallup*. Fried, *Pathways to Polling*, provides a detailed study of how political polling not only survived the 1948 disaster but went on to prosper.

36 '"Truly Blithe Spirit . . ." – Kerr', *San Francisco Examiner* (27 July 1965).

37 There are few accounts of his life, but two worth reading are Jerry Adams, 'Eugene Burdick: Writer, Teacher and Iconoclast', *San Francisco Examiner* (21 January 1962); and Chris Smith, 'Intellectual Action Hero: The Political Fictions of Eugene Burdick', *California Magazine* (Summer 2010); as is Jill Lepore's work cited below.

38 Ithiel de Sola Pool, Robert P. Abelson and Samuel Popkin, *Candidates, Issues and Strategies: A Computer Simulation of the 1960 and 1964 Presidential Elections* (Cambridge, MA, 1964), p. 1.

39 Ibid., p. 13. The limitations of the Simulmatics modelling are also clear from the book. On the major question of the electoral impact of John F. Kennedy's Catholicism, for example, the book reveals, 'The original simulation assumed that one-third of all Catholics who would otherwise have voted Republican would swing to Kennedy. That was an arbitrary figure arrived at by guess' – see p. 68.

40 Jill Lepore, 'How the Simulmatics Corporation Invented the Future', *New Yorker* (27 July 2020).

41 See Jill Lepore, *If Then: How the Simulmatics Corporation Invented the Future* (New York, 2020) and Sasha Issenberg, *The Victory Lab: The Secret Science of Winning Campaigns* (New York, 2012), pp. 116–24.

42 For an example of why Cambridge Analytica's impact, at least in Britain, should be treated with caution, see Mark Pack, 'Cambridge Analytica, Big Data, Poor Journalism and Possible Electoral Commission Probe', Mark Pack's Blog, www.markpack.org.uk, 4 March 2017.

43 The real firm inspired the novel *Simulacron-3* by Daniel F. Galouye (1964), which then inspired the German TV mini-series *World on a Wire* (1973), which, in turn, inspired *The Matrix* (1999).

44 Prior to Gallup starting up polling in Canada, there was nearly a first home-grown political poll on the Bren gun political scandal. It was cancelled before the fieldwork started: Robinson, *The Measure of Democracy*, pp. 35–7.

45 Murray Goot, 'Labor's 1943 Landslide: Political Market Research, Evatt, and the Public Opinion Polls', *Labour History*, CVII (2014), pp. 149–66.

46 For further details, see Ian McNair and Frank Teer, 'Political Opinion Polling in Australia', in *Political Opinion Polling: An International Review*, ed. Worcester, pp. 7–8.

47 Jane Stoetzel, 'Political Opinion Polling in France', ibid., pp. 21–3.

48 Elisabeth Noelle-Neumann, 'Political Opinion Polling in Germany', ibid., pp. 44–6.

49 For example, see Leo Bogart's letter to the *New York Times*, 'Professor's Own Nazi Past Accuses Her', 28 December 1991.

50 John F. Meagher, 'Political Opinion Polling in the Republic of Ireland', in *Political Opinion Polling: An International Review*, ed. Worcester, pp. 111–12.

51 The appearance of political polling even under a dictatorship is one reason why I am not persuaded by Teer and Spencer's argument that political polling did not develop sooner as it relies on a desire to understand what the whole public is thinking in a way that only goes with the spread of a mass electorate under universal suffrage. Although it is true that the larger the electorate, the greater the scope for polling to add insights which other methods cannot match, this neither requires anything very close to universal suffrage – even just for men alone – nor are elections the only reason why rulers may wish to know the state of public opinion. See F. Teer and J. D. Spence, *Political Opinion Polls* (London, 1973), p. 9. Indeed, they cite examples of polling under communist dictatorship on p. 18.

52 Juan Antonio Giner, 'Political Opinion Polling in Spain', in *Political Opinion Polling: An International Review*, ed. Worcester, pp. 178–9.

53 See 'Apparatchiks and Academics Alike Struggle to Take China's Pulse', *The Economist* (24 October 2020).

54 For a history of Gallup's early days in the UK, see Mark Roodhouse,
    '"Fish-and-Chip Intelligence": Henry Durant and the British Institute
    of Public Opinion, 1936–63', *Twentieth Century British History*, XXIV/2
    (2013), pp. 224–48.

55 The total number of votes has often been wrongly given as 11,559,165 due
    to the enterprise's own official history getting the total wrong. See Martin
    Ceadel, 'The First British Referendum: The Peace Ballot, 1934–5', *English
    Historical Review*, XCV/377 (1980), pp. 810–39.

56 Durant, Gregory and Weaver, *Behind the Gallup Poll*, p. 3.

57 Worcester, 'Political Opinion Polling in Great Britain', p. 61.

58 Quoted in Roger Mortimore, 'Political Polling in Britain – The History',
    15 December 2000, www.ipsos.com.

59 These figures are sometimes given as 57 per cent to 43 per cent, excluding
    the 10 per cent who had no opinion. That was the way in which Gallup
    and BIPO reported the figures at the time, but as subsequent convention
    has become not to recalculate leader ratings to exclude 'don't know' or 'no
    opinion', I have presented the figures in the way most comparable to other
    leader ratings readers will have come across.

60 Quoted in Worcester, 'Political Opinion Polling in Great Britain', p. 63.

61 Saul Forbes Rae, 'The Oxford Bye-Election: A Study in the Straw-Vote
    Method', *Political Quarterly*, X/2 (1939), pp. 268–79.

62 For more details of the poll figures, see my database of voting intention
    polls, PollBase, on my website: www.markpack.org.uk.

63 Derrick Gunston, House of Commons, *Hansard*, 1 August 1940, available
    at https://hansard.parliament.uk.

64 Roodhouse, '"Fish-and-Chip Intelligence"'.

65 Laura Beers, 'Labour's Britain, Fight for It Now!', *Historical Journal*, II/3
    (2009), pp. 667–95. Thank you to Iain Sharpe for bringing this article to
    my attention.

66 By 54 per cent to 38 per cent, the public expected Labour to win: R. B.
    McCallum and Alison Readman, *The British General Election of 1945*
    (London, 1947), p. 243.

67 Ibid. McCallum and Readman includes a round-up of media expectations,
    generally of a Conservative win: pp. 240–43.

68 Its first manager, Collingwood Hughes, had been an MP from 1922
    to 1925, with the unusual distinction of having rebelled against his
    own Conservative Party in order to oppose the fall of the first Labour
    government in 1924.

69 Compared with the actual election result of Labour 49 per cent to
    Conservative 39 per cent, Gallup had it at 47 per cent to 41 per cent,
    respectively, but the Centre of Public Opinion had it tied at 45 per

cent each, after excluding 17 per cent 'don't knows'. Despite its own poll showing the election tied, the *Daily Express* predicted on 6 July a majority for Churchill of over sixty seats.

70 For more details of the poll figures, see my database of voting intention polls, PollBase, on my website, www.markpack.org.uk.

71 Starting in January 1949, regular round-ups of public and private political polls were circulated in the Conservative Party. See Tim Bale, *The Conservatives since 1945: The Drivers of Party Change* (Oxford, 2012), p. 24.

72 Quoted in Worcester, 'Political Opinion Polling in Great Britain', p. 64.

73 Durant, Gregory and Weaver, *Behind the Gallup Poll*, p. 27.

74 The play was also made into an excellent film starring Henry Fonda and Cliff Robertson.

2 HOW POLITICAL OPINION POLLS WORK

1 Speaking on 'How to Make Polls Better', FiveThirtyEight Podcast, 4 December 2020. A similar point applies, of course, to methods of polling other than by the phone. Even Internet panel polls that pay are usually relying on people being willing to repeatedly do surveys for not very much money at all.

2 Miguel de Cervantes, *Don Quixote* (Madrid, 1605), Book 1, Chapter 4.

3 The authors did not name the real location on which their books were based, although people did work out that it was Muncie, Indiana.

4 Isaac Asimov, 'Franchise', *If: Worlds of Science Fiction* (August 1955), pp. 2–15.

5 The early history of Roman censuses is impeded by a shortage of documentary evidence. For an introduction to what is known, see Roger S. Bagnall, 'The Beginnings of the Roman Census in Egypt', *Greek, Roman, and Byzantine Studies*, XXXII (1991), pp. 255–65 (p. 255): 'The scarcity and ambiguity of earlier direct evidence . . . has generated an extensive controversy during the past six decades about the dates at which the Roman government instituted the census in Egypt . . . Some evidence suggests – without quite demonstrating – a . . . cycle dating back as far as 11/10 BC'. See also W. Graham Claytor and Roger S. Bagnall, 'The Beginnings of the Roman Provincial Census: A New Declaration from 3 BCE', *Greek, Roman, and Byzantine Studies*, LV (2015), pp. 637–53 (pp. 637–8): 'The provincial census was one of the most durable and pervasive institutions of the Roman Empire . . . The census reinforced imperial ideals, strengthening the notion that the emperor could "see everything and hear everything," even when ruling from the Palace in Rome.' Thank you to James Carleton Paget for these references.

6 A good overview of the origins of polling in wider social and economic surveying is given in Nick Moon, *Opinion Polls: History, Theory and Practice* (Manchester, 1999), Chapter One. See also Susan Herbst, *Numbered Voices: How Opinion Polling Has Shaped American Politics* (Chicago, IL, 1993), Chapter One.

7 Margo Anderson and Stephen E. Feinberg, *The History of the First American Census and the Constitutional Language on Census Taking: Report of a Workshop* (23 February 1999), p. 37.

8 A. L. Bowley, 'Working-Class Households in Reading', *Journal of the Royal Statistical Society*, LXXVI/7 (1913).

9 Parlin's first research for his employer was a six-month stretch of interviews, but the profession he pioneered soon moved on to more recognizable survey work based on sampling.

10 To work out the precise chance of getting five heads out of ten tosses, you can imagine writing out all the different combinations of results you could get: HHHHHHHHHH (for ten heads in a row), THHHHHHHHH (for one tail then nine heads), HTHHHHHHHH (for one head, one tail and then eight heads) and so on. If you add up all the combinations in which there are exactly five heads and compare that with the total number of combinations, you obtain the 24.6 per cent figure. In practice, rather than having to write out and tally up combinations, you can use a binomial distribution calculation to obtain the result more easily.

11 Of course, candidates can die too and therefore the dead sometimes win elections. Voting for the dead candidate makes sense not only as a tribute to them but as a tactical move if you really do not want one of the candidate's opponents to win. One of the strangest victorious dead candidates was Dennis Hof: 'a man dubbed "America's most famous pimp" was elected to Nevada's state assembly, despite owning several brothels, facing an investigation into rape allegations, and also being dead' – Rachel Gutman, 'Endorsing Dead People Is a Shrewd Political Strategy', *The Atlantic* (7 November 2018).

12 There is a distinction drawn between polling that aims to measure the public and polling that aims to measure elections in George Gallup and Saul Forbes Rae, *The Pulse of Democracy: The Public-Opinion Poll and How It Works* (New York, 1940), p. 65. However, this is a brief reference, and the distinction is not followed through. Moreover, it frames the problem as being with polls that *included* African Americans: 'The inclusion of Southern Negroes in the sample of some polls introduced still another biasing factor in their final returns, since such groups were effectively disfranchised in many Southern states.'

13 Jill Lepore, *If Then: How the Simulmatics Corporation Invented the Future* (New York, 2020), p. 104, highlights how other pollsters followed Gallup in largely ignoring the views of Black voters. This helped give Simulmatics an opening in the political field, as it was unusual in having data on and an interest in them.

14 Daniel J. Robinson, *The Measure of Democracy: Polling, Market Research and Public Life, 1930–1945* (Toronto, 1999), p. 51, including n. 60. Robinson's reanalysis of the raw Gallup data concludes that there was 'a tendency to underreport female opinion by 1 to 3 per cent'. Chapter Two of this book is the key source for understanding how women, African Americans and also those from poorer socio-economic groups were deliberately under-represented in Gallup's polling. See also Sarah E. Igo, *The Averaged American: Surveys, Citizens, and the Making of a Mass Public* (Cambridge, MA, 2007), pp. 136–49; and David W. Moore, *The Superpollsters: How They Measure and Manipulate Public Opinion*, 2nd edn (New York, 1995), p. 62.

15 Robinson, *The Measure of Democracy*, pp. 51–3, shows how there was some influential evidence in the early 1920s of very low female turnout, but this was soon superseded by evidence showing that even if it had been true, it was no longer. On Gallup's espousal of derogatory views on the role of women in political life, see p. 53.

16 Nate Silver, speaking on 'Model Talk: Trump's Electoral College Advantage', FiveThirtyEight Podcast, 3 September 2020.

17 Nate Cohn, 'We Gave Four Good Pollsters the Same Raw Data. They Had Four Different Results', *New York Times* (20 September 2016).

18 The lead was taken to be the most important figure – showing as it did who might be about to win – but looking at the lead alone magnifies the amount of variation. All five calculations put Trump in the 39–42 per cent range and Clinton in the 38–41 per cent range. Those are both respectably small ranges and yet also large enough to leave significant uncertainty in the case of a close contest.

19 'Once the survey is complete, the final data are then statistically weighted to the national profile of all adults aged 18+ (including people without Internet access). All reputable research agencies weight data as a fine-tuning measure and at YouGov we weight by age, gender, social class, region and level of education. For political work we also weight by how respondents voted at the previous election, how respondents voted at the EU referendum and their level of political interest' – 'Panel Methodology', YouGov, www.yougov.co.uk, September 2020.

20 For example, see Edward Fieldhouse and David Cutts, 'The Companion Effect: Household and Local Context and the Turnout of Young

People', *Journal of Politics*, LXXIV/3 (2012); and Alan S. Zuckerman, Josip Dasovic and Jennifer Fitzgerald, *Partisan Families: The Social Logic of Bounded Partisanship in Germany and Britain* (Cambridge, 2012).

21 Of course, you could argue that people's political views on a wealth tax are likely to be influenced not by their actual wealth but rather by what they think their wealth is. In that sense, wrong answers from people would be the most predictive. As this example shows, what counts as a relevant weight quickly becomes a matter of judgement and testing.

22 Memories change and fade in complicated ways, as data from the Netherlands in 2005 showed. People were asked in both May and October to recall how they had voted at the preceding 2003 general election. There was significant churn between both recall efforts. See Jelke Bethlehem, *Understanding Public Opinion Polls* (Boca Raton, FL, 2018), pp. 190–91.

23 Past-vote recall not matching actual past vote is an international problem. For example, see Ragnar Waldahl and Bernt Aardal, 'The Accuracy of Recalled Previous Voting: Evidence from Norwegian Election Study Panels', *Scandinavian Political Studies*, XXIII/4 (2002), pp. 373–89: 'about one in four voters will give incorrect information about their voting behaviour at the previous election'. It also occurs when people are asked about their previous political affiliations, rather than simply past vote: see Richard G. Niemi, Richard S. Katz and David Newman, 'Reconstructing Past Partisanship: The Failure of the Party Identification Recall Questions', *American Journal of Political Science*, XXIV/4 (1980), pp. 633–51. For a more optimistic set of findings about the accuracy of past-vote recall, see Douglas Rivers and Benjamin Lauderdale, 'Beware the Phantom Swings: Why Dramatic Bounces in the Polls Aren't Always What They Seem', YouGov, 1 November 2016.

24 The Institute for Democracy and Electoral Assistance (IDEA) maintains a database of where compulsory voting is in place on its website, www. idea.int. As of summer 2020, 26 countries use compulsory voting in national elections. Of those, however, eleven do not enforce it.

25 Judith Brett, *From Secret Ballot to Democracy Sausage: How Australia Got Compulsory Voting* (Melbourne, 2019).

26 Paula Surridge (@p_surridge), Twitter, 14 August 2021.

27 Author interview, 3 November 2020.

28 Jon Puleston, 'Are We Getting Worse at Political Polling?', ESOMAR conference paper (Amsterdam, 2017), Figure 11 and Figure 12. Polls conducted within seven days of an election in which turnout is at least 85 per cent average a vote share error for the top four parties or

candidates of 1.8 per cent. In contests with a turnout of 75 per cent or lower, the average error is 2.3 per cent.

29 Melvin G. Holli, *The Wizard of Washington: Emil Hurja, Franklin Roosevelt, and the Birth of Public Opinion Polling* (New York, 2002), p. 110.

30 Ann Selzer quoted in Galen Druke, 'What Iowa's Best Pollster Thinks about 2020', FiveThirtyEight Podcast, 8 August 2019.

31 For a discussion of the pros and cons of Ann Selzer's methodology, see Nate Cohn, 'Why This Is the Iowa Poll that Everyone Was Waiting For', *New York Times* (30 January 2016). Although she polls outside Iowa too, her reputation is based on political polls in the state, and there is an unanswered question about whether the success of her methodology is specific to Iowa. That was suggested, for example, by another highly rated pollster, Patrick Murray, who polls both in Iowa and elsewhere. His methodology involves many more adjustments than Selzer's: speaking on 'How to Make Polls Better', FiveThirtyEight Podcast, 4 December 2020.

32 India's political polls typically have much larger samples. If India had the same party system country-wide, it too could use standard-sized samples. But its party system varies significantly between different states, with 36 separate parties (along with four independents) winning seats at the last Indian election. A 'national' poll in India therefore is in effect a series of separate polls, one for each different local party system.

33 For example, see Moon, *Opinion Polls*, pp. 24–33.

34 Strictly speaking, three percentage points.

35 Which is why the mangled version is so common. It is simpler and easier to understand and I've yet to come across a polling situation where following the mangled version would lead you to a wrong conclusion while following the correct version would lead you to a right conclusion. It's wrong, but useful.

36 Peter Kellner, 'A Journalist's Guide to Opinion Polls', British Polling Council. Reproduced in Appendix 6, House of Lords Select Committee on Political Polling and Digital Media, *The Politics of Polling*, Report of Session 2017–19, HL Paper 106, 2018.

37 G. Elliott Morris (@gelliottmorris), Twitter, 13 September 2020.

38 Pedants note that the official version of this statement on the British Polling Council website uses 'they lie' rather than 'it lies', but grammatically aware pollsters use the version quoted here: 'British Polling Council Introduces New Rule on Uncertainty Attached to Polls', www.britishpollingcouncil.org, 1 May 2018.

39 Jon Puleston, 'Are We Getting Worse at Political Polling?', Introduction.

40 Although a more informal U.S. estimate goes further: 'a good rule of thumb is that polls have about twice as much uncertainty as you see reported' – G. Elliott Morris (@gelliottmorris), Twitter, 13 September 2020.

41 For examples featuring emeritus professor of environmental management Lynn Crowe (since deleted by her), professor of cooperative social entrepreneurship Rory Ridley-Duff (since deleted by him) and professor of psychology and gender studies Lynne Segal, see my tweets (@markpack) on Twitter, 20 November 2019. To their credit, many other professors respond to such tweets with a version of 'oh no!'

42 Kathleen A. Frankovic, 'Technology and the Changing Landscape of Media Polls', in Thomas E. Mann and Gary R. Orren, eds, *Media Polls in American Politics* (Washington, DC, 1992), p. 33. However, it was not until well after the Second World War that telephone polling took off.

43 Picking phone numbers at random requires knowing what the set of usable domestic (as opposed to business) phone numbers is or having an adequate way of approximating it. This was particularly problematic in Britain due to the varying lengths of phone numbers, the lack of up-to-date public information on the range of numbers in use and the mixing in of non-working and business numbers with domestic numbers, delaying the take-up of RDD techniques. See Gerry Nicolaas and Peter Lynn, 'Random-Digit Dialling in the UK: Viability Revisited', *Journal of the Royal Statistical Society Series A (Statistics in Society)*, CLXV/2 (2002), pp. 297–316.

44 Meredith Dost and Kyley McGeeney, 'Moving without Changing Your Cellphone Number: A Predicament for Pollsters', Pew Research Center, www.pewresearch.org, 1 August 2016.

45 One of the firm's founders defended its 1983 polls in John Clemens, 'The Telephone Poll Bogeyman: A Case Study in Election Paranoia', Chapter 21 in *Political Communications: The General Election Campaign of 1983*, ed. Ivor Crewe and Martin Harrop (Cambridge, 1986). His defence of their 1983 polling is not very convincing and uses unusual techniques such as comparing mid-campaign polls against others conducted at the same time, judging those most different from the average as being the most wrong. His point about the future then resting with phone polling over face-to-face polling was, however, right.

46 Rob Salmond, 'Weekday-Only Polling and Partisan Support Levels: Evidence from New Zealand', *Australian and New Zealand Journal of Statistics*, LI/1 (2009), pp. 63–76.

47 *The Opinion Polls and the 1992 General Election: A Report to the Market Research Society* (1994), available at ncrm.ac.uk.

48 Similarly, online pollsters tend to guard against having their polls filled up only by those who are the quickest to respond to an invitation to participate. The risk is that those who are fastest and keenest to do a survey are not typical of everyone else, and so it is better to slow down the survey in order to obtain a better mix of participants.

49 Author interview with Damian Lyons Lowe, 15 December 2020.

50 IVR (for interactive voice response) is the acronym often used to describe this technology. It should not be confused with CATI (computer-aided telephone interviews), in which a computer is helping a human pollster. For example, pollsters with computers on their desks may be calling up members of the public; the computers serve up the names and numbers to call, they then prompt for the questions to ask, and the answers are typed back into the computers. The dialling of the phone numbers may be automated too, but with CATI, it is still a human who asks the questions.

51 In analysis of different polling methods in the 2020 U.S. presidential election, Nate Silver found that hybrid polls which used IVR alongside other methods of contacting people could perform the best. He, however, continued to view pure IVR polls as performing badly: Galen Druke and Nate Silver, 'Politics Podcast: The Gold Standard for Polling Has Changed', FiveThirtyEight, 25 March 2021, www.fivethirtyeight.com.

52 See the examples in Bethlehem, *Understanding Public Opinion Polls*, p. 148.

53 Robert Worcester is probably the only political pollster to live in a castle.

54 Alas, plenty of others do indulge in such voodoo polling, including proper media outlets. A particularly poor set of examples came from recent British general elections, with voodoo polls run by serious mainstream media outlets, and then reported on as if proper data. For 2017, see 'The Constituency Opinion Polls You Should Ignore', Mark Pack's Blog, www.markpack.org.uk, 22 May 2017. For 2019, see 'General Election Poll Results: Cornwall Live Readers Say Who They Want to Be Their Next MP', CornwallLive, www.cornwalllive. com, 2 December 2019. The results were nothing like the actual results, frequently absurdly different, and were run despite the same fiasco having occurred at the previous election.

55 Following the polling failure at the 1992 British general election, there was a belief that Conservatives might feel shy about revealing their support for that party. To overcome this 'shy Tory' effect, pollster ICM tried giving people ballot papers to complete confidentially. They however later dropped this, and other pollsters did not find convincing evidence of the benefit of such an approach. See Moon, *Opinion Polls*,

pp. 186–9. Such techniques have, though, had more popularity in other countries, such as in France and Sweden; see F. Teer and J. D. Spence, *Political Opinion Polls* (London, 1973), pp. 65–6. See also Hadley Cantril, *Gauging Public Opinion* (London, 1944), pp. 77–82, for evidence from the early days of polling: 'the methods of the interview and the secret ballot do produce marked differences in answers under certain conditions'. The first use of such secret-ballot polling was probably by Gallup in a test carried out in Maine in 1940. See Harry H. Field and Gordon M. Connelly, 'Testing Polls in Official Election Booths', *Public Opinion Quarterly*, VI/4 (1942).

56 Michael Crick, *Sultan of Swing: The Life of David Butler* (London, 2018), p. 60.

57 Moore, *The Superpollsters*, p. 61. In 1946 a court ruled that Gallup's method of calculating interviewer pay had to change.

58 Courtney Kennedy et al., *Assessing the Risks to Online Polls from Bogus Respondents*, Pew Research Center (2020), available at pewresearch.org.

59 Author interview, 3 November 2020.

60 'Polls have not become markedly less accurate in recent years, [but] they did have a pretty bad 2020. Our analysis also found that a longtime truism in polling – that surveys using live callers are more accurate – is no longer true. Comparing live-caller polls with online surveys, text messaging, automated calls and mixed methods, the former is not systematically likelier to reflect the final result of an election': Galen Druke and Nate Silver, 'Politics Podcast: The Gold Standard for Polling Has Changed', FiveThirtyEight Podcast, 25 March 2021.

61 Telephone polling could only be turned around so quickly with careful advanced preparation, as shown by the description of ICM's telephone polling methodology: 'ICM Research interviewed a random sample of 505 people by telephone on 15 April 2010. It re-interviewed people who had previously been selected at random who told them they would be watching the debate and had agreed to be interviewed again' – Julian Glover and Hélène Mulholland, 'Nick Clegg Now in Contention as Potential PM, Guardian/ICM Poll Shows', *The Guardian* (16 April 2010). Internet polling can provide still faster results, and without needing as much special preparation.

62 For an example of declining telephone survey response rates, see Courtney Kennedy and Hannah Hartig, 'Response Rates in Telephone Surveys Have Resumed Their Decline', Pew Research Center, 27 February 2019: 'After stabilizing briefly, response rates to telephone public opinion polls conducted by Pew Research Center have resumed their decline. In 2017 and 2018, typical telephone survey response rates

fell to 7 per cent and 6 per cent, respectively, according to the Center's latest data. Response rates had previously held steady around 9 per cent for several years.'

63 That said, telephone polls have maintained a good record at getting elections right notwithstanding what can appear to be remarkably low response rates. Because of that record, it is hard to agree with Bethlehem in *Understanding Public Opinion Polls*, p. 120, who singles out the low response rate to telephone polls at the 2015 UK general election to conclude, 'Not surprisingly, all telephone polls failed to correctly predict the outcome of the election.' If low response rates were, on their own, so destructive of polling accuracy, then many more telephone polls just before elections should have failed. Rather, a series of Pew Center Studies and other research has found little relationship between response rate and accuracy. See Kennedy and Hartig, 'Response Rates in Telephone Surveys Have Resumed Their Decline'.

64 The defence of the standard Internet panel operators is that they – or at least the good ones among them – ask enough non-political questions to ensure that their panels are not too tilted towards the politically interested.

65 Matt Singh, 'Polling Small Areas Online', Number Cruncher Politics, www.ncpolitics.uk, 20 July 2019.

66 For example, see Claire Durand and Timothy P. Johnson, 'Review: What about Modes? Differences between Modes in the 21st Century's Electoral Polls across Four Countries', *Public Opinion Quarterly*, LXXXV/1 (2021), pp. 183–222: 'We conclude that differences between modes vary with context and over time. There are some consistent differences, however, as online polls are less likely to detect movement than are telephone or IVR polls . . . IVR polls tended to be more precise than other polls recently, but they also tended to have a conservative bias.'

67 This is done to replicate the sense of being forced to make a decision that happens when an election actually arrives. It is done as it makes results more accurate but comes with a risk that it can mask the degree of uncertainty in the minds of voters. To allow for the fact that only giving the answer when pushed is not the same as immediately offering it, it is common for pollsters to count a squeezed vote at less than full value when tallying the votes for each party or candidate.

68 This is to help ensure the sample is balanced and/or to help work out how to account for those who aren't sure who they are going to vote for.

69 The answers to these other questions can also be used to help cater for those who refused to be squeezed in the voting question. For example,

a pollster may allocate some people who prefer the leader of party A or voted for party A last time to count as voting for party A, although they did not give a party in the voting intention question. This sort of adjustment became more common in Britain following the 1992 general election polling disaster, as it looked as if those who had refused to answer voting intention questions had been disproportionately Conservative, helping create that polling miss. The rationale for making such adjustments is largely whether or not they make the final pre-election poll from a pollster more accurate. However, in doing so, such adjustments may artificially boost the support of parties on the decline, as people who have partly moved away from that party end up being allocated back as voters for it.

70 But it is a different matter for questions about issues, in which recording and reporting 'don't knows' rather than squeezing them has much more value. The ballot paper ends up forcing people to make a choice on voting; there is no equivalent mechanism for forcing issues (the occasional referendum aside, which counts as voting for these purposes). Hence you should pay full attention to such 'don't knows', as discussed further in Chapter Four.

71 Author interview, 9 December 2020.

72 For example, see Stephen Tall, 'A Rogue Poll, or Are We Kidding Ourselves?', Lib Dem Voice, www.libdemvoice.org, 25 September 2007, referring to Britain, or 'Nats Dismiss Crushing New Poll as "Rogue"', *Otago Daily Times* (26 July 2020), referring to New Zealand.

73 Other versions of the exact wording are often given, but this appears to be the wording that first appeared in print, in 1975. See A.S.C. Ehrenberg, 'The Teaching of Statistics: Corrections and Comments', *Journal of the Royal Statistical Society Series A (General)*, CXXXIV/4 (1975), pp. 543–5. This reference comes from Ronny Kohavi, 'Twyman's Law and Controlled Experiments', EXP Platform, www.exp-platform. com, 5 July 2017. The eponymous Twyman is not the twenty-first-century pollster Joe Twyman, but twentieth-century TV and radio audience measurement pioneer Tony Twyman.

74 Author interview, 9 December 2020.

75 Andrew Gelman et al., 'The Mythical Swing Voter', *Quarterly Journal of Political Science*, XI/1 (2014), pp. 103–30.

76 Author interview, 29 December 2020.

77 Molly Ball, 'Friday Interview: The Polling Guru of the Iowa Caucuses', *The Atlantic* (25 November 2011).

78 Clare Malone, 'Ann Selzer Is the Best Pollster in Politics', FiveThirtyEight, www.fivethirtyeight.com, 27 January 2016.

79 Ball, 'Friday Interview: The Polling Guru of the Iowa Caucuses'.

80 Although she would have been justified in defending the polling miss given the closeness of the vote shares, she actually ran an article titled, 'Iowa Poll Was a Miss, and I Don't Like It', and said, 'For me, it was the first time my final poll numbers showed the wrong candidate in front in a presidential race, and I don't like it. The easy explanation would be that although Kerry led in the poll, the numbers were within the margin of error. I don't like this answer. The findings published in the Register are our best estimate of what will happen': *Des Moines Register* (10 November 2014), p. 11.

81 Malone, 'Ann Selzer Is the Best Pollster in Politics'.

82 The 2008 caucus poll is sometimes described as making her reputation, but her polling was already called 'gold standard' before it. For example, see 'Pols Struggle to Spin Final Iowa Polls', CBS News, www.cbsnew.com, 2 January 2008.

83 Speaking on 'How to Make Polls Better', FiveThirtyEight Podcast, 4 December 2020.

84 Author interview, 15 December 2020.

85 For example, see the 2019 Australian federal election post-mortem: D. Pennay et al., *Report of the Inquiry into the Performance of the Opinion Polls at the 2019 Australian Federal Election* (2020), available from https://apo.org.au, Section 6.5.

86 Lord Ashcroft (@lordashcroft), Twitter, 19 October 2014.

3 THE RIGHTS AND WRONGS OF POLLING QUESTIONS

1 This was first attributed to him in a slightly different form in the 'Currents' column, *Publishers Weekly*, 11 November 1968.

2 Norman Bradburn, Seymour Sudman and Brian Wansink, *Asking Questions: The Definitive Guide to Questionnaire Design – For Market Research, Political Polls, and Social and Health Questionnaires*, revd edn (San Francisco, CA, 2004), p. 4.

3 Quoted in W. Joseph Campbell, *Lost in a Gallup* (Oakland, CA, 2020), p. 12.

4 'Polls and the Use of Leading Questions' – letter by Dick Leonard, Politico, www.politico.com, 2 May 2007. Research by NOP for the *Daily Mail* before this referendum also showed a significant variation in the majority in favour of Britain's membership of what was then called the Common Market, depending on the question wording. See Nick Moon, *Opinion Polls: History, Theory and Practice* (Manchester, 1999), pp. 67–9.

5 Thank you to the 'Britain Elects' (@BritainElects) Twitter account, whose tweet drew my attention to the poll, Twitter, 27 October 2019.

6 Lord Ashcroft, 'Where the Parties Stand – And More on That Second EU Referendum...', Lord Ashcroft Polls, www.lordashcroftpolls.com, 17 January 2018.

7 Rob Johns, 'Slippery Polls: Why Public Opinion Is So Difficult to Measure', in *Sex, Lies and Politics: The Secret Influences that Drive Our Political Choices*, ed. Philip Cowley and Robert Ford (London, 2019), Chapter One.

8 Cited in Jelke Bethlehem, *Understanding Public Opinion Polls* (Boca Raton, FL, 2018), p. 33.

9 'Questionnaire Design', Pew Research Center, www.pewresearch.org, accessed 1 August 2021.

10 ComRes had a still higher figure, but that was on the basis of 'I would be prepared to vote tactically.' For details of all these polls, see Mark Pack, 'Proportion of Voters Saying They'll Vote Tactically Rises (Probably)', Mark Pack's Blog, www.markpack.org.uk, 20 November 2019.

11 For some examples of the research from different countries, see Barry C. Edwards, 'Alphabetically Ordered Ballots and the Composition of American Legislatures', *State Politics and Policy Quarterly*, XV/2 (2015), pp. 171–91; Mark Pack, 'What Do the Academics Say? Ballot Paper Ordering', Mark Pack's Blog, 12 September 2009; John Regan, 'Ballot Order Effects: An Analysis of Irish General Elections', MPRA Paper 38304, University Library of Munich, Germany (2012); and Richard Webber et al., 'Ballot Order Positional Effects in British Local Elections, 1973–2011', *Parliamentary Affairs*, LXVII/1 (2014), pp. 119–36.

12 Galina Borisyuk, 'What's in a Name: Ballot Order Effects', in *Sex, Lies and Politics*, ed. Cowley and Ford, p. 112.

13 Shaun Bowler and Bernard Grofman, eds, *Elections in Australia, Ireland, and Malta under the Single Transferable Vote: Reflections on an Embedded Institution* (Ann Arbor, MI, 2000), p. 58.

14 There is a related form of problematic questions, which come in the form of 'push polling'. This is the use of slanted questions designed to change the views of the person being polled. As a result, push polling does not restrict itself to simply hitting a certain sample size. Rather, push polling is done as widely as a campaign thinks will be useful and it can get away with.

15 Moon, *Opinion Polls*, p. 41, edited slightly to read clearly in this context.

16 House of Lords Select Committee on Political Polling and Digital Media, *The Politics of Polling*, Report of Session 2017–19, HL Paper 106 (2018), p. 4.

17 Philip E. Converse, 'The Nature of Belief Systems in Mass Publics', in *Ideology and Discontent*, ed. David E. Apter (New York, 1964), pp. 206–61.

18 See also another classic study on this topic, the ambitious general theory of how public opinion forms in John R. Zaller, *The Nature and Origins of Mass Opinion* (Cambridge, 1992), p. 1: 'citizens do not typically carry around in their heads fixed attitudes on every issue on which a pollster may happen to inquire; rather, they construct "opinion statements" on the fly as they confront each new issue.' Zaller's work generated much debate and Zaller himself has since modified his theory. It is, however, possible to draw the more modest conclusions in this chapter without having to get deep into those debates.

19 This example and the rule of thumb come from Anthony Wells, 'Why You Should Be Wary of Agree/Disagree Statements', UK Polling Report, http://ukpollingreport.co.uk, 2 April 2019. Among the other examples he quotes is a poll which had at least 11 per cent of people both agreeing that 'divorce should not be made too easy' and also that it should be 'as quick and easy as possible'.

20 Laura Wronski, 'Let's Agree Not to Use Agree/Disagree Questions', SurveyMonkey, www.surveymonkey.co.uk, accessed 1 August 2021.

21 This five-option approach is often called a five-point Likert scale, named after pioneering American social scientist Rensis Likert.

22 Jonathan Martin and Sheryl Gay Stolberg, 'Roy Moore Is Accused of Sexual Misconduct by a Fifth Woman', *New York Times* (13 November 2017).

23 The bigger picture reinforces this point. Democrat Doug Jones won the solidly Republican seat in the election, but then went on to lose it again by the hefty margin of 60 per cent to 40 per cent in 2020, when up against a normal Republican opponent. Voters had really taken against Roy Moore.

24 There is a good, brief discussion of such questions by Keiran Pedley, Leo Barasi and Matt Singh in 'Why the Polls Are Not Moving, Brexit Regret (or Not) and Alabama', Polling Matters Podcast, 15 November 2017.

25 Anthony Wells, 'Why People Don't Know What They Are Going to Do: Meaningless Polling Questions', in *Sex, Lies and Politics*, ed. Cowley and Ford, p. 19.

26 Ibid., p. 21.

27 Hadley Cantril, *The Invasion from Mars* (Princeton, NJ, 1940).

28 Stuart Oskamp and P. Wesley Schultz, *Attitudes and Opinions* (New York, 2005), p. 314.

29 Robert McG. Thomas Jr, 'Lloyd A. Free, 88, Is Dead; Revealed Political
    Paradox', *New York Times* (14 November 1996).

30 Hadley Cantril, *Gauging Public Opinion* (London, 1944), pp. 14–17.

31 David W. Moore, *The Superpollsters: How They Measure and
    Manipulate Public Opinion*, 2nd edn (New York, 1995), p. 96.

32 Philip Cowley and Dennis Kavanagh, *The British General Election of
    2017* (London, 2018), p. 189. The details of the policy tested were actually
    less generous than the version that ended up causing so many problems
    in the election and 'nothing in the polling indicated problems.'

33 Robert M. Worcester, 'Political Opinion Polling in Great Britain',
    in *Political Opinion Polling: An International Review*, ed. Robert M.
    Worcester (London, 1983), p. 80.

34 Anthony Wells, 'How We Design Election Polling Questions', YouGov,
    www.yougov.co.uk, 7 June 2019.

35 Quoted in Mark Pack, 'Does It Matter Which Parties Are Named by
    Opinion Pollsters in Voting Intention Questions?', Mark Pack's Blog,
    25 August 2019.

36 There is a side issue about whether the opinion polls overstated the
    Liberal Democrat support levels during this election, as the party under-
    performed the late campaign polls. In the polls that came out on the
    final day, the party averaged 27.2 per cent, but it only secured 23.6 per
    cent. However, because the Liberal Democrats finished neither first nor
    second, this possible polling error did not receive the sort of attention
    that polling problems in the 1970, 1992 and 2015 general election
    secured. Why it happened remains unexplained.

37 Mark Pack, 'Exclusive Poll: Newspaper Hostility Makes Voters More
    Likely to Back Lib Dems', Lib Dem Voice, www.libdemvoice.org,
    28 April 2010. The rest of the editorial team were not to blame; it is
    all on me.

38 Anthony Wells (@anthonyjwells), Twitter, 23 September 2019.

39 Diane Lowenthal and George Loewenstein, 'Can Voters Predict
    Changes in Their Own Attitudes?', *Political Psychology*, XXII/1 (2001),
    pp. 65–87.

40 For an example of other evidence, see 'Your Regular Reminder that
    Hypothetical Polls Can Be as Accurate as an American War Film',
    Political Betting, www.politicalbetting.com, 1 December 2019.

41 Lee Sigelman et al., 'Hair Loss and Electability: The Bald Truth',
    Journal of Nonverbal Behavior, XIV/4 (1990), pp. 269–83.

42 Caitlin Milazzo, 'Looking Good for Election Day: Do Attractive
    Candidates Do Better?', in *Sex, Lies and Politics*, ed. Cowley and Ford,
    p. 66.

43 Winston Churchill, House of Commons, *Hansard*, 11 November 1947, available at https://hansard.parliament.uk.

44 For example, see Gert Stulp et al., 'Tall Claims? Sense and Nonsense about the Importance of Height of U.S. Presidents', *Leadership Quarterly*, XXIV/1 (2013), pp. 159–71.

45 For example, see Rosie Campbell and Philip Cowley, 'The Impact of Parental Status on the Visibility and Evaluations of Politicians', *British Journal of Politics and International Relations*, XX/3 (2018), pp. 753–69.

46 Will Jennings, 'Wrong about Nearly Everything, but Still Rational: Public Opinion as a Thermostat' and Geoffrey Evans, 'The People Are Perceptive: Immigration and the EU', both in *Sex, Lies and Politics*, ed. Cowley and Ford.

47 'Spreadsheet Snafu, "Long Covid" Quantified, and the Birth of Probability', *More or Less*, Radio 4, 7 October 2020. See also D. Landy, B. Guay and T. Marghetis, 'Bias and Ignorance in Demographic Perception', *Psychonomic Bulletin and Review*, XXV (2018), pp. 1606–18: 'In countries around the world, people massively overestimate the size of minority groups while dramatically underestimating the size of majority groups . . . Small values are overestimated, and large values are underestimated, regardless of the topic'.

48 David Landy, Noah Silbert and Aleah Goldin, 'Estimating Large Numbers', *Cognitive Science*, XXXVII/5 (2013), pp. 775–99: 'While about half of people did estimate numbers linearly over this range, nearly all the remaining participants placed 1 million approximately halfway between 1 thousand and 1 billion, but placed numbers linearly across each half, as though they believed that the number words "thousand, million, billion, trillion" constitute a uniformly spaced count list' (p. 775).

49 1961, Africa and no, he was real.

50 He pioneered this concept in his book *An Economic Theory of Democracy* (New York, 1957).

51 Thomas Scotto et al., 'We Spend How Much? Misperceptions, Innumeracy, and Support for the Foreign Aid in the United States and Great Britain', *Journal of Experimental Political Science*, IV/2 (2017), pp. 119–28.

52 There is also evidence that the public is rational in giving more attention to issues as they become more important. One study found that the worse – and so more important – the state of the U.S. economy, the more attention people gave to economic information: Georgia Kernell and Samuel Kernell, 'Monitoring the Economy', *Journal of Elections, Public Opinion and Parties*, XXXI/2 (2021), pp. 199–219.

53 George F. Bishop, *The Illusion of Public Opinion: Fact and Artifact in American Public Opinion Polls* (Lanham, MD, 2005), pp. 55–8.

54 See, for example, ibid., Chapter Two (which also includes discussion of Philip Converse's two seminal essays on such 'nonattitudes') and David W. Moore, *The Opinion Makers: An Insider Exposes the Truth behind the Polls* (Boston, MA, 2008).

55 Karl-Heinz Reuband, '"Pseudo-Opinions" in Population Surveys: How Citizens Judge Fictional Politicians', *ZA-Information/Zentralarchiv für Empirische Sozialforschung*, XLVI (2000), pp. 26–38.

56 For example, see Patrick Sturgis and Patten Smith, 'Fictitious Issues Revisited: Political Interest, Knowledge and the Generation of Nonattitudes', *Political Studies*, LVIII/1 (2010), pp. 66–84.

57 George F. Bishop et al., 'Pseudo-Opinions on Public Affairs', *Public Opinion Quarterly*, XLIV/2 (1980), pp. 198–209; Mark Blumenthal and Emily Swanson, 'Beware: Survey Questions about Fictional Issues Still Get Answers', *Huffington Post*, www.huffpost.com, 11 April 2013.

58 It is worth noting caveats about two other studies often cited on this topic. The fictitious Metallic Metals Act, on which apparently 70 per cent of people were willing to express a view, comes from an article that presents no substantive data on how the finding was achieved, leaving the possibility that it is more of an anecdote about a group of people rather than a serious survey finding. In addition, the Agriculture Trade Act, for which 25–30 per cent of people offered an opinion, was a real piece of legislation, albeit obscure. In this case, the researchers felt it unethical to ask about something fictional and so chose a piece of legislation it was very unlikely people had heard of. For details of both, see Howard Schuman and Stanley Presser, 'Public Opinion and Public Ignorance: The Fine Line between Attitudes and Nonattitudes', *American Journal of Sociology*, LLXXV/5 (1980), pp. 1214–25.

59 Sturgis and Smith, 'Fictitious Issues Revisited: Political Interest, Knowledge and the Generation of Nonattitudes', p. 66.

60 Ibid. I have recalculated the polling figures in the text that follows in order to follow modern convention and include those with 'no opinion'. Gallup and Rae presented the headline percentages with 'no opinion' excluded.

61 For example, see Timothy Frye et al., 'Is Putin's Popularity Real?', *Post-Soviet Affairs*, XXXIII/1 (2017), pp. 1–15. In this case, the list test was used to see if people were afraid to give an honest answer about their views of an authoritarian leader. For an example of the list test being used to test whether people were afraid of giving a potentially socially embarrassing answer, see J. R. Lax, J. H. Phillips and A. F. Stollwerk,

'Are Survey Respondents Lying about Their Support for Same-Sex Marriage? Lessons from a List Experiment', *Public Opinion Quarterly*, LXXX/2 (2016), pp. 510–33.

62 A variant on this is to give the interviewees cards with two questions on them and a random selection device for deciding which question to answer. Interviewees only give their answers, without revealing which questions they are answering. In each pair, one question is on a sensitive topic and the other is a question to which the true results are known. See Bradburn, Sudman and Wansink, *Asking Questions*, pp. 90–91 and 101–3.

63 'The Ministerial Broadcast', *Yes, Prime Minister*, series 1, ep. 2, BBC (1986).

64 See Moon, *Opinion Polls*, pp. 73–6, including NOP's own tests of the different approaches to question ordering.

65 Richard Rose, ed., *The Polls and the 1970 Election*, Occasional Paper No. 7 University of Strathclyde Survey Research Centre (Glasgow, 1970; repr. with corrections 1975), pp. 19–20. ICM's polls in the 1997–2001 Parliament also gave the Lib Dem higher ratings than others due to prompting their name as an answer option.

66 Alec Tyson and Carroll Doherty, 'Polling on the Deficit: Why Question Order Matters', Pew Research Center, www.pewresearch.org, 20 December 2013. For other American examples, see Bishop, *The Illusion of Public Opinion*, pp. 60–64.

67 For an example of when it was not possible to randomize the order of answer options and the impact that had on an exit poll's findings on which issues were most important to voters, see Sheldon R. Gawiser and G. Evans Witt, *A Journalist's Guide to Public Opinion Polls* (Westport, CT, 1994), pp. 76–7.

68 For examples of this from U.S. political polling, see Bishop, *The Illusion of Public Opinion*, Chapter Four.

69 Such hope is important because, as research shows, not only can the ordering of questions alter the results, so too can whether a question appears in a survey that is non-political or whether it appears after political questions. See Jack Bailey, 'Political Surveys Bias Self-Reported Economic Perceptions', *APSA pre-print*, January 2021, https://preprints. apsanet.org, which found that having questions asking people's perception of the economy appear in a political survey results in greater partisan bias in the answers than if the same questions appear in an otherwise non-political survey (questions about dental hygiene in this case). This is likely due to a priming effect – asking people about politics gets them into a partisan mindset. Arguably the priming effect more accurately reflects what happens at voting time – people thinking more

about politics – so this may both distort the results but also give us more useful results.

70 As a result of the controversy over Clinton's use of polling, his successor, George W. Bush, made great play in public of paying less attention to polls. He did, however, still use political polling heavily, albeit more discreetly. See, for example, Joshua Green, 'The Other War Room', *Washington Monthly* (April 2002).

4 IS IT ALL ABOUT VOTING INTENTION?

1 Quoted in Robert M. Worcester, 'Political Opinion Polling in Great Britain', in *Political Opinion Polling: An International Review*, ed. Robert M. Worcester (London, 1983), p. 83. He was referring to the February 1974 general election.

2 For example, see Mark Pack, *Bad News: What the Headlines Don't Tell Us* (London, 2020), pp. 32–5.

3 George Gallup and Saul Forbes Rae, *The Pulse of Democracy: The Public-Opinion Poll and How It Works* (New York, 1940), p. 80.

4 Mike Smithson (@MSmithsonPB), Twitter, 30 August 2020.

5 Mike Smithson, 'Disastrous Favourability Ratings for Johnson in Scotland but a Glimmer of Hope for Starmer', Political Betting, www.politicialbetting.com, 31 July 2020. His site published another analysis in 2021 by a guest contributor under the nickname 'Fishing'. It came to a much weaker conclusion: 'three years out, the government's and the PM's approval ratings are a slightly better predictor of the result of the next general election than the opinion polls, but the difference is fairly marginal and from a small sample size; two years away, no indicator is robust; in the last year of the Parliament, the government's opinion poll lead is a better predictor of the result of the next general election than approval ratings' – 'Leader and Government Approval Ratings and Voting Intention as a Guide to General Election Results', Political Betting, www.politicalbetting.com, 18 February 2021.

6 Robert Andersen and Geoffrey Evans, 'Who Blairs Wins? Leadership and Voting in the 2001 Election', *British Elections and Parties Review*, XIII/1 (2003), pp. 229–47.

7 Jack Blumenau, 'Do Party Leader Approval Ratings Predict Election Outcomes?', British Politics and Policy at LSE, https://blogs.lse.ac.uk, 17 February 2015.

8 Author interview, 1 December 2020.

9 This is why I find unconvincing the critique of leadership ratings as being ephemeral and an illusion in George F. Bishop, *The Illusion of*

Public Opinion: Fact and Artifact in American Public Opinion Polls (Lanham, MD, 2005), Chapter Five. Changing views of what you want from a leader in the face of changing circumstances is reasonable.

10 Dan Pfeiffer, The Message Box, https://messagebox.substack.com, 30 August 2020.

5 OTHER TYPES OF POLLS

1 Sidney Verba, 'The Citizen as Respondent: Sample Surveys and American Democracy – Presidential Address, American Political Science Association, 1995', *American Political Science Review*, XC/1 (March 1996), pp. 1–7.

2 George Gallup and Saul Forbes Rae, *The Pulse of Democracy: The Public-Opinion Poll and How It Works* (New York, 1940), p. 45.

3 Roosevelt and Hurja were therefore 28 years ahead of the candidate (John F. Kennedy) and pollster (Louis Harris) pairing from 1960, which is sometimes cited as the first combination of candidate and campaign pollster.

4 David Greenberg, 'FDR's Nate Silver', Politico, www.politico.com, 16 January 2016, is a highly readable profile of the 'Wizard of Washington'. Hurja is also the subject of a biography: Melvin G. Holli, *The Wizard of Washington: Emil Hurja, Franklin Roosevelt, and the Birth of Public Opinion Polling* (New York, 2002).

5 Quoted in Holli, *The Wizard of Washington*, p. 41.

6 Ibid.

7 It was more a half-break, as he only got taken on by the campaign by agreeing to work for it without pay.

8 The data from bookmakers' surveys, briefly mentioned in *Time Magazine*'s 2 March 1936 profile of Emil Hurja, is an intriguing loose end from history: how much political data did they gather, how good was it and when did it start? This aspect of the early history of political polling and straw polls awaits exploration.

9 How influential Straus's efforts really were in helping Roosevelt win the nomination is disputed. See Holli, *The Wizard of Washington*, p. 45.

10 Ibid., p. 53.

11 Ibid., p. 60.

12 The exception is the simplicity of his statistics. Hurja did not use complicated regressions or factor analysis, for example.

13 'Roosevelt's Ballot Expert Predicts Landslide for Ike', *Detroit News* (19 October 1952).

14 Holli, *The Wizard of Washington*, p. 132 n. 46.

15 Internal campaign polls have the advantage that campaigns usually have access to the official list of who is qualified to vote in an election and sometimes also official records of who voted in previous elections, something that pollsters usually do not use in drawing up their samples. Therefore, internal campaign polls could sometimes have an advantage thanks to superior sampling and turnout modelling. It is an argument covered by Sasha Issenberg regarding U.S. political polling specifically in '"Likely Voters" Lie: Why Private Campaign Polls Get Such Different Results from Public Media Polls', Slate, www.slate.com, 15 December 2011. However, as Issenberg's piece acknowledges, there are good arguments both for and against polling methodologies that rest heavily on information that is available to campaigns but not pollsters. There is no simple pattern of one being better than the other.

16 This is my experience in Britain with media reports of internal polling from the Liberal Democrats. It's far from uncommon for such reports to fail to distinguish clearly between polling on the one hand and canvassing and other data on the other.

17 Especially as sometimes a story comes to light such as the 2021 Irish polling scandal: 'Earlier this week, it emerged that Sinn Féin, Fine Gael, Fianna Fáil and the Green Party had all conducted private polling on voter intentions using members or activists who purported to be working for companies that didn't exist. In some instances, business cards (Fine Gael) or fake ID badges (Sinn Féin) were distributed to them' – Jack Horgan-Jones, 'Q&A: Why Were Political Party Members Posing as Pollsters?', *Irish Times*, 11 June 2021. If parties are willing to produce fake identity documents, a bit of artistic licence with numbers given to journalists would be pretty small beer.

18 Ben Hall, 'Saatchi Claims Labour Cannot Win Again', *Financial Times* (5 October 2004).

19 'Marginal Success?', Ipsos MORI, www.ipsos.com, 6 January 2005.

20 Lord Ashcroft, *Smell the Coffee: A Wake-Up Call for the Conservative Party* (London, 2005), pp. 9–10. Ashcroft presents a range of other evidence that points against the internal poll being accurate on pp. 8–14, including his own marginal seat poll.

21 My own reporting of internal Liberal Democrat constituency polls ahead of the 2015 election fell foul of this. Each was a decently conducted poll, with proper data tables available. But the selection of which to pass around was not a neutral or random one.

22 Take this example from the 1984 U.S. presidential election: 'In the final days when Peter Hart, the Democrats' pollster, forecast a Reagan victory and recommended a redirection of the campaign's efforts to help other

candidates, his report was quashed out of fear that it would destroy the morale of party workers and the loyalty of contributors': Leo Bogart, *Polls and the Awareness of Public Opinion*, 2nd edn (New Brunswick, NJ, 1985), p. xiii.

23 Harry Enten, 'What Republican Internal Polling Can Actually Tell Us', CNN, https://edition.cnn.com, 22 October 2020.

24 David Broughton, *Public Opinion Polling and Politics in Britain* (Hemel Hempstead, 1995), p. 109.

25 Tim Shipman, 'Panicking No 10 Dumps Donald Trump and Woos Joe Biden', *Sunday Times* (11 October 2020).

26 Author interview, 27 October 2020.

27 David W. Moore, *The Superpollsters: How They Measure and Manipulate Public Opinion*, 2nd edn (New York, 1995), p. 198, credits Republican pollster Richard Wirthlin with pioneering tracking polling in this contest for Ronald Reagan, borrowing a technique he had previously used for Maxwell House Coffee in the 1960s.

28 There is one exception: regular, full polls are sometimes called 'tracking' polls. These are fine.

29 For example, YouGov decided not to poll the 2008 Glasgow East parliamentary by-election because it had only around one hundred panel members in the constituency, and they were overwhelmingly public sector workers – i.e. a very atypical cross-section: Mark Pack, 'YouGov's Polling Panels: An Interesting Snippet from Peter Riddell', Mark Pack's Blog, www.markpack.org.uk, 24 February 2009. There have been some recent experiments with river sampling in order to generate enough online participants in a particular constituency, as discussed earlier.

30 He subsequently ate an edible hat on the BBC, after previously declining to eat a non-edible hat on another BBC show.

31 Lenore Taylor, '"Mercenary Voters" Decided UK Election, Says Pollster Who Predicted Tory Victory', *The Guardian* (5 August 2015).

32 See Chris Cook, 'Labour Leadership Thought Public Polls Were Too Optimistic', BBC, www.bbc.co.uk, 11 May 2015, although note that Labour's polling did not get it all right: Patrick Wintour, 'Miliband So Confident of Election Gains He Had Full Plan to Oust Cameron', *The Guardian* (3 June 2015).

33 There is one small exception: if there are smaller, geographically concentrated parties in a small number of marginal seats, then a marginal seats poll that looks at that party's chances specifically can add something to a national poll.

34 British parliamentary by-elections have often been so volatile – at least in the comparison between the previous result and that of the by-election

– that one major study of them uses the word in its title: Pippa Norris, *British By-Elections: The Volatile Electorate* (Oxford, 1990).

35 Bogart, *Polls and the Awareness of Public Opinion*, p. xvi.

36 Stephan Shakespeare, 'How to Measure a Debate', YouGov, www.yougov.co.uk, 16 May 2011. Although dated 16 May 2011, the piece reads as if written partway through the 2010 general election, between the second and third TV debates.

37 For a good introduction to what happened, see David A. Graham, 'The Myth of Gerald Ford's Fatal "Soviet Domination" Gaffe', *The Atlantic* (2 August 2016).

38 For example, Lionel Marquis, 'The Psychology of Quick and Slow Answers: Issue Importance in the 2011 Swiss Parliamentary Elections', *Swiss Political Science Review*, XX/4 (2014), pp. 697–726.

39 The first MRP election analysis using polling data was done for the 2012 U.S. election, published in 2014. Most unusually it used data from an opt-in poll on the Xbox gaming platform with a huge sample size (750,148 responses from 345,858 different people). It was an exercise to show how MRP could be used to extract meaningful results even from very skewed sampling, and so this was not an exercise in showing how the support in small geographic areas could be predicted from otherwise insufficiently large national samples: Wei Wang, David Rothschild, Sharad Goel and Andrew Gelman, 'Forecasting Elections with Non-representative Polls', *International Journal of Forecasting*, XXXI/3 (2014), pp. 980–91. In 2015 an MRP analysis was published using British political data from 2010 to 2014 to estimate constituency opinion on a range of topics: Nick Vivyan and Chris Hanretty, *Estimated Political Opinion in Westminster Parliamentary Constituencies* (2017), UK Data Archive, Colchester, Essex. They also published MRP election forecasts online at www.electionforecast.co.uk (now archived at www.archive.org) during the 2015 general election. The model did not perform well, saying Conservative seat losses were almost certain. Perhaps thankfully given this, the innovativeness of the model mostly went unnoticed. A YouGov MRP model did get the 2016 European referendum right, but that too went mostly unremarked: Douglas Rivers and Benjamin Lauderdale, 'Introducing the YouGov Referendum Model', YouGov, 21 June 2016. Academics had also published online MRP models for that referendum, the 2016 U.S. presidential election and the 2017 UK general election, but they too went mostly unnoticed. These were written up in Benjamin E. Lauderdale et al., 'Model-Based Pre-Election Polling for National and Sub-National Outcomes in the U.S. and UK', *International Journal of Forecasting*, XXXVI/2 (2020), pp. 399–413. Therefore although the 2017

general election was not the first outing for MRP, it was the moment that made its public reputation, or could have broken it.

40 Lord Ashcroft, 'Election 2017: The Ashcroft Model', Lord Ashcroft Polls, www.lordashcroftpolls.com, 12 May 2017.

41 YouGov supplied the polling data for both the MRP model and its own conventional opinion polls. Although the MRP model performed well, YouGov's final conventional poll did not, despite sharing that data source. Partly this was due to bad luck, with random sampling variation making the final YouGov poll less accurate. Partly also it was due to a methodological adjustment turning out badly. The final conventional poll did some reallocation of those who said 'don't know' to their former parties. Although such reallocations can work well for other pollsters and have often been done by YouGov, YouGov pollster Anthony Wells himself explains, 'They have always made my polls worse.'

42 There was a third MRP model, by academic Chris Hanretty. It too was wrong, ending up pointing to a Conservative majority of 82. It is, however, a special case as, unlike the other two MRP models, it did not use its own up-to-date national polling sample. Instead, it reused polling from a variety of other sources, along with historical election results. The model deserves plaudits for the frank 'frequently asked questions' (FAQ) section on its website, electionforecast.co.uk (now archived at www.archive.org). It included, 'Were you wrong in 2015?' and 'Will you be wrong again?'. For a comparison of how the three MRP models performed, see Ron Johnston et al., 'Exploring Constituency-Level Estimates for the 2017 British General Election', *International Journal of Market Research*, LX/5 (2018), pp. 463–83.

43 Stephan Shakespeare, 'Two Methods, One Commitment: YouGov's Polling and Model at the 2017 Election', YouGov, 7 June 2017.

44 Sam Coates, 'Poll Firm Predicts Shock Losses for Theresa May's Tories at General Election', *The Times* (31 May 2017). The online headline was a little tamer than the print version, though only a little: 'Poll Firm Predicts Shock Losses for Theresa May's Tories at General Election', www.thetimes.co.uk.

45 Alan Travis, 'YouGov's Poll Predicting a Hung Parliament Is Certainly Brave', *The Guardian* (31 May 2017).

46 Martin Boon (@martinboon), Twitter, 30 May 2017.

47 Ben Page (@benatipsosmori), Twitter, 30 May 2017.

48 Will Jennings (@drjennings), Twitter, 30 May 2017.

49 Jim Messina (@messina2012), Twitter, 31 May 2017.

50 Alix Culbertson, 'Holes in the Poll EXPOSED: Why the YouGov Panel Predicting Tory Loss Shouldn't Be Believed', *Daily Express* (1 June 2017).

51 For a full description of the methodology, see Lauderdale et al., 'Model-Based Pre-Election Polling for National and Sub-National Outcomes in the U.S. and UK'.

52 Author interview with Jack Blumenau, 9 October 2020.

53 More accurately, MRP models usually work out both likely party support and likelihood to vote, combining those to obtain an estimate that is cognizant of turnout.

54 Cheaper versions of MRP have started being offered up by others, with sample sizes much smaller than this. There is a trade-off between how many variables can be sensibly explored and sample size, but in my experience cheaper MRP analyses are notably quiet on what they are sacrificing in order to keep to their smaller samples.

55 As YouGov explained for its 2017 MRP work, which involved a set of seat estimates that were regularly updated during the election campaign: 'Every day YouGov interviews approximately seven thousand panellists about their voting intentions in the 2017 General Election. Over the course of a week, data are collected from around fifty thousand panellists. While this is a much larger sample than our usual polls, the samples in each of the 650 Parliamentary constituencies are too small (on average, only 75 voters per constituency per week) to produce reliable estimates' – Doug Rivers, 'How the YouGov Model for the 2017 General Election Works', YouGov, 31 May 2017. This use of a rolling sample added another factor to the model – how much weight to give to the most recent data compared with older data still being used.

56 One of the key brains behind the YouGov MRP model in 2017 and 2019, Ben Lauderdale, responded on Twitter to my description of this rule of thumb with: 'That is generally the calculation I do as well!': Ben Lauderdale (@benlauderdale), Twitter, 28 November 2018.

57 This is one of the two key factors influencing how well MRP models perform, as identified in Matthew K. Buttice and Benjamin Highton, 'How Does Multilevel Regression and Poststratification Perform with Conventional National Surveys?', *Political Analysis*, XXI/4 (2013), pp. 449–67.

58 Author interview with Jack Blumenau, 9 October 2020.

59 The polls close at 10 p.m. in British general elections, and the publication of exit polls is always held off until the polls have closed both to allow for late data and to avoid the chance that the results of an exit poll might have an impact on how people vote. By contrast, publication and leaking of data from exit polls before the polls have closed is a regular feature of American politics, often raising concerns about its impact on voting, especially given that the number of time

zones in the USA means that polls close in some parts of the country many hours before they close elsewhere.

60 There is an adulatory Twitter account: 'Is Sir John Curtice on TV?', @JohnCurticeOnTV.

61 This company name no longer survives, but through a series of corporate changes, it is one of the antecedents of current pollster Kantar TNS.

62 See David Butler and Michael Pinto-Duschinsky, *The British General Election of 1970* (London, 1971), pp. 337 and 417. The Gravesend constituency had 'remarkable typicality . . . by all kinds of criteria'. The national swing figure here is slightly different from that given in this book due to the difference between calculating results including or excluding Northern Ireland (that is, on a Great Britain vs United Kingdom basis).

63 Figures from Richard Rose, ed., *The Polls and the 1970 Election*, Occasional Paper No. 7, University of Strathclyde Survey Research Centre (Glasgow, 1970; repr. with corrections 1975), p. 62.

64 ITN used ORC to carry out an exit poll in marginal seats, and the BBC used Louis Harris to do exit polling in English and Scottish seats. The former was pretty accurate, while the latter was well off due to a faulty choice of sampling locations and differential participation, with Conservative voters less willing to take part. See David Butler and Dennis Kavanagh, *The British General Election of October 1974* (London, 1975), p. 195.

65 'Britain's Exit Poll Has an Exceptional Record', *The Economist* (11 December 2019).

66 This is sort of accurate. With the rise in voting before polling day – via either the post or early voting locations, depending on the country and the rules – exit polling has become more complicated. This was a particular issue in the 2020 U.S. presidential election, in which the significant increase in pre-polling-day voting provided a challenge for exit pollsters. For example, see Laura Bronner and Nathaniel Rakich, 'Exit Polls Can Be Misleading – Especially This Year', FiveThirtyEight, www.fivethirtyeight.com, 2 November 2020.

67 Exit polling for parliamentary by-elections had a spurt of popularity in the 1990s but has long since ceased. See Broughton, *Public Opinion Polling and Politics in Britain*, p. 133, for details of those 1990s exit polls. Their demise is a shame, as exit polls offer the chance not only to predict the result promptly at 10 p.m. but to gather data, such as on vote-switching patterns, that helps explain why a by-election result has turned out the way it has. Punditry on by-election results is still extensive, but such data is now missing. Comment is cheap and data is costly.

68 The size of Parliament had grown between these elections, but only from 651 to 659.

69 John Curtice, 'Rash Promises and Tears: Exit Polls', in *Sex, Lies and Politics: The Secret Influences that Drive Our Political Choices*, ed. Philip Cowley and Robert Ford (London, 2019), p. 39. This emphasis on vote share change also helps the exit poll deal with the rise of postal voting. Postal voters are not caught by exit polling at polling stations, but as long as the vote share changes among postal voters match those among non-postal voters, the right results will be produced even if the absolute level of party support is different between postal and in-person voters. As postal voters tend to vote earlier in the election, there is still a risk that a major change in levels of support between the start of postal voting and polling day may cause a problem for the exit poll. However, the large changes in party support during the 2017 general election did not derail that election's exit poll.

70 Sam Wang, 'The Mailbag', Princeton Election Consortium, https://election.princeton.edu, 5 September 2020.

71 This was possibly supplemented by data about absent or early voting.

72 Most accounts of the origins of exit polling overlook this 1940 effort. Those that do not overlook it mislocate it in Denver, citing the work of Kathleen Frankovic as the source (for example, Kathleen A. Frankovic, 'Technology and the Changing Landscape of Media Polls', in *Media Polls in American Politics*, ed. Thomas E. Mann and Gary R. Orren (Washington, DC, 1992), p. 33). Thank you to Kathleen Frankovic for her kind correspondence, which helped to identify the location as Boulder rather than Denver. It appears that an error slipped into one of her works, which others have then cited.

73 Harry H. Field and Gordon M. Connelly, 'Testing Polls in Official Election Booths', *Public Opinion Quarterly*, VI/4 (1942), pp. 610–16. As that piece goes on to add, 'Probably never before in American history had representatives of an unofficial organization been permitted to operate in any way whatsoever within an official polling station.'

74 Nick Moon, *Opinion Polls: History, Theory and Practice* (Manchester, 1999), p. 137.

75 Various sources give slightly different timings. I have gone with 23 minutes, as that is the time stamp given by Walter Cronkite when he read out the decision to call the race for Goldwater.

76 Moon, *Opinion Polls*, pp. 95–107, for additional detail. See also Rick Perlstein, *Before the Storm: Barry Goldwater and the Unmaking of the American Consensus* (New York, 2009), p. 354. Thank you to Ashton Ellett for bringing this reference to my attention.

77 For the VPA's methodology, based on partial vote returns from around a state, see 'Vote Projection Proves Accurate; V.PA. Method Also Holds for Regional Returns', *New York Times* (5 November 1964). Projecting and even calling results based on early voter data after the polls have closed have become an increasingly sophisticated operation and are now a normal part of U.S. election night. For example, see Mark Sullivan, 'How a 4-Year-Old Startup Will Call the Winners on Election Night', *Fast Company*, fastcompany.com (30 October 2020).

78 Quoted in Bill Leonard, *In the Storm of the Eye: A Lifetime at CBS* (New York, 1987), p. 104.

79 Sheldon R. Gawiser and G. Evans Witt, *A Journalist's Guide to Public Opinion Polls* (Westport, CT, 1994), p. 134; and John G. Geer, ed., *Public Opinion Polling around the World: A Historical Encyclopaedia* (Santa Barbara, CA, 2004), vol. I, p. 399. The full story of the invention of exit polls is a little more complicated than just these key dates. The 1964 contest had been preceded by the use of pollster sampling techniques to extrapolate from early actual election returns to projected full results and also by the use of polling carried out on polling day itself. But, save for the Denver exception, 1964 looks to have been the first case of interviewers standing at a polling place, asking people questions after they had finished voting. That is the distinctive feature of an exit poll. For more details showing why the NBC 1964 activity does not count as an exit poll, see Moore, *The Superpollsters*, p. 255.

80 Dutch political scientist, later turned politician, Marcel van Dam is sometimes credited with the first exit poll. However, this did not come until February 1967, though it was commendably accurate and garnered some attention on television. For details of his poll, see Jelke Bethlehem, *Understanding Public Opinion Polls* (Boca Raton, FL, 2018), pp. 198–200.

81 Warren J. Mitofsky and Murray Edelman, 'Election Night Estimation', *Journal of Official Statistics*, XVIII/2 (2002), p. 171.

82 There are a few rare exceptions for elections involving unusually large geographies, such as in London-wide elections for the mayor and assembly, in which vote totals are declared on a borough-by-borough basis with ward-by-ward data released later.

83 Warren J. Mitofsky, 'Voter News Service after the Fall', *Public Opinion Quarterly*, LXVII/1 (2003), p. 45.

84 Florida was the most embarrassing moment for the exit polls, but they indicated the wrong winner in seven other states too.

85 For example, see Mark Blumenthal, 'Is RFK, Jr. Right about Exit Polls? – Part II', Mystery Pollster, https://mysterypollster.com, 8 June 2006. Robert F. Kennedy Junior was a believer in the exit polls being right in

2004 and the election result therefore being a result of fraud. He later became a vocal opponent of vaccinations.

86 Kerry's defeat following exit polls indicated he would win spun up some conspiracy theories about electoral fraud. This led to the unusual situation of leading exit pollster Warren Mitofsky arguing against the accuracy of his own polls in order to reject the conspiracy theories: 'I just don't believe in conspiracies. I'm much more a believer in something practical, like incompetence': Richard Morin, 'The Pioneer Pollster Whose Credibility You Could Count On', *Washington Post* (6 September 2006).

87 Robin Sproul, 'Exit Polls: Better or Worse since the 2000 Election?', Joan Shorenstein Center on the Press, Politics and Public Policy Discussion Paper Series, #D-42 (2007).

88 For example, see Nate Cohn, 'Trump Losing College-Educated Whites? He Never Won Them in the First Place', *New York Times* (27 February 2018); and Thomas B. Edsall, 'The 2016 Exit Polls Led Us to Misinterpret the 2016 Election', *New York Times* (29 March 2018). The reference to national elections in the quote includes congressional elections and not only presidential election years.

6 POLLING GETS IT RIGHT

1 Leo Bogart, *Polls and the Awareness of Public Opinion*, 2nd edn (New Brunswick, NJ, 1985), p. 39.

2 Quotes taken from the live blog 'What Went Down in the March 8 Presidential Primaries', FiveThirtyEight, www.fivethirtyeight.com, 8–9 March 2016.

3 The eight were ComRes (53 per cent for 'Remain' to 47 per cent for 'Leave'), Ipsos MORI (52 per cent to 48 per cent), Opinium (49 per cent to 51 per cent), ORB (54 per cent to 46 per cent), Populus (55 per cent to 45 per cent), Survation (51 per cent to 49 per cent), TNS (49 per cent to 51 per cent) and YouGov (51 per cent to 49 per cent). These figures exclude 'don't knows'.

4 We saw earlier that in UK general elections, two-thirds of the time the polls are within two points of the result. There are not enough referendums and referendum polls in the UK for a similarly robust calculation specific to them, but if we apply the general election error rate instead, and assume there is a 50:50 chance of an error being in favour or against the 'Remain' side, then you obtain the one in six figure.

5 'Brexit Poll Tracker', *Financial Times*, https://ig.ft.com, as updated on 23 June 2016. Missing from this table is a NatCen poll which

put 'Remain' ahead. For its first poll in June, Opinium changed its methodology, with the old methodology putting 'Leave' ahead and the revised putting 'Remain' ahead.

6 Ipsos MORI, 'June 2016 Final Referendum Poll' slide deck, available at Ipsos.com.

7 Nate Silver, 'The Real Story of 2016', FiveThirtyEight, 19 January 2017.

8 Christian Endt and Julian Hosse, 'Umfragen sind besser als ihr Ruf' ('Polls Are Better than Their Reputation'), *Süddeutsche Zeitung* (27 October 2019).

9 This comment appears to have been based on Andreas Graefe, 'Accuracy of German Federal Election Forecasts, 2013 & 2017', *International Journal of Forecasting*, XXXV/3 (2019): 'The present study reviews the accuracy of four methods (polls, prediction markets, expert judgment, and quantitative models) for forecasting the two German federal elections in 2013 and 2017. On average across both elections, polls and prediction markets were most accurate, while experts and quantitative models were least accurate. However, the accuracy of individual forecasts did not correlate across elections. That is, the methods that were most accurate in 2013 did not perform particularly well in 2017. A combined forecast, calculated by averaging forecasts within and across methods, was more accurate than three of the four component forecasts.'

10 Will Jennings and Christopher Wlezien, 'Election Polling Errors across Time and Space', *Nature Human Behaviour*, 11 (2018), pp. 276–83. More recently, polling in the 2020 U.S. presidential primaries was also similarly good, once you factor in that fieldwork often stopped so far before polling day that late swing will have undone some of the polls. See Nathaniel Rakich, 'We've Updated Our Pollster Ratings ahead of the 2020 General Election', FiveThirtyEight, 19 May 2020. There is also no declining trend in the accuracy of U.S. election polls: 'Election polls sometimes get the answer wrong – but they're about as accurate as they've always been' – Nate Silver, 'The Polls Are All Right', FiveThirtyEight, www.fivethirtyeight.com, 30 May 2018. This cites Jennings and Wlezien but also uses other data.

11 Author interview, 9 December 2020.

12 The elections analysed from that period were those in the UK in May 2015, Denmark in June 2015, Greece in September 2015, Canada in October 2015, Ireland in February 2016, Spain in June 2016, Australia in July 2016, Iceland in October 2016, the USA in November 2016, France in March and April 2017, and the UK in June 2017. The Quebec 2018 election does not break this pattern of polling accuracy, as shown by C. Durand and A. Blais, 'Quebec 2018: A Failure of the Polls?',

Canadian Journal of Political Science, LIII/1 (2020), pp. 133–50. Its conclusion is, 'Our post-election poll shows that changing voter behaviour – last-minute shifts and the vote of non-disclosers – explains most of the discrepancy.' In other words, the polls did not get it wrong in the Quebec elections so much as the voters changed their minds between being polled and voting.

13 Jennings and Wlezien also found that polling errors tend to be lower in elections using proportional representation and in presidential systems.

14 Jon Puleston, 'Are We Getting Worse at Political Polling?', ESOMAR conference paper (Amsterdam, 2017), Introduction.

15 Ibid., Figure 4.

16 For another example of how the polls provide a useful guide to the likely winners even in the USA, see Nate Silver, *The Signal and the Noise*, updated edn (New York, 2020), Figure 2-4, p. 63. This shows the percentage chance of a Senate candidate winning based on the size of their polling lead and how far ahead of polling day the polling figures are taken. Even a one-point lead one year out from polling day got the winner right 52 per cent of the time. A five-point lead a week out got the winner right 89 per cent of the time.

17 Ibid., Figure 14.

18 'An example of declining face-to-face response rates comes from the British Election Study. The response rate for the first British Election Study (BES) in 1963 was 79.4 per cent ... This dropped to 55.9 per cent for the 2015 BES ... Response rates for telephone polls declined even more dramatically than face-to-face surveys': Christopher Prosser and Jonathan Mellon, 'The Twilight of the Polls? A Review of Trends in Polling Accuracy and the Causes of Polling Misses', *Government and Opposition*, LIII/4 (2018), pp. 757–90 (pp. 758–9).

19 Puleston, 'Are We Getting Worse at Political Polling?', Figure 23. It is worth noting that this is significantly better than an analysis of 423 American polls in 1979–84 found: Irving Crespi, *Public Opinion, Polls, and Democracy* (Boulder, CO, 1988), pp. 51–2.

7 POLLING GETS IT WRONG

1 Quoted in Richard Hodder-Williams, *Public Opinion Polls and British Politics* (London, 1970), p. 80.

2 Adapted from an old Liberal Party saying that elections are the punctuation marks in community politics.

3 The final polls in 1966 had Labour with leads of between 8 per cent and 17 per cent. Labour won with a lead of 7 per cent, so although the actual

numbers were rather off, the big picture – Labour comfortably ahead – was correct. For more details, see my database of voting intention polls, PollBase, on my website, Mark Pack's Blog, www.markpack.org.uk.

4 Marplan had reported figures of Labour at 50 per cent and Conservatives at 42 per cent. But unlike most general election voting-intention polls which are carried out for Great Britain (that is, England, Scotland and Wales, excluding Northern Ireland and its different party system), this one was carried out on a UK-wide basis, including Northern Ireland. If the figures are recalculated to exclude Northern Ireland, Labour's lead in the poll was 9.6 per cent, rounded up to 10 per cent.

5 Robert M. Worcester, 'Political Opinion Polling in Great Britain', in *Political Opinion Polling: An International Review*, ed. Robert M. Worcester (London, 1983), p. 74.

6 David Butler and Michael Pinto-Duschinsky, *The British General Election of 1970* (London, 1971), p. 185. See note 4 above regarding the Marplan figure cited in the tables.

7 One source gives NOP's fieldwork as ending on 14 June: Richard Rose, ed., *The Polls and the 1970 Election*, Occasional Paper No. 7, University of Strathclyde Survey Research Centre (Glasgow, 1970; repr. with corrections, 1975), p. 30.

8 That is even without getting into questions about the dates in the first table. Both the dates given for the NOP and ORC polls are questionable with other sources giving fieldwork middle dates as either 13 or 14 (NOP) and 14, 15 or 16 (ORC, depending on how you account for their two waves of fieldwork). Such adjustments would disrupt the neat trend even when using the middle date of fieldwork.

9 This and the following quotes are from Butler and Pinto-Duschinsky, *The British General Election of 1970*, p. 185.

10 Rose, *The Polls and the 1970 Election*, p. 26. Curiously, despite that, Harris concluded that late swing was a factor but does not quote evidence other than the chronology of the final polls, debunked above – Rose, *The Polls and the 1970 Election*, p. 21.

11 This exercise compared post-election re-interviews with the answers the same people had given in late May.

12 Butler and Pinto-Duschinsky, *The British General Election of 1970*, p. 186.

13 The Conservatives appear to have had a good campaign at least since its midpoint, perhaps: NOP and Harris had a rising and then falling Labour lead, as did ORC to a lesser extent. Gallup had Labour's lead falling and then rising, while Marplan had it steadily rising.

14 The four points were that poll reports should include fieldwork dates, sampling method and sample size; significant changes in the number

of 'don't knows' should be highlighted; further details of survey design and sampling work should be available on request; and any unpublished findings from a poll should be available to others in the media. These good intentions were not always reflected in how the polls were reported – so much so that tracking down the fieldwork dates of the final Harris poll cited above quickly runs into problems of unclear, questionable or silent sources.

15 Moreover, that decline was despite two potentially turnout-raising reforms introduced in 1969: easier applications for postal votes and an extension in polling hours until 10 in the evening. Their impact, however, may have been muted by the cut in the voting age from 21 to 18.

16 Oddly, Rose, *The Polls and the 1970 Election*, includes examples of other pollsters speaking about turnout adjustments yet also has ORC claiming they were the only ones to adjust for differential turnout.

17 Worcester, 'Political Opinion Polling in Great Britain', p. 75.

18 From the foreword to *The Opinion Polls and the 1992 General Election: A Report to the Market Research Society* (1994), available at ncrm.ac.uk. David Butler was not only the British Nate Silver of his generation; he was that of several generations, dominating British polling analysis for half a century and inventing with colleagues basic concepts of how elections are understood, including 'swing'.

19 *The Opinion Polls and the 1992 General Election: A Report to the Market Research Society*.

20 Usually swing and turnout are treated as separate concepts. However, the MRS post-mortem treated them as parts of the same issue – the actual behaviour of voters varying from what they had previously told pollsters they would do.

21 This was partly because its sampling finished six days ahead of the general election.

22 However, the existence, or not, of shy voters, beyond any simple survey non-response effect – especially shy Tories in the 1990s and shy Trump supporters later in the USA – continues to be a matter of dispute. Adjustments for shy Tories worked well for ICM's polls 1997–2010, although not subsequently, and other research has failed to find evidence of shy voters. See the exchange between Jon Mellon (@jon_mellon) and Martin Boon (@martinboon) on Twitter, 4 November 2020.

23 However, the post-mortem also found that the poll tax was, at most, only a very small contributor to the polling miss. This highly controversial new tax was linked to a decline in people's willingness

to be on the electoral register. It became a popular theory that the poll tax put off Labour-leaning people in particular, with a result that the polls (sampling the public) found more Labour voters than were on the electoral register. It was a popular theory, but one the evidence showed was highly marginal at best.

24 Nick Moon, *Opinion Polls: History, Theory and Practice* (Manchester, 1999), pp. 76–80.

25 For an analysis of some of the other factors commonly wrongly claimed to help explain the polling errors, see Moon, *Opinion Polls: History, Theory and Practice*, pp. 115–30.

26 Damian Lyons Lowe, '"Yer Jaiket Is Hanging by a Shooglie Peg!":
Fear, Groupthink and Outliers', in *Political Communication in Britain: Campaigning, Media and Polling in the 2017 General Election*, ed. Dominic Wring, Roger Mortimore and Simon Atkinson (London, 2019), p. 221.

27 For example, see John Curtice, 'Who Is Right? YouGov or Survation?', What Scotland Thinks, www.whatscotlandthinks.org, 16 July 2014, and Peter Kellner, 'Measuring UKIP's support', YouGov, www.yougov.co.uk, 15 January 2013.

28 Author interview, 15 December 2020.

29 Interviewed by Galen Druke on 'Political Podcast: How to Make Polls Better', FiveThirtyEight Podcast, 4 December 2020.

30 David Cowling, 'Election 2015: How the Opinion Polls Got It Wrong', BBC, www.bbc.co.uk, 17 May 2015.

31 Matt Singh, 'Is There a Shy Tory Factor in 2015?', Number Cruncher Politics, www.ncpolitics.uk, 6 May 2015.

32 Author interview, 1 December 2020.

33 Ibid.

34 P. Sturgis et al., *Report of the Inquiry into the 2015 British General Election Opinion Polls* (2016), available at eprints.ncrm.ac.uk.

35 'By a process of elimination, then, we are led to conclude that unrepresentative samples – the ways the poll samples were collected and adjusted – must have been the primary cause of the 2015 polling miss . . . We are not limited, however, to basing our key conclusion solely on elimination of plausible alternatives', ibid., pp. 47–8.

36 Do not be too kind to Australian pollsters, however. As the industry post-mortem reported, there was significantly less cooperation from the pollsters than on similar post-mortems in other countries. For example, D. Pennay et al., *Report of the Inquiry into the Performance of the Opinion Polls at the 2019 Australian Federal Election* (2020), p. xi and p. 5: 'despite our requests, the pollsters provided no raw data to enable

us to attempt to replicate their results . . . For the most part, pollsters were reluctant to fully cooperate with the Inquiry; some refused. This reluctance seemed mainly to stem from a concern that they would be asked to disclose what they regard as proprietary or 'commercial in confidence' information or because they were embarking upon their own reviews.' Most remarkably to eyes used to British levels of polling transparency, only two of the Australian pollsters were willing to release the full wording of their polling questionnaires and only one provided cross-tabs. The culture of secrecy, including among Australian polling firms that are part of international groups whose outlets in the UK follow standard transparency requirements, is perhaps a consequence of the near-thirty-year monopoly that Gallup had in the early days of Australian political polling. This generated a sense of secrecy about polling rather than the sense of community between pollsters that grew up in countries with a more diverse early polling history. There is at least a hopeful recent sign with some Australian pollsters signing up in 2020 to a new Australian Polling Council with strong transparency rules: www.australianpollingcouncil.com.

37 These figures are for the two-party preferred-vote shares. Australia uses preferential voting, so the two-party preferred measure captures vote shares after the preferences for those finishing outside the top two have been redistributed.

38 Some used this measure prior to 1993, but as 1993 was the first election at which all the pollsters used it, this election is the convenient starting point from which to measure the accuracy of modern polling.

39 There was a partial exception in 2004, during which Morgan had two final polls, using different survey modes. Both got the election winner wrong. Counting Morgan once, the majority of pollsters got the election right. But if you count these two polls separately, half the final polls were wrong.

40 *Report of the Inquiry into the Performance of the Opinion Polls at the 2019 Australian Federal Election*, p. xi.

41 Quoted in the presentation 'An Evaluation of 2016 Election Polls in the United States', AAPOR 72nd Annual Conference (2017).

42 See the table posted by Derek Thompson (@DKThomp), Twitter, 15 October 2020. The RCP averages vary a little by source, with W. Joseph Campbell, *Lost in a Gallup* (Oakland, CA, 2020), p. 184, giving them as Clinton 45.5 per cent and Trump 42.2 per cent, for a lead of 3.3 per cent.

43 For example, see Ad Hoc Committee on 2016 Election Polling, *An Evaluation of 2016 Election Polls in the U.S.*, American Association for Public Opinion Research (2017), available from www.aapor.org.

44 The figure of 98.2 per cent is given in Natalie Jackson, 'HuffPost Forecasts Hillary Clinton Will Win with 323 Electoral Votes', *HuffPost*, www. huffingtonpost.co.uk, 7 November 2016, although 98.3 per cent is cited in some other places, and in the regularly updated 'Election 2016 Forecast', *HuffPost* finalized on 98.0 per cent.

45 Alexandra King, 'Poll Expert Eats Bug after Being Wrong about Trump', CNN, https://edition.cnn.com, 12 November 2016, and Campbell, *Lost in a Gallup*, p. 171.

46 Claude E. Robinson, *Straw Votes: A Study of Political Prediction* (New York, 1932), pp. 81–5, has a good discussion about the risks of pre-1936 straw polls being deliberately manipulated by fraudulent returns or analysis, including how the *Buffalo Courier Express* caught fraudulent returns in 1929 by having 'Buffalo' deliberately mistyped on the return address for legitimate participants in its straw poll.

47 Andrew Gelman, 'So, What's with That Claim that Biden Has a 96 per cent Chance of Winning? (Some Thoughts with Josh Miller)', Statistical Modelling, Causal Inference, and Social Science, https:// statmodeling.stat.columbia.edu, 2 November 2020.

48 Ibid.

49 What's more, the highest-profile poor polling performance came in the California recall election, where the polls under-reported Democrat support – the opposite of the problem that occurred in 2020.

50 Nate Silver, 'The Death of Polling Is Greatly Exaggerated', FiveThirtyEight, www.fivethirtyeight.com, 25 March 2021.

51 One other reassurance about the extent of the polling miss in 2020 is that polling on policy issues does not appear to have been impacted significantly. Research by Pew found that reworking previous issue polls to take into account the sort of errors seen at the 2020 election did not undermine the headline findings from such issue polls: 'Using the national tally of votes for president as an anchor for what surveys of voters should look like, analysis across 48 issue questions on topics ranging from energy policy to social welfare to trust in the federal government found that the error associated with underrepresenting Trump voters and other Republicans by magnitudes seen in some 2020 election polling varied from less than 0.5 to 3 percentage points, with most estimates changing hardly at all. Errors of this magnitude would not alter any substantive interpretations of where the American public stands on important issues' – Scott Keeter et al., 'What 2020's Election Poll Errors Tell Us about the Accuracy of Issue Polling', Pew Research Center, www.pewresearch.org, 2 March 2021.

52 James Kanagasooriam, 'Voter Distrust and Non-Stop Polling Shocks', Politico, www.politico.com, 15 April 2021.

53 'The overstatement of Democratic support was larger in races that did not involve Trump (i.e., senatorial and gubernatorial contests)': American Association for Public Opinion Research, *Task Force on 2020 Pre-Election Polling: An Evaluation of the 2020 General Election Polls* (2021), available at www.aapor.org, p.4.

54 ALG Research et al., 'Revisiting Polling for 2021 and Beyond', Democracy Docket, www.democracydocket.com, 13 April 2021. This was a joint statement by five Democratic polling firms: ALG Research, Garin-Hart-Yang Research Group, GBAO Strategies, Global Strategy Group and Normington Petts.

55 American Association for Public Opinion Research, *Task Force on 2020 Pre-Election Polling: An Evaluation of the 2020 General Election Polls*, p. 5.

56 Jennifer Agiesta, 'CNN Launches New Polling Methodology', CNN, cnn. com, 10 September 2021. See also NBC's changes set out in Chuck Todd, Mark Murray and Ben Kamisar, 'Trump's Rough Day Hints at Limits of His Power over GOP', NBC News, www.nbcnews.com, 28 July 2021.

57 Correspondence with author, 14 April 2021.

58 An example is how some pollsters in Britain 'improved' their polls after the 1970 election by adding in adjustments for differential turnout for both the February and October 1974 elections. These made their results worse in February but then better in October. Attempting to correct for polling errors is often a frustrating business. See David Butler and Dennis Kavanagh, *The British General Election of October 1974* (London, 1975), pp. 195–6.

59 Although by the 1980s the perils of finishing fieldwork too soon and being caught out by late swing were very well established in American polling lore, thanks to the 1948 experience, most pollsters got the 1988 Republican presidential primary in New Hampshire wrong by finishing their fieldwork too soon, missing the late swing to George H. W. Bush. Gallup itself got the result wrong by 17 percentage points for this reason. See Irving Crespi, *Public Opinion, Polls, and Democracy* (Boulder, CO, 1988), p. 56.

60 If you disagree with this, and think the polls are hopelessly wrong, here is a simple get-rich-quick scheme. Always bet against the polls. If you're right, you'll end up rich, and then you can invite me to fly out in your helicopter to meet on your luxury yacht for a caviar and champagne celebration as you lord it over me and this book.

61 Henry Durant, William Gregory and Denis Weaver, *Behind the Gallup Poll* (London, 1951), p. 5.

8 REGULATING OPINION POLLS

1 House of Commons, *Hansard*, 22 October 1985, available at https://hansard.parliament.uk. Freud was an MP from 1973 to 1987 and a national celebrity through his skill with food and humour, including the long-running *Just a Minute* quiz show. However, his legacy has been severely tarnished by credible evidence of child sex abuse. This resulted in his widow saying she was, 'deeply saddened and profoundly sorry for what has happened to these women': Ben Quinn, 'Sir Clement Freud Accused of Abusing Two Girls between the Late 1940s and '70s', *The Guardian* (14 June 2016).

2 More precisely, it is the first attempt I have managed to track down.

3 Walter M. Pierce, 'Climbing on the Bandwagon', *Public Opinion Quarterly*, IV/2 (1940).

4 For a discussion of some of the more respectable arguments used to support banning straw polls, see Claude E. Robinson, 'Recent Developments in the Straw-Poll Field – Part 2', *Public Opinion Quarterly*, I/4 (1937).

5 This appears to be his first bill, but in some of his correspondence, Pierce makes reference to time spans that imply his first bill was earlier than this. For example, in 1939 he wrote, 'I have repeatedly introduced two different bills over a period of seven years': Walter M. Pierce to General Hugh S. Johnson, 19 October 1939, Walter M. Pierce Papers, University of Oregon, Collection 68, Box 25, Folder 15.

6 Postmaster General to James Mead, 12 March 1935, Congressional Archives, HR74A-D30 Box 310.

7 He returned to the issue in Congress in 1936, 1937, 1939, 1940 and 1941, but these efforts did not get very far. Thank you to Anne L. Washington of NYU Steinhardt School for helping me track down this congressional activity and other information related to him.

8 Postmaster General to James Mead, 17 February 1937, Congressional Archives, HR75A-D29 Box 289.

9 Walter M. Pierce, *Congressional Record*, LXXXVI/2 (21 February 1940), p. 2163, available at www.congress.gov.

10 'Anti-Straw Vote Bill to Be Pushed', *Evening Star* (Washington, DC) (30 December 1935) and 'Seeks to Bar Polls from Nation's Mails', *Indianapolis Times* (2 January 1936). The then-head of the Post Office was James Farley, mentioned in Chapter Five for his role as boss of the first campaign pollster. Thank you to David Smith of Northeastern University for helping me locate these references.

11 For example, in Britain the Speaker's Conference on Electoral Law in June 1967 recommended banning publishing polls for 72 hours before polling day, but this did not make it into the subsequent Representation of the People Act 1969.

12 Erik Gahner Larsen and Zoltán Fazekas, *Reporting Public Opinion: How the Media Turns Boring Polls into Biased News* (Cham, 2021), p. 110 concludes, 'in a complex information environment, the number of wasted votes increases when laws prohibit the publication of opinion polls.'

13 Wolfgang Donsbach, *Who's Afraid of Election Polls? Normative and Empirical Arguments for the Freedom of Pre-Election Surveys* (Amsterdam, 2001), p. 1. Donsbach's work includes a lovely example of a poll showing that which party you support heavily influences which party you think was ahead in the polls you have seen reports of.

14 Banning only publication – that is, allowing fieldwork close to polling day but banning publishing the results – does not circumvent this problem, as without the potential for publicity for a pre-election poll, the ability to get funding for such polling is greatly reduced. Media outlets are a major source of funding for political polling, in particular, and which media outlet is going to commission a poll it then cannot publish?

15 WAPOR/ESOMAR, *Freedom to Conduct Opinion Polls: A 2017 Worldwide Update*, pp. 7 and 10, available at www.esomar.org.

16 Restricting interference with people coming and going at polling stations protects their freedom and convenience of voting. Exit pollers are very much the benign end of the problem, and their location appears to matter for the accuracy of exit polling: 'In Washington State . . . after the 1980 election . . . news organisations submitted relevant research [to the courts] linking the accuracy of the estimate of each polling place's vote totals to how close interviewers were to the polling station itself': ibid., p. 20.

17 Ibid., p. 7 and p. 10.

18 Ibid., p. 13. These are median figures.

19 Ibid., p. 25.

20 'Objects and Rules', British Polling Council, www.britishpollingcouncil.org, accessed 1 August 2021.

9 ALTERNATIVES TO OPINION POLLS

1 Leo Bogart, *Polls and the Awareness of Public Opinion*, 2nd edn (New Brunswick, NJ, 1985), p. 4.

2 See Susan Herbst, *Numbered Voices: How Opinion Polling Has Shaped American Politics* (Chicago, IL, 1993), Chapter Three, especially the

useful table on p. 48. Herbst discusses who the 'public' in 'public opinion' was seen as being. Exclusionary definitions that omitted, for example, people with less money and less education were common.

3 I skip over the occasional claims made about how sales of cookies, cakes or other confectionery will predict an election result. But if you really need some evidence that food sales are not a substitute for polling, see evidence about Joe Biden and cookie sales: 'Remember that story about cookies that said Biden was going to lose? The county it's in is voting 63–37 for him' – Matt Singh (@mattsingh), Twitter, 6 November 2020.

4 The UK Parliament petition system has a little sub-genre of petitions calling for an investigation into multiple signatures on petitions on the UK Parliament petition system. See petition.parliament.uk. For a brief description of the preventative measures an online petition system can take, see 'Is It Possible to Repeatedly Sign a Parliamentary Petition Using the Same Email Address?', Full Fact, www.fullfact.org, 25 March 2019.

5 For some examples from the UK of such petitions, see Tom Baker, 'Is #RevokeArticle50 the Biggest Petition in UK History?', Thoughtful Campaigner, www.thoughtfulcampaigner.org, 24 March 2019.

6 This was the case at least when he was at the White House. Obama usually did not do the ten-letters-a-day cycle when he was travelling.

7 Ashley Parker, 'Picking Letters, 10 a Day, that Reach Obama', New York Times (19 April 2009). See also Jeanne Marie Laskas, 'To Obama with Love, and Hate, and Desperation', New York Times Magazine (17 January 2017).

8 Ibid.

9 Mark Pack, Bad News: What the Headlines Don't Tell Us (London, 2020), pp. 84–5.

10 Bogart, Polls and the Awareness of Public Opinion, pp. 53–4.

11 For examples of politicians judging public opinion by quantifying incoming correspondence and editorial columns, see Herbst, Numbered Voices, pp. 99–100.

12 Philip Cowley, 'Why MPs' Postbags Have Been So Important in the Cummings Row', The Times (29 May 2020). 'Foxes' is a reference to fox hunting, a topic on which public opinion is very strongly on one side of the issue, but MPs' postbags in some parts of the country are dominated by the minority.

13 Peggy Noonan, 'Monday Morning', Wall Street Journal Blogs, http:// blogs.wsj.com 5 November 2012.

14 Data from canvassing can be an effective way of tracking political fortunes. However, it requires considerable skill to reliably produce accurate analysis. Most people who talk about the feedback from the doorsteps do not even have access to all their campaign's data from that contest, let alone the historic data and analytical skills to do analysis well.

15 For a brief introduction to the problems of counting crowds, see Rob Goodier, 'The Curious Science of Counting a Crowd', *Popular Mechanics* (12 September 2011).

16 'Reagan and Mondale Are Ending Drives with Contrasting Strategy; Democrat Acts to Keep Backers Solid, Saying Polls Ignore Shifts', *New York Times* (30 October 1984).

17 Bogart, *Polls and the Awareness of Public Opinion*, p. vii.

18 Nathaniel Rakich, 'Don't Let Crowd Sizes Mislead You', FiveThirtyEight, www.fivethirtyeight.com, 5 September 2019.

19 Peter Kellner, 'The Labour Campaign', in *Britain at the Polls 1983: A Study of the General Election*, ed. Austin Ranney (Des Moines, IA, 1985), p. 77. A similar fate befell one of Foot's successors as Labour Party leader, Jeremy Corbyn, in the 2017 general election. Although Corbyn secured a large and surprising increase in support for his party, he still lost the election and never became prime minister despite his crowds completely dwarfing the public reaction to Prime Minister Theresa May's occasional forays into meeting the public.

20 Barbara Sommer, 'Front Yard Signs as Predictors of Election Outcome', *Political Methodology*, VI/2 (1979), pp. 237–40. See also Darcy Henton, 'Study Finds Number of Political Yard Signs an Indicator of Final Election Results', *Calgary Herald* (1 November 2014). However, see also Sasha Issenberg, 'High Stakes: Do Campaign Signs Work?', Slate, www.slate.com, 10 January 2012.

21 See Donald Green et al., 'The Effects of Lawn Signs on Vote Outcomes: Results from Four Randomized Field Experiments', *Electoral Studies*, XLI (2015), pp. 143–50. See also as an example of why posters and signs may work: Mark Pack, 'This Is Why the Posters, Avatars, Status Updates and More Matter', Mark Pack's Blog, www.markpack.org.uk, 27 April 2010. There is also some evidence that they may raise turnout: Costas Panagopoulos, 'Street Fight: The Impact of a Street Sign Campaign on Voter Turnout', *Electoral Studies*, XVIII/2 (2009), pp. 309–13.

22 For what can be learnt about politics from poster displays, see Todd Makse, Scott Minkoff and Anand Sokhey, *Politics on Display: Yard Signs and the Politicization of Social Spaces* (New York, 2019).

23 Former work colleagues insist I have been spotted wearing a suit to the beach.

24 The classic modern statement of the wisdom of crowds is James Surowiecki, *The Wisdom of Crowds: Why the Many Are Smarter than the Few* (New York, 2005). For some illustrations of when this theory does and does not work, see Philip Ball, '"Wisdom of the Crowd": The Myths and Realities', BBC Future, www.bbc.com, 8 July 2014.

25 As with financial markets, you also get the problem with prediction markets and spread betting of people placing bets based on how they think the prices will move rather than what they expect reality to turn out to be. For example, I have one suit made from the proceeds of placing a spread bet in a leadership contest. I did not particularly expect the person I backed to win. But I did expect that person to announce an intention to stand. By placing a bet ahead of that announcement, I was able to pocket a nice little profit from the market moves in response to that announcement when it was made.

26 For traditional betting, odds are offered and you pay up your money and wait for the outcome. For prediction markets, a price is quoted that can move up or down, and you can buy or sell in the market at any point. If you buy low and sell high, you can bank a profit before the event has happened.

27 Nate Silver, *The Signal and the Noise*, updated edn (New York, 2020), p. 334.

28 Oddly, Richard Holden used both of those polling failures as examples of why the betting markets might be better in his piece 'Vital Signs: For the Best Election Predictions, Look to the Betting Markets, Not the Opinion Polls', The Conversation, www.theconversation.com, 17 May 2019. He went on to say, 'What are betting markets saying about the May 18 Australian federal election? They're saying Labor has a roughly 85 per cent chance of winning'. Labor, however, lost the election the following day.

29 J. James Reade and Leighton Vaughan Williams, 'Polls to Probabilities: Comparing Prediction Markets and Opinion Polls', *International Journal of Forecasting*, XXXV/1 (2019), pp. 336–50; Robert S. Erikson and Christopher Wlezien, 'Are Political Markets Really Superior to Polls as Election Predictors?', *Public Opinion Quarterly*, LXXII/2 (2008), pp. 190–215.

30 Thomas Wood, 'Do Betting Markets Outperform Election Polls? Hardly', Monkey Cage Blog – *Washington Post*, www.washingtonpost.com, 9 August 2016; Kelsey Piper, 'Why Prediction Markets Are Bad at Predicting Who'll Be President', Vox, www.vox.com, 15 February 2020.

31 Matthew Wall, Maria Laura Sudulich and Kevin Cunningham, 'What Are the Odds? Using Constituency-Level Betting Markets to Forecast

Seat Shares in the 2010 UK General Elections', *Journal of Elections, Public Opinion and Parties*, XXII/1 (2012), pp. 3–26.

32 Chris Hanretty, Ben Lauderdale and Nick Vivyan, 'If Not Polls, then Betting Markets?', British Politics and Policy at LSE, https://blogs. lse.ac.uk, 18 May 2015. For some older data, see Matt Wall, 'Racing Certainties: The Value of Political Gambling', in *More Sex, Lies and the Ballot Box*, ed. Philip Cowley and Robert Ford (London, 2016), Chapter Fourteen.

33 Sveinung Arnesen and Ole Bergfjord, 'Prediction Markets vs Polls – An Examination of Accuracy for the 2008 and 2012 U.S. Elections', *Journal of Prediction Markets*, VIII/3 (2014), pp. 24–33; and David Rothschild, 'Forecasting Elections: Comparing Prediction Markets, Polls, and Their Biases', *Public Opinion Quarterly*, LXXIII/5 (2009), pp. 895–916.

34 Sveinung Arnesen and Oliver Strijbis, 'Accuracy and Bias in European Prediction Markets' (research paper for The European Prediction Market Infrastructure for Political Events – EPIPE, 2015).

35 Andreas Graefe, 'Political Markets', in *The SAGE Handbook of Electoral Behaviour*, ed. Kai Arzheimer, Jocelyn Evans and Michael S. Lewis-Beck (London, 2017), Chapter 37.

36 Graefe, 'Political Markets', p. 879.

37 Author interview with Deborah Mattinson, 4 November 2020.

38 Ibid. She also makes the point that other forms of qualitative research, such as ethnographic research and getting people to keep diaries, provide additional valuable qualitative insight.

39 Lord Ashcroft (@LordAshcroft), Twitter, 29 December 2017.

40 Lord Ashcroft, 'Where the Parties Stand – And More on That Second EU Referendum . . .', Lord Ashcroft Polls, www.lordashcroftpolls. com, 17 January 2018. The details of the different question wordings are discussed in Chapter Three. There were no events in the Brexit saga that triggered a major shift in public opinion between the two polls.

41 Mark Pack, 'Are the Voters on Twitter Typical of the Rest of Us?', Mark Pack's Blog, 10 April 2017.

42 Mark Pack, 'Political Views of Twitter Users Do Not Match the Wider Population, but That Matters Less than You Might Think', Mark Pack's Blog, updated 1 September 2020.

43 The availability of such data depends on what permissions social networks grant for use of their data (policy decisions) and also how easy social networks make it to pull such data into other systems (technical decisions). Twitter does well on both fronts compared with other social networks.

44 Javier Sajuria and Jorge Fábrega, 'Do We Need Polls? Why Twitter Will Not Replace Opinion Surveys, but Can Complement Them', in *Digital Methods for Social Science*, ed. Helen Snee et al. (London, 2016); Beppe Karlsson, 'Tweeting Opinions: How Does Twitter Data Stack Up against the Polls and Betting Odds?', student thesis, Linnaeus University (2018); Daniel Gayo-Avello, Panagiotis T. Metaxas and Eni Mustafaraj, 'Limits of Electoral Predictions Using Twitter', Proceedings of the Fifth International AAAI Conference on Weblogs and Social Media (2011); and Daniel Gayo-Avello, 'A Meta-Analysis of State-of-the-Art Electoral Prediction from Twitter Data', *Social Science Computer Review*, XXXI/6 (2013), pp. 649–79. This meta-analysis includes the apparently successful use of Twitter to predict Dutch elections in 2011. In context it shows it is not convincing evidence for the superiority of Twitter over opinion polls, on which see also Erik Tjong Kim Sang and Johan Bos, 'Predicting the 2011 Dutch Senate Election Results with Twitter', paper presented at the 13th Conference of the European Chapter of the Association for Computational Linguistics, 23–27 April 2012.

45 Citation required.

46 A run of good luck means that just occasionally it takes a long time for the success to end, as with the Robinsons Bakery in Manchester whose use of muffin sales to predict election results worked from 1964 until at least 1992. See Maggie Fox, 'Why the Pollsters Got It Wrong', *Reuters* (10 April 1992), available at reuters.com; and Bronya Smolen, 'Manchester Bakery Gives Election Views to BBC', *British Baker* (30 April 2015).

47 W. E. Binkley and M. C. Moos, *A Grammar of American Politics* (New York, 1958). Quoted in Herbst, *Numbered Voices*, p. 107.

10 EVEN GOOD POLLS MISLEAD

1 Ithiel de Sola Pool, Robert P. Abelson and Samuel Popkin, *Candidates, Issues and Strategies: A Computer Simulation of the 1960 and 1964 Presidential Elections* (Cambridge, MA, 1964), p. 38.

2 Nate Cohn, 'Why This Is the Iowa Poll that Everyone Was Waiting For', *New York Times* (30 January 2016).

3 PollBase, at Mark Pack's Blog, www.markpack.org.uk.

4 Ariel Edwards-Levy (@aedwardslevy), Twitter, 7 October 2020. She specializes in covering polling and is the subject of the tribute song 'Ariel Edwards-Levy Is an Important Person' by Papa Razzi and the Photogs.

5 Thank you to Jack Bailey for producing the data with noise. The data was produced as 45 random draws from a normal distribution, with a mean of 0.42 and a standard deviation of 0.015 (that is, we assume that

the party is really on 42 per cent but that the polls have a margin of error of 3 per cent), along with then a second set of 45 random draws on the same basis but with a mean of 0.38. I then took data from each column in turn based on what the 'true' figures were for each party at each point.

6　Nate Silver, 'The Misunderstanding of Momentum', FiveThirtyEight, www.fivethirtyeight.com, 20 October 2010. For other examples of evidence, see 'Swings Swing Back Again, or Why You Should Not Get Excited by the Next Opinion Poll', Mark Pack's Blog, 4 April 2015; and Leo Barasi, 'Why Neither Side in the EU Referendum Will Ever Have Momentum'; Noise of the Crowd, www.noiseofthecrowd.com, 3 March 2016.

7　Barasi, 'Why Neither Side in the EU Referendum Will Ever Have Momentum'.

8　The one exception to this is when the polls are being put into a projection model. Good models can look at the past trends in polling data and so make a reasonable extrapolation as to how significant it is that X months out from polling day party C is G per cent ahead in the polls. There are some consistent patterns over time, such as how the closer you are to polling day, the smaller the likely gap between a poll finding and the actual election result. See Christopher Wlezien, 'The (Mostly) Pre-Baked Cake: Polls and Votes', in *More Sex, Lies and the Ballot Box*, ed. Philip Cowley and Robert Ford (London, 2016), Chapter Three. This is also a key part of U.S. models such as FiveThirtyEight's.

9　Leo Bogart, *Polls and the Awareness of Public Opinion*, 2nd edn (New Brunswick, NJ, 1985), p. 104.

10　'When a Leader of a Country Falls Ill, Do You Think the Public Have a Right to Know Their Full Condition?', YouGov, www.yougov.co.uk, 6 October 2020.

11　If in doubt, believe the away fans, as the evidence is that sports referees favour the home team unless there is effective remedial action to cancel out such bias: Thomas Dohmen and Jan Sauermann, 'Referee Bias', *Journal of Economic Surveys*, xxx/4 (2016), pp. 679–95.

12　'Tory Immigration Policy Is Popular; Its Brand Name Is Not', *The Times* (10 March 2005). Thank you to Professor Tim Bale for helping me find this story.

13　The question formulation falls foul of the agree–disagree question format problems discussed in Chapter Three. However, what matters in the analysis here is the difference in answers between the options. Although the agree–disagree format problems may well have skewed the overall levels of net agreement, this does not undermine the conclusions drawn about the differences between those levels.

14 Lord Ashcroft, *Smell the Coffee: A Wake-Up Call for the Conservative Party* (London, 2005), p. 52.

15 Philip Cowley, 'Don't Believe in Tribal Politics? Take a Look at How People Respond to Downing Street's Cats', *The Spectator* (4 November 2014).

16 Ibid.

17 See in particular James Tilley and Sara Hobolt, 'Is the Government to Blame? An Experimental Test of How Partisanship Shapes Perceptions of Performance and Responsibility', *Journal of Politics*, LXXIII/2 (2011), pp. 1–15 (p. 1): 'Our findings show that partisan loyalties have pervasive effects on responsibility attributions [whether people think the government is responsible for something], but somewhat weaker effects on evaluations of performance [how well people think the government is doing at something]'.

18 Thank you to Sunder Katwala, whose tweet drew my attention to the poll: Sunder Katwala (@SunderSays), Twitter, 11 September 2020, the day the poll was conducted.

19 Jesse Lopez and D. Sunshine Hillygus, 'Why So Serious? Survey Trolls and Misinformation', Social Science Research Network (SSRN), https://papers.ssrn.com, 14 March 2018: 'Survey trolls appear significantly more likely to endorse absurd political claims as being fact, and make up a large proportion of those who report believing that recent instances of misinformation are definitely true'.

20 David W. Moore, *The Opinion Makers: An Insider Exposes the Truth behind the Polls* (Boston, MA, 2008), pp. 5–8. Moore interprets these figures rather differently, claiming they showed public opinion was equally split: 'as many people opposed the war as supported it . . . the public didn't support the war before it was launched but was in fact evenly divided'. But the split of 30 per cent versus 8 per cent between the second and fourth categories, which he lumps together without presenting these individual figures, shows that there was a clear tilt, albeit one not as strong as the simple headline figure from the first question implied. Moreover, being in favour of something but also not being sad if that thing doesn't happen still counts as supporting something. Just as someone may, say, support a tax rise but also not be sad if the tax rise doesn't happen, because they think that the tax rise is right but also know it would cost them money personally. Although the follow-up question is a useful one to tease out where public opinion really stands on an issue, Moore's rhetoric goes further than his evidence justifies. His rhetoric also outruns the evidence in other examples he uses, such as when he says that supporting something but not being sad if it doesn't happen 'hardly

qualifies as a view that elected officials should treat with deference'. That is unnecessarily dismissive of people with nuanced views or views that pull between self-interest and the wider interest.

21 Mark Pack, *Bad News: What the Headlines Don't Tell Us* (London, 2020).

22 For example, for the 1992 general election, the *Daily Mail* decided against spending money on polls because its editor could not see any sales benefit: Nick Moon, *Opinion Polls: History, Theory and Practice* (Manchester, 1999), p. 46.

23 Ivor Crewe, '"Improving, but Could Do Better": The Media and the Polls in the 1979 General Election' in *Political Communications: The General Election Campaign of 1979*, ed. Robert Worcester and Martin Harrop (London, 1982), p. 124. The rise of social media has made this worse, with polls that appear to show dramatic change getting amplified more than those which show little change, even if the former are suspect outliers. Erik Gahner Larsen and Zoltán Fazekas, *Reporting Public Opinion: How the Media Turns Boring Polls into Biased News* (Cham, 2021), p. 5, shows how polls showing greater change get more attention at all steps of the process from conceiving a poll through to audience reactions to it. As a result, 'the polls that people engage with are *not* representative of what all opinion polls show.'

24 Keiran Pedley (@keiranpedley), Twitter, 29 August 2020.

25 Crewe, '"Improving, but Could Do Better"', p. 115.

26 The age bands used in this example are those typically found in YouGov polls in the UK.

27 The huge expansion of university education in the UK in recent decades, in particular, means there is a correlation between someone's age and someone's likely level of education attainment. As the correlation is strong but not perfect, that means that the conclusions you draw if you assume age is the explanatory factor can lead you into error.

28 Fred Backus, 'Four in 10 Think Time Travel Will Someday Be Possible', CBS News, www.cbsnews.com, 16 April 2021.

29 For simplicity, I have left out another set of numbers that are relevant: how answers to the question varied by political partisanship. In particular, were older people less likely to say they thought they will die because they tended to be more Conservative and so more favourable in their estimate of the Conservative government's efforts to combat coronavirus? It could be partisanship rather than age that was the real factor. In this case, that seems unlikely, as the net scores were nearly identical between Conservative (–51) and Labour (–53) voters.

30 For example, see Mary-Kate Lizotte and Andrew H. Sidman, 'Explaining the Gender Gap in Political Knowledge', *Politics and*

Gender, V/2 (2009), pp. 127–51 (p. 147): Lizotte and Sidman conclude, 'Men are far more likely to hazard guesses than women, which leads to inflated estimates of their political knowledge relative to that of women.'

31 A similar point applies to questions in which people are not given 'don't know' as an option but are asked to rate something on a 0–10-point scale. A bump in people answering '5' can be a disguised version of 'don't know', and again, it is only a fuller set of figures than a simple average score that reveals the full story. Similar, but messier, things can happen with 1–10-point scales, with people also picking 5 as if it was the midpoint, though it is not.

32 Even when pollsters record 'don't know' as an answer and you pay attention to these numbers, the results may hide the degree of uncertainty behind them, as shown by a 1999 experiment: 'Half the respondents were asked standard "favour or oppose" questions about school vouchers and charter schools, and the questioners recorded a "don't know" response only if respondents volunteered it. The other half received parallel questions with the added phrase, "or haven't you heard enough about that to have an opinion?" On the voucher questions, the 4 per cent volunteered "don't know" response ballooned into a 33 per cent explicit "'haven't heard enough" . . . [for] the charter school results . . . only 9 per cent volunteered "don't know" in the standard favor/oppose version, [but] 63 per cent in the other form said they had not heard enough to have an opinion' – Richard Morin, 'Who Knows?', *Washington Post* (10 September 2001).

33 For more on how to make sense of numbers in the news, including more on this particular effect, see Pack, *Bad News*, Chapter Eleven.

34 Scott Malone, 'Trump? Clinton? Many Young Americans Prefer Giant Meteor, Poll Finds', Reuters, www.reuters.com, 18 October 2016. The report concluded that the poll 'had a margin of error of 3.2 percent', highlighting one of the limitations of such calculations.

35 The extent to which 'expressive responding' explains results showing apparent belief in misinformation and conspiracy theories is a matter of debate among political scientists. Absurd answers such as the meteor one and one cited elsewhere in this chapter about future election results illustrate, however, that this is a factor to consider when analysing polling about elections and political preferences. Thank you to Will Jennings for highlighting to me the debate over expressive responding.

36 Jennifer C. Whitman and Todd S. Woodward, 'Evidence Affects Hypothesis Judgments More if Accumulated Gradually than if Presented Instantaneously', *Psychonomic Bulletin and Review*, XVIII (2011), pp. 1156–65.

37 Simple monthly averages of support for the Conservatives only varied between 38 per cent and 42 per cent and for Labour between 37 per cent and 41 per cent, for example.

38 Survation is excluded from this list as it only asked a leader-rating question about Theresa May once during the year, and so any difference between its figures and the year-long averages of others may simply reflect when its one poll was done.

39 Robert Ford (@robfordmancs), Twitter, 31 August 2020.

40 'Polling Explainer: Is the Race for the White House Tightening?', *Financial Times* (4 September 2020).

41 Followers of polling have it easier than followers of economic statistics, as GDP growth rates are presented in a still more different way between countries such as the USA and the UK. In the USA, quarterly figures are presented in annualized form, which is not the tradition in the UK. That makes U.S. figures look around four times as good (or bad) as UK figures to the untrained eye.

42 As indeed may the headline numbers, given the differences in the ways 'don't knows' are treated in them – see Chapter Four. Usually, poll reports are all done in the convention of one country, but sometimes the conventions cross over, as with the pollster Redfield & Wilton in 2020, who used UK conventions for the plus and minus figures but U.S. conventions for 'don't knows' in reporting its polling on the U.S. presidential election in 2020.

43 This is from the interview section at the end of his talk '120 Years of the Labour Party: In Conversation with Tony Blair' to King's College, London, 20 February 2020.

44 Deborah Mattinson, *Beyond the Red Wall* (London, 2020), p. 167.

45 Karl Marx, *Selected Writings in Sociology and Social Philosophy*, ed. T. B. Bottomore and Maximilien Rubel (London, 1956), pp. 210–18.

46 Nate Silver, 'Calculating "House Effects" of Polling Firms', FiveThirtyEight, www.fivethirtyeight.com, 22 June 2012.

47 This is a risky adjustment to make if your wishes for a particular outcome make you see skewed data where there isn't any. This was the fate of the Republican fashion for 'unskewing the polls' in the 2012 U.S. presidential election. People claimed they were unskewing the polls to make them more accurate. But they were actually taking polls accurately showing Obama beating Romney and twisting them into inaccurate figures showing Romney ahead. He wasn't and he lost. See Harry Enten, 'The Polls Aren't Skewed', FiveThirtyEight, www.fivethirtyeight.com, 9 August 2016.

48 For example, see 'FAQ: Are the Liberal Democrat Voice Surveys of Party Members Accurate?', Mark Pack's Blog, 18 August 2012. The run of decent Lib Dem Voice poll results came to an end in the 2014 Liberal Democrat party president contest. I was no longer involved in those polls by then but make no claim that was the cause of their failure. See Stephen Tall, 'That LibDemVoice Survey on the Party Presidency (Which, Ahem, Called It Wrong): 8 Thoughts from Me', Lib Dem Voice, www.libdemvoice.org, 30 November 2014.

49 In particular, the 2020 contest saw an MP of many years from London up against a much newer MP from outside London. My methodology would likely have produced samples skewed towards longer-standing members and members from London, where I have been most active in the party.

50 The route is number 603 in London. Lynne Featherstone often credited the bus route for being a large part of the reason for her election to Parliament. Because she became an MP, in 2010 she became a minister. Because she became a minister, she was able to make the government legalize same-sex marriage. Bad data can go a long way.

11 JUDGING POLLING FIRMS

1 Herbert Morrison, House of Commons, *Hansard*, 11 March 1959, available at https://hansard.parliament.uk.

2 This table is based on published polls and so uses the final Survation poll published ahead of the 2015 general election, rather than the more accurate later one that was not published until after polling day. TNS has variously been TNS-BMRB and Kantar TNS. For 2010, the Conservative–Labour gap is used, though some pollsters had the Liberal Democrats in second. In 2001 Ipsos MORI had two final polls, one telephone and one face-to-face. The figure given is the average of the leads shown in the two (12 per cent and 15 per cent for Labour, respectively).

3 For example, Nate Silver tweeted in October 2020, 'This interview with Trafalgar Group really worried me, for instance. These are not conventional polling methods and it sounds like they provide a lot of room for subjectivity or frankly confirmation bias in how one constructs a voter universe': Nate Silver (@NateSilver538), Twitter, 19 October 2020. He also raised questions about polling cross-tabs from Trafalgar: 'I'm not a Let's Delve Into The Crosstabs guy, but some of the shit here is just crazy. Trump is not going to win 30 per cent of the Democratic vote in Michigan. Biden is not going to win 25 per cent of Republicans. Trump is not going to win independents by 32 points', and 'I am not sure

what's happening, but now the links to these Trafalgar polls with the dubious crosstabs have gone dead'. On the same day, he also said, 'I don't know exactly what they're doing, but it's not a good sign that I always know what a Trafalgar Group poll is going to say without having to open the link' – Nate Silver (@NateSilver538), Twitter, 25 October 2020.

4 Author interview, 22 December 2020.

5 See its press release, 'AtlasIntel Is Confirmed as the Most Accurate Pollster of the 2020 Presidential Election', 7 November 2020. Independent analysis came to the same conclusion: 'Politics Podcast: The Gold Standard for Polling Has Changed', FiveThirtyEight Podcast, 25 March 2021.

6 Matt Singh (@MattSingh), Twitter, 2 November 2020.

7 Harry Enten, 'Fake Polls Are a Real Problem', FiveThirtyEight, www.fivethirtyeight.com, 22 August 2017.

8 Unattributed comment made in 1937 or 1938. Versions of this quote are attributed to a wide range of people including Yogi Berra, Niels Bohr and, of course, Mark Twain. For its origin, see 'It's Difficult to Make Predictions, Especially about the Future', Quote Investigator, www.quoteinvestigator.com, 20 October 2013.

9 W. Joseph Campbell, *Lost in a Gallup* (Oakland, CA, 2020), p. 104. A polling consultant said of him, 'He thinks he is always right. He *never* makes a mistake' – ibid., p. 106.

10 Quoted in Will Lester, '"Dewey Defeats Truman" Disaster Haunts Pollsters', *Los Angeles Times* (1 November 1998).

11 Campbell, *Lost in a Gallup*, p. 150.

12 See, in particular, Philip Tetlock and Dan Gardner, *Superforecasting: The Art and Science of Prediction* (New York, 2015).

12 MAKING SENSE OF THE POLLS

1 Peter Hitchens, 'My First Epistle to the Corbynites – Don't Get Me Wrong about the Polls', MailOnline, www.dailymail.co.uk, 22 May 2017.

2 Mark Pack, 'Aspects of the English Electoral System, 1800–50, with Special Reference to Yorkshire', PhD thesis, University of York, 1995.

3 Sidney Verba, 'The Citizen as Respondent: Sample Surveys and American Democracy – Presidential Address, American Political Science Association, 1995', *American Political Science Review*, XC/1 (March 1996), pp. 1–7.

4 For a useful – and more favourable to Bourdieu – discussion of the epistemological debates behind the concept of public opinion and

whether treating opinions equally is a good thing, see George F. Bishop, *The Illusion of Public Opinion: Fact and Artifact in American Public Opinion Polls* (Lanham, MD, 2005), Chapter One.

5 Brandon Keim, 'Real-Time Debate Feedback Distorts Democracy', *Wired* (4 August 2011). This includes links to a variety of other relevant pieces of research, including from the USA. The differences in the results are comfortably large enough to be outside the sampling margins of error discussed earlier.

6 Author interview, 22 December 2020.

7 Quoted in David Epstein, *Range: How Generalists Triumph in a Specialized World* (New York, 2019), frontispiece.

8 Author interview, 30 December 2020.

9 Except possibly John Curtice and Ann Selzer.

10 'There is a long history of the direction of polling error being unpredictable: If the polls miss in one direction – say, the Republican direction – in one year, then they're equally likely the next year to miss again in the Republican direction or the Democratic direction' – Nate Silver, quoted in Ezra Klein, 'Nate Silver on Why 2020 Isn't 2016', Vox, www.vox.com, 30 October 2020.

11 Quoted in W. Joseph Campbell, *Lost in a Gallup: Polling Failures in U.S. Presidential Elections* (Berkeley, CA, 2020), p. 205.

THANK YOU

1 Nate Silver (@natesilver), Twitter, 14 October 2020.

FURTHER READING

1 House of Lords Select Committee on Political Polling and Digital Media, *The Politics of Polling*, Report of Session 2017–19, HL Paper 106, 2018, p. 17.

ACKNOWLEDGEMENTS

1 House of Commons, *Hansard*, 30 September 1941, available at https://hansard.parliament.uk.

FURTHER READING

'For the discerning reader, there is an awful lot
of political intelligence in the opinion polls.'
– JOHN CURTICE, political scientist[1]

An inspiration for this book is Nick Moon, *Opinion Polls: History, Theory and Practice* (Manchester, 1999). It's still a valuable source on British political polling and if there had been a recent edition of the book, I would most likely have concluded there wasn't a gap for this book to try to fill.

The best study of the pre-1936 history of political polling, which shows how much more there was to straw polls than most polling histories give credit for, is Claude E. Robinson, *Straw Votes: A Study of Political Prediction* (New York, 1932). Emil Hurja's seminal contribution to the development of polling both pre- and post-1936 is covered in Melvin G. Holli, *The Wizard of Washington: Emil Hurja, Franklin Roosevelt, and the Birth of Public Opinion Polling* (New York, 2002).

An excellent account of how choices over political polling design shaped politics, as well as being the key source for the bias towards better-off white men in Gallup's early polling, is Daniel J. Robinson, *The Measure of Democracy: Polling, Market Research and Public Life, 1930–1945* (Toronto, 1999). For more on how the media frequently misreport polls (and political campaigns in general), see my earlier book, *Bad News: What the Headlines Don't Tell Us* (London, 2020).

A useful summary of the arguments in favour of the positive impact of political polls on the health of democracy, and the reasons not to ban or heavily constrain them through regulation, is Wolfgang Donsbach, *Who's Afraid of Election Polls? Normative and Empirical Arguments for the Freedom of Pre-Election Surveys* (Amsterdam, 2001).

A fun history of polling missteps in the United States is W. Joseph Campbell, *Lost in a Gallup* (Oakland, CA, 2020) and still more fun round-ups of insights into voter behaviour, many derived from polls, are Philip Cowley and Robert Ford, eds, *More Sex, Lies and the Ballot Box* (London, 2016), and Philip Cowley and Robert Ford, eds, *Sex, Lies and Politics: The Secret Influences That Drive Our Political Choices* (London, 2019).

Finally, there are a couple of books that expound topics only tangentially touched upon in this book but which are so interesting that they deserve mention. For a fuller and brilliant history of Simulmatics and its contribution to the development of political polling, see Jill Lepore, *If Then: How the Simulmatics Corporation Invented the Future* (New York, 2020). For the history of the compulsory vote, and that Möbius strip ballot paper suggestion, see Judith Brett, *From Secret Ballot to Democracy Sausage: How Australia Got Compulsory Voting* (Melbourne, 2019).

ACKNOWLEDGEMENTS

'Nothing is more dangerous in war-time than to live in the
temperamental atmosphere of a Gallup Poll, always
feeling one's pulse and taking one's temperature.'
– WINSTON CHURCHILL, prime minister[1]

I have experience with polling, both conducting and commissioning polls, and I have less fear of numbers than most. But I am neither an expert pollster nor an advanced statistician. What I hope this book shows I am is someone able to collate, simplify and then sprinkle history over it all. To borrow James Clear's words from the Introduction to his book *Atomic Habits: An Easy and Proven Way to Build Good Habits and Break Bad Ones*, 'What I offer you is a synthesis of the best ideas smart people figured out . . . Anything wise in these pages you should credit to the many experts who preceded me. Anything foolish, assume it is my error.'

Speaking of smart people who have helped this book, several thank yous are in order. Thank you to my brother Peter for checking and simplifying my attempts at explaining the maths of samples. His pupils are lucky to have such a great teacher. Thank you to Tim Bale, Jack Blumenau, Philip Cowley, John Curtice, Bobby Duffy, Murray Goot, Will Jennings, Ben Lauderdale, Darren Lilleker, Damian Lyons Lowe, Deborah Mattinson, Matt Singh, Patrick Sturgis, Paula Surridge, Joe Twyman, Anne L. Washington and Anthony Wells for their help with my research, my writing and answering so many of my questions. Thank you also to Jim Williams for his wise feedback on parts of my earlier drafts (but when you're out walking, Jim, you really should look where you're going rather than be reading printouts of book drafts).

Thank you to the Center for Legislative Archives at the U.S. National Archives and Records Administration and the Special Collections service at the University of Oregon Libraries for providing copies of their holdings on Pierce's early attempts to regulate political polling. The Internet Archive's book collection was invaluable in letting me look up references in obscure books when COVID-19 lockdowns prevented the use of traditional libraries.

Acknowledgements

Thank you also to the many in the British polling profession who have answered my questions over the years, and occasionally been quiz-winning teammates on the Saturday night at the Election, Public Opinion and Parties (EPOP) annual conferences. For a profession with commercial competitiveness underpinning it, its members are remarkably open to answering questions and sharing information.

Thanks are further due to the now long since defunct telephone market research firm that gave me a summer placement many years ago and to colleagues in the Liberal Democrats I worked with for many years both on proper polling and on the collection of the sort of skewed survey data discussed in this book. Prior to that, I first got into looking up the details of polls on the microfilm readers at Camden Public Library. The legacy of the staff's helpfulness has been a long one, and one for which I am very grateful.

The team at Reaktion Books have worked wonders to turn my drafts into a proper book. Special thanks goes to Amy Salter and commissioning editor Dave Watkins, who had the idea of asking me to write this book at just the right moment for me to say yes.

Mistakes, omissions and bizarre judgements that remain in the book despite all the above are, of course, on me. I hope not too many of them have annoyed you.

Finally, thank you to Dominic Mathon for, several years ago, giving me the idea for the 'Polling UnPacked' title pun. I hope my book lives up to the quality of his punning.

347

INDEX